Going Deeper

with

GOD

Addressing Challenging Issues in
Our Relationship with God

DOUGLAS L. MEAD, MSSW

ISBN 978-1-0980-8721-0 (paperback)
ISBN 978-1-0980-8722-7 (digital)

Christian Faith Publishing, Inc.
832 Park Avenue
Meadville, PA 16335
www.christianfaithpublishing.com

Printed in the United States of America

CONTENTS

INTRODUCTION

When the question "What kind of a relationship do you want to have with God?" is asked, one way to tell what the answer will be is to look at where people go to church. At least this is one indicator.

As I look at many of the large churches, I see people drawn to the Word of Faith movement (to be discussed in chapter 1) and similar messaging churches that talk of a God who allegedly promises great things and is outwardly very active in people's lives and will provide, protect, and speak to people regularly. It seems that a great many people are drawn to a God who controls all things, who has a specific plan for each one's life, who will welcome the opportunity to solve people's problems if they can just let go and let him handle them. We can then add a little health and prosperity to this offering.

I know most Christians love to hear how powerful God is because we want him to use his power to help us. Many seem to think that faith is a superpower. We love to hear how God will answer audacious prayer requests as demonstrations of his power. We love to envision a God who will do mighty miracles on a regular basis, where the idea of being filled with the Spirit means speaking in tongues and healing people.

Just the other day, I heard a preacher declare in the pulpit with certainty that God did a miracle the previous week. It was about a man who had COVID-19 and was healed. This is a person who was hit hard by this virus and had most of the worst symptoms. Many questioned if he would make it. But he did. He recovered from the terrible grip of this virus and left the hospital walking without needing assistance. Now is this a miracle? Maybe, but how can anyone really know?

What about the skilled doctors who carefully treated this person, the compassionate nurses who provided twenty-four-seven care, the effective medications he took, and the amazing medical machines used to help him? Should one assert a miracle occurred when there is a lot of evidence to show that it's more likely that terrific medical care was the primary reason for his recovery? What we can suspect is that God used people to heal this man. I like to think of this as an example of a pattern, or even a doctrine, of God's partnership with people. We can't take people out of the equation in this situation. We can also keep God in the equation. God used people to help heal this man. We can praise God for his healing.

I believe when this situation was declared a miracle, the basic assumption of the preacher was to imply that God did this alone, by himself. After all, a miracle is a supernatural occurrence. People don't do supernatural things. I believe this situation was framed as a miracle because Christian people want a God who does miracles, especially in answer to prayers. We look for evidence of this, even if it is a stretch.

I believe this kind of thinking about God is spreading into all faith traditions to a certain degree, at least through the people if not the leadership. We see evidence of this in the songs we sing and the phrases we use as we talk about God.

There seems to be a great appetite, indeed, a longing for a God who is all about doing high and mighty things on a regular basis. These are people who want God to protect them and their loved ones from harm and provide for them in every context, including enabling them to become prosperous. How do others who see God differently compete with this theology?

Hopefully, everyone can understand that there are alternative views on how to have a relationship with God. In contrast to the Word of Faith movement and similar teachings, there are many others who genuinely seek God and center their expectations based more upon the scriptures than emotions.

It is one thing to know how great and powerful God is, but it is another thing to know how God restrains himself from being over-powering. This relates to the debate about God's sovereignty versus the free will of man. Yes, God has the ability to be in control of all, but he delegates much power to mankind to work in partnership with him. This concept will be addressed in this book.

As we consider the impact of those who want to see a God very actively intervening in our world, it's like we are being given a clear contrast. It appears as if we must either align with those who equate a relationship with God as a daily thrilling experience with having tremendous benefits, similar to ideas such as skydiving, river rafting, sunset cruises, and five-star hotel dining, or we align with those who choose a boring relationship with God with similar ideas such as taking bicycle rides in neighborhoods, eating nutritious crackers, and consuming sugar-free drinks.

We all need to understand that there is another dimension to this situation which is authentic, reality-based, scripturally sup-ported, and exhilarating. I believe it's a false dichotomy to say we must display mighty faith such as those in the Word of Faith move-ment and those with similar thinking or we are then weak in the faith and dishonoring to God. It's a deceptive argument and not based on an honest analysis.

It's a false argument to say that either God does it all and we just need to get out of the way versus we do it all and God needs to get out of the way. Neither of these options is the scriptural way.

I will be proposing in this book that the way to a meaningful, purposeful, and authentic relationship with God is to engage ear-nestly in the partnership relationship we have with him. It is us in conjunction with God. This is the way God designed it from the very beginning. It is where we base our actions and expectations on scriptures—the whole of scriptures—not just picking and choosing selective verses here or there.

I am proposing in this book that God, our creator, has made us with having godlike qualities which come with tremendous skills and abilities. Given this, he delights in us using our skills and abilities in partnership with him and how he helps us. He ultimately gets the glory as it is totally the way he designed things to be.

This Book Is Written for You

So are you ready to be challenged? I am writing this book to hopefully cause you to think deeper about what a personal relationship with God means. As a result of reading this material, I hope it will motivate you to do further study on topics and issues which are being raised and, ultimately, to seek him and the more intimate personal relationship into which he invites us all.

I have written this book with the hope it could be a good resource for those who are searching, open-minded, and willing to consider faith in Jesus. I am also writing this book in hopes it will be a source of spiritual encouragement for those new in the faith. I have kept in mind how a searching person and a new Christian would react as I wrote each chapter. I'm hoping what I've included in this book relates to the kinds of questions you have.

I believe this book will be challenging and helpful to many who are mature in the faith. I also believe that preachers and teachers can use much of the information in this book as an aid as they do their ministry work.

We all know there are so many unbiblical, contradictory, and confusing concepts being advanced by Christians and Christian groups of many kinds these days. This seems to be spreading throughout the Christian community like wildfire. It's reaching people in many ways, including by word of mouth, as people share their faith through Christian music, books, Internet searches, preaching, etc. It is so easy to access all kinds of information. No one is able to escape the barrage of false and questionable doctrine that is challenging everyone's thinking.

What to Expect from This Book

I believe everyone needs to be more aware of the variety of questionable viewpoints out there which are based on questionable scriptural support. Most assuredly, I'm not the only one who thinks this way. I've been receiving words of caution about these groups from scholarly people for years.

I encourage you to be careful and wary as you absorb and interpret many of the conflicting messages coming your way. I have tried to provide a contrast to many of these misguided doctrines and offer reasonable and positive alternative teachings based on a strong biblical view of the issues. I hope this book will encourage your faith.

When I teach Bible classes in church, I find that experienced Christians still mention ideas I think are flawed. When I hear people who are speaking up in class and expressing ideas I find misguided, that's an awkward situation. Unfortunately, it seems to happen fairly regularly. I try to be careful how I handle this. I don't want to put people in an uncomfortable position or embarrass them. I often prefer to let many comments slide. Sometimes I will try to deal with them in a more private setting, sometimes not. This is another reason why a book like this can be so helpful!

As mentioned in chapter 1, disagreements can be good for us if they cause us to study further and grow deeper in our knowledge and faith. Sometimes the only way we do this is because of disagreements. Yes, I've been disappointed with teachings I don't agree with at times. However, due to my critical thinking mind, I usually attain greater clarity because those disagreements cause me to do additional study. They often become a topic of discussion with my Christian friends as I process these ideas.

I realize many people's views are well entrenched. Others are not. It reminds me of politics. There are those who are strong Democrats, and it doesn't matter what is going on. They will vote for the Democrats. The same is true for a certain amount of Republicans. Those who are more open-minded appear to be the independents and those new to politics.

From a similar point of view, I realize many who are well entrenched in their doctrines will not budge at all. I'm hoping this book will reach the independents, so to speak, as well as those who are open-minded and willing to explore a deeper relationship with God.

I suspect some of the views I will promote in this book will be new, and some of the ways I address topics will provide fresh and helpful ideas.

One of the topics I present which may have a different twist is my emphasis on the partnership relationship I believe we have with God. I think this concept explains more accurately how we walk with God in our journey throughout life. It has broad and practical application as to how we view our interactions with God. I explain this in detail in the chapter on "Our Relationship with God—a Partnership."

I will bring up the idea of worldview many times in this book. To me, one's worldview has a huge influence on how one understands what others say about their relationship with God and what they expect God to do. I interpret so much about what is said through the filter of my worldview. If I have not seen evidence through my worldview of experiences to support concepts being mentioned, I almost instinctively question their validity. I will then be quick to talk to other seasoned Christians about the issues and process my thinking that way.

For example, I often hear Christian pastors, ministers, and leaders teach about how God provides for us and how he will take care of our problems if we will just give them to him. Just today, as I was writing this section, someone sent me a video message from a pastor in Florida asserting that "Jesus is about fixing broken people, fixing broken situations, and mending that which has been damaged." His purpose in doing the video was to encourage everyone to humble themselves and pray for God to take away the coronavirus from the world. He saw this as a real possible solution to this problem. He believed with enough prayer from all over the country that God would intervene and end this plague.

However, as I understand the teachings of Jesus, he was more focused on people coming to know him as their Lord and Savior so they can have eternal life with him. That is why he came into the world (John 3:16). That was Jesus's primary message by far. Yes, Jesus did heal people in amazing ways. His healings came as a secondary benefit. He did not come to earth for that primary reason.

Regarding that situation with the pastor from Florida, my worldview does not give me a reason to believe that God would do what he said. I've never seen this happen before, ever. Therefore, what am I to think about what he was saying?

Philip Yancey in his book *Reaching for the Invisible God: What Can We Expect to Find?* Relates to this. He says, "A Christian who expects God to solve all family problems, heal all diseases, and thwart baldness, gray hair…is pursuing childish magic, not mature religion."

Philip describes the idea of feel-good Christianity as pursuing childhood magic. As much as people want to believe God will jump to make life easier for everyone based on a simple request, the scriptures are full of examples of hardships and suffering people will have to endure in this life. Mature Christians grounded in the scriptures focus on more important issues.

Moving on.

In one of the chapters, I try to persuasively offer several solid reasons why people should consider believing that God does exist. In reality, what I share is just the tip of the iceberg. There are a lot of materials on Christian apologetics available for the seeking mind. I believe we all would benefit to have knowledge in this area so we can more confidently relate to the skeptics around us. They are everywhere. I wish there was a prepackaged core course which churches could access in order to teach as a Sunday morning Bible class on these issues. Everyone needs it!

I address many other issues and topics I think will be helpful in growing and enhancing our personal relationship with God. One is to have a deeper appreciation for what it means to be made in God's image. A big insight from this concept is how God made people with free will, independent free will. Once he did so, he can't take it back. Having free will is huge. It explains a lot. I believe what we find all over in the New Testament scriptures are passages about us voluntarily harnessing the free will we have so that we choose out of love and obedience to conform to the will of God.

Another topic relates to how so many people like to say the phrase "God has a plan for our lives." I think they likely mean a specific plan for our lives. I question if most really understand what they are saying. We'll explore this issue.

I know there are many Christians who want so desperately to experience God's presence in their lives. This makes many vulnerable to some of the unbiblical teaching out there among the Word of Faith groups and Calvinists, to name a few. I've addressed this by identifying many of the ways we can identify that God is with us. I'm sure many could add to the list I came up with on this.

Another of the sayings I frequently hear people express is "God is in control." I also wonder if many understand what they mean when they say this. I suspect that the way I explore this will be in more depth than the way most have considered this before. I've spent a lot of time studying this issue.

One of the big issues I hear Christians talk about wanting more information on is how to understand how God fits into all the evil, pain, and suffering in the world. I hope you will find this chapter very interesting and helpful.

I have told many of my friends that I began this project as an effort to prepare material for an upcoming Sunday morning Bible class I would teach. As I got further into writing the material, I sensed it might be book worthy. If you are reading this, then it did work out! I hope you enjoy it and find it well worth your time.

I come to writing on the topics addressed in this book from a unique background compared with many other Christian authors. Several years ago I completed a 40 year career in the social service field. I was a state licensed clinical social worker and provided professional counseling during those years to those struggling with marital, family and personal problems from a Christian point of view. For the last 32 years of working, I was also an Executive Director for non-profit agencies providing foster care, adoption and counseling services. My focus will be grounded in the scriptures, full of common sense and guided by practical principles reflecting the capabilities of people to learn, change, develop skills and abilities and interact with God and things spiritual.

My goal is for Jesus to be prominently displayed in his rightful place as we pursue a relationship with God.

God bless you all!

CHAPTER 1

Confusion Abounds in How to Have a Relationship with God

> For by him all things were created, in heaven and on earth,
> visible and invisible, whether thrones or dominions or rulers or
> authorities—all things were created through him and for him.
> —Colossians 1:16

One of the phrases we hear frequently in the Christian community is having "a personal relationship with God." This is mentioned in a variety of contexts, but what does it mean?

We hear this phrase often when a discussion is about encouraging one to become a follower of Christ. In this context, it can simply mean the process of becoming a believer and accepting Jesus as one's Lord and Savior. Becoming "born again" is how one enters into a relationship with God.

For mature Christians, the phrase "having a personal relationship with God" is heard quite often also. However, there can be many questions as to what this phrase may mean because there are many perspectives as to how this relationship works.

To those outside of the Christian environment, there are likely many questions as well as to what this phrase means.

Given all the differing views out there in Christian circles about what a relationship with God entails, determining what to believe is a real challenge. It can be very confusing. That is why I chose this topic to write about.

Just consider the many ways we receive conflicting messages about biblical topics and spiritual issues. It can be difficult to find congruent and consistent thoughts and ideas being expressed among the resources which can be so easily accessed. We find all kinds of perspectives from the variety of churches there are, from the Internet where any idea can be found, from Christian bookstores which feature many faith perspectives, from Christian-based radio stations, etc. There are tremendous differences of opinion and viewpoint.

I've learned long ago that I cannot just choose a Christian book to read or an article with a Christian message to read without first understanding the religious orientation of the writer. I can then filter the message as needed and appropriate. However, not everyone is able to see these distinctions if they are not familiar with the differences in views.

I'm concerned for how confusing all this can be for those open-minded people who are searching for the truth and exploring the merits of becoming a Christian. I'm concerned for those who are skeptics, cynics, and doubters who may find all the diversity and disunity among believers regarding Christian messaging as just another stumbling block to faith.

I'm concerned about those who are young in the faith and can get discouraged by all the conflicting ideas. I'm also concerned about seasoned Christians who are having differing and conflicting viewpoints being thrown in their faces daily. This can throw some off-balance, causing questions and confusion. All of that is also why I chose this topic to write about.

Phrases Can Be Confusing

The use of Christian lingo is similar to the use of lingo in other particular types of subcultures. It is lingo which is intrinsic and distinctive to their communities and needs explaining for others outside the communities to understand what is being said. Simply stated, words and phrases used by Christians can be confusing.

I find there are many Christian phrases that are frequently uttered in which it is assumed that everyone understands and agrees with what is being said when, in actuality, the meaning of the phrase is not clear. Many phrases can have multiple meanings, and many phrases are packed with meaning.

I believe it would be helpful and most often best to define what a phrase means when it is being uttered. Listeners need to be clear on what is being meant when something is stated, especially regarding phrases with multiple possible explanations.

One such phrase is "God is in control," which appears to be a very commonly used phrase these days. That is a phrase which has deep roots into various Christian doctrines and can mean differing things to different people. However, most utter this phrase without providing any explanation of what they mean when they say it.

Another phrase we hear often is "everything happens for a reason." The same concerns mentioned above apply here. Another phrase is "we need to listen to the voice of God." This is often mentioned by many in the Christian community. The same concerns mentioned above apply here.

We hear phrases such as "Let go and let God" and "Give all of your concerns to God to handle." Again, these are vague concepts that need explanation.

The phrase "a personal relationship with God" can have similar dynamics. There are many differing views by Christians about how God works in our world today and in the lives of his people. Because of this, having a relationship with God is as subjective and varied as the person on the other end.

The Need to Question Teachings

As you will see, I will address many topics and ask many probing questions. To dig deeper into issues requires one to pause, reflect on the topic, create a list of questions about the topic, and do research to explore the topic further. Without questioning what we are being taught, we can easily get caught up into accepting a teaching as being true when it may not be true. Without questioning, we can miss out

on considering various and diverse viewpoints which may be important. Without questioning, we are not being critically-minded learn-
ers. Without questioning, what is being said gives a lot of power to
the teacher, too much power.

I began doing more questioning in my life when I was in graduate school. This is one of the skills and techniques graduate students
are expected to learn. I came to live by the axiom, to question is to
care. Questioning things will cause us to open our minds to see more
sides of an issue. This is what I hope to do in this book.

As a result of the questions presented, I hope you will be able
to think more deeply about the challenging issues addressed in this
book. I'm sure my comments and analysis will cause you to generate
questions of your own.

Many Dynamics Involved

Philip Yancey, one of my favorite Christian authors, has written a book to explore the many dynamics of how to understand what
is meant by having a personal relationship with God. It is entitled
Reaching for the Invisible God: What Can We Expect to Find? We read in
Colossians 1:15, "He [Jesus] is the image of the invisible God." Yancey's
book deals with the challenges of having a relationship with a God who
is invisible and not experienced through our five senses (touch, sight,
hearing, smell, and taste). Nothing in the material and physical side of
life is like the relationship we must have with God. It is unique indeed.

As Philip Yancey is known to do in his books, he addresses many
of the tough questions people have with Christianity associated with
the topic he is writing about. In his book above, Philip asks, "What
is a relationship with God supposed to look like anyway?" and "How
does a relationship with God truly work?"

Also in his book, Philip says that there are many believers who
struggle with faith and say that what they experience in person seems
so different from what they hear so confidently described from the
pulpit. Philip mentions the struggles people have as they try to add a
dose of realism to the spiritual propaganda that promises more than
it can deliver.

I think the same thing when I hear preachers talk about the need for everyone to "expect a miracle" and "expect the impossible" as if these happen regularly. These are also phrases which could have differing meanings to different people.

Most people filter what is being said through their personal experiences and their worldview—their understanding of how the world works by what they've seen and experienced.

In my attempt to be genuine in my faith, I try not to speak on topics I have not studied or learned through the world I've experienced. I admit, what I don't know is vast! I also admit that I could be wrong in the conclusions I make about topics.

I love to read and study spiritual topics I'm interested in. I do a fair amount of study and investigation, especially now that I am retired. We all know we can't expect to experience everything in order to accept it as truth. So that is why we study and investigate. The more we know, the more we have to share. The more we know, the more it can empower us.

Many Differing Views on a Relationship with God

Based on my experience and training, I know something about how relationships work. I've had a clinical license in social work for over thirty years and have done a good amount of marriage, premarital, and relationship counseling, beginning this work in 1985. I will use this background to bring to bear some insights into the kind of relationship we can have with God.

We all know there are differing ways one could explore the topic of how to have a relationship with God. One way is similar to how Philip Yancey approaches topics. He shares concerns and struggles people have had with the topic. He looks more deeply into the topic. He deals with the tough questions many prefer to avoid. He shares information from his life's experiences, how he has personally struggled with issues, and then comes to his conclusions. With Philip, one gets more than just pat answers.

Another way to address this topic is similar to those who are motivational type of presenters. These are often those who try to appeal to the emotions and are what I call touchy-feely kind of people. They know we are all drawn to hope, exciting possibilities, stories of those who have overcome adversities, and those who have beat the odds and transcended the negativity of naysayers. Because of our limitations and wants in life, we are eager to hear about a God who will do more than we can ask or imagine and take control to protect us and our loved ones from harm. Again, these are presenters who get people charged up by emotional appeals.

A Note of Caution about Questionable Doctrines

For anyone to address the topic of how to have a relationship with God requires an honest and open acknowledgment that there are erroneous pseudo-Christian movements, questionable preaching, and incorrect doctrines. I believe many are being misguided by deceitful and false teaching. Unfortunately, this is having a huge impact in our country (and our world) as many seek to live as God would have them live. These groups and movements are competing for the hearts and minds of people with what we can call mainline Christian groups anchored in the truths of scripture.

Charismatic Movement

There are many established belief systems reflective of the many denominations and independent groups which each have their own perspectives on how to relate to God today. Those in the Pentecostal and Assemblies of God denominations, as well as those in the charismatic movement in general, have developed systems of beliefs which embellish and exaggerate the outward showing of spiritual power and present God as one who is constantly doing bold and miraculous things. This can allegedly include prophesying, healing, and speaking in tongues.

Word of Faith Movement

Then there are those in the Word of Faith movement which I understand grew out of the Pentecostal movement in the late twentieth century. This is a movement which is deceiving countless numbers of people, causing them to grasp for a way of life and unbiblical faith which promises God will do tremendous things in people's lives. This can be characterized as feel-good Christianity. This is also known as the wealth and prosperity gospel. Preachers and followers in this movement say things like the following:

- The more money you give, the more God will do for you.
- Serve God to get more from God.
- Jesus died so we can have an abundant life (meaning material abundance).
- Just name it and claim it.
- Speak things into existence.
- God will give you the desires of your heart.
- Sow a seed to reap a harvest.
- Your destiny is on the horizon.
- God called you to be greater.

The supporters of this movement believe that faith works like a mighty force. Through faith, we can obtain anything we want, including health, wealth, success, or whatever. To them, this force is only released through the spoken word. They believe as they speak the words of faith, power is then discharged to accomplish their desires.

What we find in this movement is the desire and effort to make God into what we want him to be. All this results in a distorted view of God. How can this be good?

The Word of Faith movement is said to be the fastest-growing "Christian" movement in the world. The question is, Why does something so obviously wrong have such a huge following? Why are so many people drawn to this teaching? (See appendix A for more information on the Word of Faith movement.)

Andy Stanley, in his book *Irresistible: Reclaiming the New that Jesus Unleashed for the World*, says "The prosperity gospel is rooted in God's covenant with Israel rather than the teaching of Jesus." They should limit the basis of their doctrine on the New Covenant scriptures, the New Testament.

Calvinism/Reformed Theology

Then there are those in the Calvinist or reformed church movement which seems to be growing in America these days. The Calvinist doctrine believes in their own version of predestination, does not accept that mankind has independent free will, asserts that God does not love everyone the same, and that Jesus came to earth to save only "the elect." They don't believe that Jesus came to offer salvation to everyone.

Their view of predestination teaches that God chooses who will go to heaven before anyone is born. This would mean that God has predestined some people to go to hell. Many Calvinists believe in an extreme notion of God's sovereignty, which means God is in control of everything that happens, including having his hand in all the evil, pain, and suffering in the world. The plan of salvation they present is not supported by the simple truths frequently stated in the scriptures. For instance, they believe salvation (regeneration) comes before having faith and repentance. There are many other features to their beliefs and doctrines which are troubling to many.

I wonder why the Calvinists build so much of their doctrine based on Old Testament scripture. I wish Calvinists would not do this and focus just on the New Testament to make their case for scriptural support for their positions. (See appendix B for reasons to be concerned about Calvinism.)

The Need for Clarity

It is all of these kinds of influences and more that complicate Christianity and make understanding the truth extra challenging. I believe there is a fair amount of confusion in the Christian community about what we can expect from God in a relationship with him. Again, this is not a surprise given the many views promoted by all kinds of faith traditions.

The bottom line is that we must come to an accurate view of who God is and how he interacts with humans. Do we have any say in determining the nature of God? No, we don't get to choose the kind of God we get to have here on earth. Do we have any say in determining the nature of mankind? No again. God has determined this when he created us. Would it be appropriate for us to wish that God would be different? What gives us the right to do that? Our challenge is to come to understand who God is as much as we can and to accept and embrace this reality.

We must be careful not to develop a distorted view of God. Unfortunately, this is easy to do. Of first importance is to get this right. Unfortunately, this is where there are tremendous differences of opinion. Many have it wrong. It's up to each individual to be very careful and seek to come to a full and accurate understanding as much as possible as to the nature and attributes of God, as well as the nature of the relationship God wants to have with mankind. This book offers much to think about regarding all this.

It is not the purpose of this book to take heretical and misguided groups on in a frontal confrontation. I'm not fully qualified to do this, nor is it appropriate for what I am offering in this book. I mention this as a word of caution and to acknowledge that it is out there prominently displayed for all to see. For many unsuspecting people, it may be difficult to even identify where this is happening. However, there are pastors, ministers, and biblical scholars who are addressing these issues and exposing this heresy. Some of this can be found in messages provided on YouTube.

How Important Is truth?

- Nothing else matters as much as the truth.
- If faith is built on false premises and realities, how good is that faith?
- If a relationship is built on false premises, how good is that relationship?
- We must be continual seekers of the truth.

The apostle Paul said in Philippians 4:8: "...whatever is true... whatever is right...think about such things."

Characteristics of Sound Teaching

The apostle Paul tells Titus, one of his converts and fellow missionaries, "You must teach what is in accord with sound doctrine" (Titus 2:1). Scattered throughout his letter to Titus are descriptions of sound doctrine. Sound doctrine is the only basis for putting obligations on mankind for what we are to believe and how we are to act. Sound doctrine is true, accurate, and consistent with the scriptures. It's the only doctrine that matters.

Unfortunately, as it was true in biblical times, many Christian groups and denominations today stray from sound doctrine. It is really up to each individual person to determine which churches align themselves the most with the teachings of the Bible. Sound teaching would be based on being able to cite book, chapter, and verse for all doctrine. Sound teaching takes into consideration what all of the Bible teaches. It does not only use verses which are cherry-picked to support a particular doctrine while leaving out other relevant passages of scripture. Sound preaching doesn't manipulate scripture to make a point by using paraphrased versions which stray from the true meaning of the Greek words used in the New Testament.

Dealing with Disagreements

It is one thing to have biblical disagreements with those who are in what we can call mainline Christian groups versus having disagreements with heretical groups.

I have realized that although I find issues I disagree on with Calvinists and others, this does not mean that scholarly people within those groups don't have a lot of helpful things to say about the scriptures in other areas. We should be careful not to simply and broadly dismiss the godly thoughts of others just because we may disagree with them on some issues. To do that would be like doing what an old adage says not to do: "Don't throw the baby out with the bathwater."

Having some disagreements with other Christians does not mean I have any sense of superiority over them. On the contrary, I know my place well. Anyone can disagree with the leaders of the faith (highly educated, experienced, and knowledgeable pastors, ministers, and teachers) on a variety of issues. These disagreements do not take away from the value and breadth of the good teaching they do have to share with us. We all need to approach issues of disagreement with discernment, humility, and grace. I maintain the greatest respect for all authentic Christian leaders, even those with whom I may disagree on some issues.

I say this because discussing the topics and issues in this book will inevitably lead to those who will agree and those who will disagree. Some of this will be evident in how the issues are addressed.

Pursuing a genuine personal relationship with God is, indeed, a tough and tricky topic to write about. Since there are so many differing ways Christian people speak of experiencing a personal relationship with God, it is unlikely that anyone can write on this topic and have agreement across the board. When people disagree, there is usually controversy.

Again, we all know that disagreements on things biblical and spiritual are many. One can likely find smart, highly educated, and respected people to defend almost any position or doctrine. In addition, anyone can choose to believe what they want, regardless of what others may say. We can then add the reality that most of us have our biases, whether they are conscious or unconscious. These are all reasons why many disagreements are difficult to resolve.

We also know many people hold strong opinions on things spiritual. There are many who come across very strong, assertive, and sometimes aggressive as they share their views. Even so, I would think we can all surmise that no one has it all figured out perfectly.

Some of My Struggles with Controversial Concepts

My journey has been one of struggle for many years in coming to terms with many concepts that just do not sit well with me. They do not fit with the experiences I've had personally, nor do they fit with the experiences I've seen in others. All of this is based on my worldview. Some of the concepts I've wrestled with include the following:

- Does God have a specific plan for our lives as many insist he does based on Jeremiah 29:11?
- Is God in control of everything? This is a phrase I hear stated all the time.
- We are to trust God, but for what? Everything? Or do we have to be more specific in what we say we trust God for?
- Do we have to listen for the voice of God, whatever that means?
- Do we apply scriptures in the Old Testament as if they have similar meaning for us today?
- Are we to let go and let God take care of things? Are we to just get out of the way and let God handle our problems and deal with the situations we are in?
- Are we to expect God to do miracles regularly?

Again, we know any time someone shares an idea with which others disagree, it can become controversial. Well, I expect to share some ideas with which some or many may not agree. I do this with a desire to share what I see as truth or what appears to me to be more likely to be true. If there are disagreements between well-meaning people, we need to be kind, courteous, self-disciplined, compassionate, understanding, and loving as we deal with them.

It Is Good to Be Challenged by Disagreements

I think we do well to remember that there is a sense in which it is good to be challenged. It is good to disagree in the proper way. When we have disagreements, they can serve as a motivation for us to study further and clarify our thinking.

No matter who would write this book, I believe it will most certainly be greeted by those who will agree and others who will disagree on items.

I don't share this material under the guise that I have it all figured out or claim to have a unique connection to God. None of us have the brainpower to comprehend everything. We can learn together. That is the beauty of sharing ideas together. We just don't have to have it all figured out.

You may have heard the concept that we all have our blind spots. There are things about me that I don't see and others see (and vice versa). There are also things I don't fully understand. I may not know I don't understand, but others who know more can see I don't fully understand. We don't know what we don't know.

Philip Yancey in his book *Reaching for the Invisible God: What Can We Expect to Find?* states, "Everyone who believes in God carries around a basic assumption of how God acts in relation with us." He goes on to say, "Yet the more personal conception of God we have, the more unnerving are the questions about him. Shouldn't a loving God intervene more often on our behalf? And how can we trust a God we can never confidently count on to come to our aid."

Philip's quote above identifies some of the challenges we have in our relationship with God. This book is an attempt to explore many questions which inevitably arise for those seeking a deeper relationship with God. These questions will be posed, and answers to them will be pursued.

We need to remember that to believe in God is one thing. To know perfectly and comprehensively how God works in our world is another. We'll be relating to both of these issues in this book. Read on!

Let Us Think Deeper about a Relationship with God

When we become Christians, we receive the Holy Spirit and over time come to know God better because of this. We also interact with Christian people. We can be encouraged and challenged by their faith and the comments they make about their relationship with God.

As we build a relationship with God, we need to constantly seek to know God more and more through the Bible. We need to dig deeper looking for truth and learn to stand on faith. We need enough knowledge that enables us to trust God based on our understanding of who he is and what he does based on the Bible. We need to know what we can understand about him from his characteristics and attributes and from how we experience him interacting with us personally.

Again, there are some who believe mistakenly about how God operates in our lives. Some are misguided on what is true doctrine.

A relationship with God may likely be characterized on the one hand by mystery, uncertainty, challenges, doubts, and unconventional ways. On the other hand, a relationship with God can also be characterized as aligning with the truth, eternal principles, enduring values, and a being whose traits are unchanging and logical.

I share this material to help us think more deeply about all of these subjects. This book is ideal for those who don't currently have a relationship with God but are searching to understand what the Christian life is about. It applies well to the new Christian who wonders about the same issues. It can be helpful for those who have been Christians for some time and want to have information regarding differing viewpoints on topics that are challenging to understand.

As you read this book, keep in mind the many differing topics which will be addressed. Read the table of contents. It is likely that one will want more discussed under one particular chapter when in actuality it will be addressed at a later time under another chapter.

Let's Get Started!

So with this as our backdrop, let's begin our study on how to have a genuine personal relationship with God.

CHAPTER 2

❧

Relationships Matter with Others and with God

There is only one happiness in this life, to love and be loved.
—George Sand

Relationships matter immensely. They are an instrumental part of life. They help shape us. It is in relationships where our social, emotional, and spiritual needs are met. As we know, we have relationships in all significant areas of our lives, such as family relationships, parent-child relationships, sibling relationships, friendship relationships, coworker relationships, church family relationships, sports teams, school, neighborhood, recreational, business, career, governmental, etc.

Strong and vibrant relationships are a vital component of one's health and well-being. There is compelling evidence that strong relationships contribute to a long, healthy, and happy life. Conversely, the health risks from being alone or isolated in one's life are comparable to the risks associated with cigarette smoking, blood pressure, and obesity. Research shows that healthy relationships can help you live longer, deal with stress, and be physically healthier.

Relationships are imperative for many different reasons, such as increasing our emotional well-being, creating stability, learning how to be a good friend or mate, having someone to count on and trust in times of need, someone to vent to when we face challenges, and friends who help take away loneliness and make us feel included.

Each of our relationships elicits different responses within us which help us to grow and learn more about ourselves. Relationships oftentimes are the glue that holds us together during stressful situations and when we face life's difficulties. Without relationships, we would have a deadened spirit and a lack of connection to our true selves.

Some Relationships Are Not Easy

So yes, we know that all the significant relationships we have in life are impactful to us in some way. Some of the close relationships we have, such as family and marital relationships, determine much about who we are and what we become.

Hopefully, most of the relationships we've had in our lives have been positive, helpful, encouraging, and healthy. However, we know that most of us have had relationships which were very hard, hurtful, and discouraging.

Unfortunately for some, they began their journey in life in a highly dysfunctional family with unhealthy relationships. This presents many extra challenges for them, which can take many years to a lifetime to overcome.

Given the multitude of relationships we have over the years, no one can escape from having experienced difficult ones which have caused us to struggle in order to cope with their impact. As strange as this may sound, this is often a good experience for us even though it was hard because we grow and mature through these experiences (see Romans 5:1–5 and James 1:2–4). We learn how to cope with life in general because of both the positive and challenging experiences we've had.

All of this underscores that human beings in many ways are defined by their relationships more than anything else.

J. Paul Getty, at the time perhaps the richest man in the world, said, "I hate and regret the failure of my marriages. I would gladly give all my millions for just one lasting marital success." He possessed the money to live whatever lifestyle gave him the most satisfaction, but at the end of his life, he came to realize that a good, enduring marriage meant more to him than riches. He died feeling like a failure at what life is really all about—having meaningful relationships, especially the ones that are the closest.

The company we keep is one of the most telling indicators of who we truly are. However, when all is said and done, the only relationship in life that deals with meaning, morality, and destiny and defines who we are for eternity is our relationship with God.

The Importance of a Relationship with God

Having a personal relationship with God is considered incredibly important in all Christian circles and faith traditions. Some say that Christianity is not a religion but a relationship with God.

In this book, I'm going to refer to this relationship with the phrase "a relationship with God," as a relationship with Jesus being also inferred and included in that phrase.

"A relationship with God" is one of the most frequently uttered phrases used by Christians to encourage spiritual growth. The need for this relationship is mentioned regularly to non-Christians in the process of evangelism as establishing a relationship with God begins with being born again. Based on its broad meaning, many would say the phrase "a relationship with God" captures the very heart of what it means to be a Christian.

Yes, relationships define us. We need to make sure the relationship which defines us best is the one we have with God. When that's true, every other relationship will be blessed by God's presence. If God is a part of our lives, if we are keeping company with God, then he's also a part of our marriage, our friendships, our random encounters with strangers, and every other relationship the world uses to define us. When God is a part of who we are, the world learns a little more about who he is.

Given all of this, it is interesting to note that the phrase "a personal relationship with God" is not found anywhere in the scriptures. However, this does not nullify its relevance. This phrase is used to describe in human terms the broad nature of how we respond and interact to the God of the Bible. This phrase is derived from how the scriptures speak about who God is, what God has done, and what response God wants from people.

As we look at this deeper, and as we've clearly mentioned earlier, we will find there are varying perspectives among Christians as to how a personal relationship with God works. It's a concept which seems to be understood differently between well-meaning people.

We know there is no formula in the scriptures for how this relationship is to play out. Therefore, there is no basis to say that anyone has this figured out perfectly. There is also no basis to say that one person's relationship with God will look the same as others. We need to be careful about comparing ourselves to others and judging others whose relationship with God looks different or doesn't seem to match up with our own.

While seeking a deeper relationship with God, our capacity to understand him will expand. We will find this to be a worthy pursuit which can bring tremendous blessings and insight. As our knowledge of God increases, so will our desire to keep his commandments and our ability to see ourselves through his eyes.

We would do well to continuously be aware of the eternal context in which our current circumstances are playing out. We would also do well to recognize that through being made in God's image, the seed of divinity is within each of us.

Questions about a Personal Relationship with God

All of this causes us to acknowledge there are many questions when it comes to truly understanding the nature of the relationship we should have with God. Posing questions and seeking answers to questions is a great way to explore deeper what a relationship with God entails. The following are some questions which have come to my mind.

1. Whose responsibility is it to initiate and pursue a relationship with God?

2. Is there a universal reason why people can be attracted to a relationship with God?
3. Does God want to have a personal relationship with people? How do we know?
4. Who determines what this relationship is to look like and the terms of this relationship?
5. What does it mean to have an intimate relationship with God?
6. Is everyone to have the same kind of relationship with God, or do different people have different relationships with God?
7. How is the relationship with God similar and dissimilar to relationships we have with other people?
8. Is it normal and acceptable if one's relationship with God fluctuates over time? Should we expect and insist that it be constant and ever growing instead?

Building a strong relationship with God is said to be the highest priority of life. However, there are many secular, non-spiritual people who don't see a need for this and won't agree with that statement.

There are some non-Christian people who are searching for the truth. They may have a lot of questions and may be open to consider establishing a relationship with God. However, other basic questions about God and faith must first be addressed to their satisfaction. This is also what this book is designed to offer.

Scriptures with Inferences to a Relationship with God

As Christians, we believe the Bible is God's inspired word and provides what we need to guide us through life's journey. However, we need to understand the nature of scriptures and a general sense of what we can expect to find in them.

As we consider the topic of how to have a personal relationship with God, we can question whether there are scriptures which clearly and explicitly make the case about how God wants to be in a relationship with us and also describe the nature of this relationship.

Will we find scriptures like this? As much as many of us would love this to be the case, it just isn't so. Therefore, we are left with finding scriptures which make inferences to all of this.

Even so, we should not be discouraged or disappointed about this. One reason is because of what we understand about the nature and purpose of the scriptures.

We should not look to the Bible to be a policy and procedures manual for how the Christian movement should function. We won't find this. We also will not find sections of scriptures providing a thesis, essay, exposé, or specific articles which address and explain important doctrinal or ethical issues of our day.

Gordon Fee and Douglas Stewart in their book *How to Read the Bible Book by Book: a Guided Tour* start our stressing that the challenge in reading the Bible is to be aware of how each book fits into the larger story. They say in the opening chapter:

> First, let's be clear: The Bible is not merely some divine guidebook nor is it a source of propositions to be believed or a long list of commands to be obeyed. True, one does receive plenty of guidance from it, and it does indeed contain plenty of true propositions and divine directives. But the Bible is infinitely more than that. Here we have the greatest narrative of all—God's own story. That is, it does not purport to be just one more story of humankind's search for God. No, this is God's story, the account of his search for us, a story essentially told in four chapters: Creation, Fall, Redemption and Consummation (Fulfillment, Completion).

What I'd like to do now is to look at a smattering of scriptures which bear upon our relationship with God and enlighten us to how God views this dynamic. I've identified sixteen passages, but we all know there are many others.

Ephesians 2:10

"For we are his workmanship, *created in Christ Jesus for good works*, which God prepared beforehand, that we should walk in them."

The point: We exist to do good works which will glorify God which indicates what God wants from us.

Colossians 1:16

"For by him all things were created, in heaven and on earth, visible and invisible, whether thrones or dominions or rulers or authorities—all things were *created through him and for him*."

The point: We exist for God's pleasure.

Romans 5:8

"But God shows his love for us in that while we were still sinners, *Christ died for us*."

The point: Christ dying for us indicates how valuable we are to God and how much he cares about us.

Matthew 5:16

"In the same way, let your light shine before others so that they may see your good works and *give glory to your Father who is in heaven*."

The point: Giving glory to God keeps God important to us. It indicates a priority of our lives.

1 Corinthians 1:9

"God is faithful, by whom *you were called into the fellowship* of his Son, Jesus Christ our Lord."

The point: Having fellowship with Jesus indicates a friendly relationship.

Matthew 22:37–39

"Jesus replied: **'Love the Lord your God with all your heart and with all your soul and with all your mind.'** This is the first and greatest commandment. And the second is like it: 'Love your neighbor as yourself.'"

The point: This relates to a deep relationship with God for which we give our all in pursuing it.

1 Corinthians 10:31

"So, whether you eat or drink, or whatever you do, *do all to the glory of God.*"

The point: God must be on our minds a lot, and we hold him always in the highest esteem.

John 15:11

"These things I have spoken to you, that *my joy may be in you*, and that your joy may be full."

The point: The relationship is a positive and happy relationship.

1 John 4:8

"Anyone who does not love does not know God, because *God is love.*"

The point: To know God is to love God.

John 4:24

"God is spirit, and those who worship him must *worship in spirit and truth.*"

The point: God is so great that we are to worship him.

2 Corinthians 13:14

"The *grace* of the Lord Jesus Christ and the *love of God* and the *fellowship of the Holy Spirit* be with you all."

The point: The Holy Trinity is united in their love and desire for a relationship with us.

John 14:6

"Jesus said to him, 'I am the way, and the truth, and the life. *No one comes to the Father except through me.*'"

The point: Jesus is incredibly important in our lives and provides us access to God.

Matthew 6:33

"But *seek first the kingdom of God* and his righteousness, and all these things will be added to you."

The point: A relationship with God should be our number one priority in life.

2 Peter 3:9

"The Lord is not slow to fulfill his promise as some count slowness, but *is patient* toward you, *not wishing that any should perish*, but that all should reach repentance."

The point: How great it is that God loves us this much. We should all be eager to respond.

John 14:3

"And if I go and prepare a place for you, I will come again and will take you to myself, *that where I am you may be also.*"

The point: Jesus wants us to be with him for eternity.

John 6:40

"For my Father's will is that everyone who looks to the Son and believes in him shall have eternal life, and I will raise him up at the last day."

The point: What more can we want? We have an eternal relationship with God.

Man Was Created to Be in a Relationship with God

What is of tremendous importance and encouragement is to consider the question, "Why did God decide to create mankind?" What was his motivation?

We know we can only come to an opinion on any of this from the Bible, which provides God's revelation to mankind. God reveals so much about himself in the scriptures. Without the scriptures, there is no way anyone could find any answers to these questions.

Genesis 1 tells us we are the only creatures made in God's image. We can also surmise that since God made us in his image, this provides the means from which God is able to relate to us in the best way possible. The way God made us seems a perfect setup for him having a relationship with us. We can also infer from Genesis 1 that we are the only created beings on earth fit for a relationship with God. We're the only creation Jesus was willing to die for.

Being made in God's image also would seem to validate that God gave mankind free will as this is the only basis for mankind to authentically relate to God. Otherwise, mankind would just be puppets manipulated by God.

We learn from the scriptures that God is love (1 John 4:8), and there are many places throughout all of scripture revealing his love. We also know from the new covenant scriptures that the most important and the greatest commandment given to man is to love God with all of our being (Matt. 22:37–38). As we understand what love is and does, it requires a meaningful relationship in which it can be expressed. For love to be the most meaningful, it needs to be reciprocal in nature.

All of this appears to me to be the obvious reason why God created us. The most likely scenario is that God made a plan to be in a meaningful relationship with mankind from the very beginning. It appears that having a relationship with mankind was the whole purpose of creating all that was created.

When God's Relationship with Mankind Started

In the beginning, man enjoyed full fellowship with God. With Adam and Eve disobeying God in the garden, this changed things. All of mankind has since been impacted by them. God knew this would happen, so he implemented his plan for creation to fulfill his intended purpose. This plan was developed before the foundations of the world were in place.

Ephesians 1:3–4:

> Praise be to the God and Father of our Lord Jesus Christ, who has blessed us in the heavenly realms with every spiritual blessing in Christ. For he chose us in him before the creation of the world to be holy and blameless in his sight.

Titus 1:2:

> In the hope of eternal life, which God, who does not lie, promised before the beginning of time.

We know that God began with a special relationship with the Jewish people. However, when God originally called Israel, he didn't call Israel to be the end and the final goal of his purpose of salvation. He called them to be the means of salvation for the whole world. God has always determined he would save people from every tongue, tribe, and nation in the world.

We see this when God set up his agreement with Abraham in Genesis 12:1–3:

> [1] The LORD had said to Abram, "Go from your country, your people and your father's household to the land I will show you.
>
> [2] "I will make you into a great nation, and I will bless you;
>
> I will make your name great, and you will be a blessing.
>
> [3] I will bless those who bless you, and whoever curses you I will curse; and all peoples on earth will be blessed through you.

This was repeated in Genesis 22:18, 26:4, and 28:14, so it is not an obscure truth. It was well-known.

The problem with this plan is that the Jewish people would not sustain their belief in God and be obedient to the covenant they had with God. They failed in their charge to be the ones to bring salvation to the world.

When Jesus was born, we know the Jews had been waiting for their Messiah for centuries. They had been through a lot of hardships and harsh treatment over the centuries. They had a succession of conquerors. They had been mistreated throughout their history. This was because they were continually under the judgment of God for their unbelief and apostasy, which had gone on for generations.

Because the Jews had experienced hostility from the nations around them, they had grown to dislike the people around them very much. This hostility caused them to turn inward and become very Israel-centric. Because of this, they had nothing but disdain for the nations around them. If they traveled out of Israel and came back, they shook the Gentile dust off their garments and shoes. They couldn't eat with Gentile utensils. They couldn't enter a Gentile home. All of this had developed into a way to insulate themselves from the nations around them.

The Jewish people saw God as the God of Israel. They did not see themselves as a nation to be missionaries to the world even though there were individual Jews who reached out and brought Gentiles into belief in the one true God.

So due to their difficult times with other nations, the Jews had no interest in going beyond themselves. To them, they were God's people, and the blessings stopped with them.

We see this in their attitudes toward the Samaritans. They hated them for many reasons and called them half-breeds in a derogatory way, meaning part Jew and part Gentile.

The Israelites rejected God over and over in the Old Testament. In *2 Chronicles 36:16*, we read, "But they mocked God's messengers, despised his words and scoffed at his prophets until the wrath of the LORD was aroused against his people and there was no remedy."

God Transitions to Using Gentiles for His Mission Work

Because of all of this, God had to carve out a new channel. He transitioned away from the Jewish nation to using the Gentiles to reach the world for Christ.

The apostle Paul relates to this in several passages of his writings. One is in Galatians 3:6–9:

> [6] So also Abraham "believed God, and it was credited to him as righteousness."
>
> [7] Understand, then, that those who have faith are children of Abraham. [8] Scripture foresaw that God would justify the Gentiles by faith, and announced the gospel in advance to Abraham: "All nations will be blessed through you." [9] So those who rely on faith are blessed along with Abraham, the man of faith.

God knew that Israel would fail him. He would turn to the Gentiles. This is what the apostle Paul says in *Romans 9:23–25*:

> [23] What if he did this to make the riches of his glory known to the objects of his mercy, whom he prepared in advance for glory—[24] even us, whom he also called, not only from the Jews but also from the Gentiles? [25] As he says in Hosea:
>
> "I will call them 'my people' who are not my people; and I will call her 'my loved one' who is not my loved one."

We know that the apostle Peter as well as other Jewish Christians back then struggled with accepting their Gentile brothers and sisters as co-equals in the faith. God came to Peter in a vision in Acts 10 to deal with this.

And then later in that passage, Peter says the following:

> [34] Then Peter began to speak: "I now realize how true it is that God does not show favoritism [35] but accepts from every nation the one who fears him and does what is right. (Acts 10:34–35)

Later in Acts, the apostle Paul speaks to this.

> [44] On the next Sabbath almost the whole city gathered to hear the word of the Lord. [45] When the Jews saw the crowds, they were filled with jealousy. They began to contradict what Paul was saying and heaped abuse on him.
>
> [46] Then Paul and Barnabas answered them boldly: "We had to speak the word of God to you first. Since you reject it and do not consider yourselves worthy of eternal life, we now turn to

the Gentiles. [47] For this is what the Lord has commanded us:

"'I have made you a light for the Gentiles, that you may bring salvation to the ends of the earth.'"

[48] When the Gentiles heard this, they were glad and honored the word of the Lord; and all who were appointed for eternal life believed. (Acts 13:44–48)

So from the very beginning, from Creation, God had in mind a plan to be in relationship with all of mankind. It began with the Jewish nation and was transitioned to involve the Gentiles (all non-Jewish people).

CHAPTER 3

God's Covenant Relationships

*The biblical covenants form the unifying thread of God's
relationship with mankind and His saving
action through Scripture.*

The covenants are crucial because they are the backbone of the storyline of the Bible. The Bible isn't a random collection of laws, moral principles, and stories. It is a story of redemption and a story of God's kingdom. And the story unfolds and advances through the covenants God made with his people.

If we don't understand the covenants, we will not understand the Bible because we won't understand how the story fits together. The best way to see this is by quickly reviewing the covenants in the scriptures.

As we noticed in the last chapter, part of God's plan for mankind involved choosing the Jewish people with whom he would establish a special one-of-a-kind relationship...a covenant relationship with just them for a time.

The word in Hebrew for covenant is *Berith* (pronounced "Berreeth"), which simply means "a covenant." The Greek word for covenant is *Diathēke (*pronounced dee-ath-ay'-kay) and means "a set agreement having complete terms determined by the initiating party, which also are fully affirmed by the ones entering the agreement."

At its most basic level, a covenant is an oath-bound relationship between two or more parties. In a covenant with God, there are no bargaining, bartering, or contract negotiations regarding the terms of the covenant. God alone dictates the terms.

No other nation in the world would have this relationship with God in Old Testament times. The goal of all divine-to-human covenants is summed up in the words found throughout the Bible: "I will be your God and you will be my people, and I will dwell among you" (Exod. 6:7, 29:45; Ezek. 11:20; 2 Cor. 6:16; Rev. 21:3).

The biblical covenants form the unifying thread of God's saving action throughout scripture, beginning explicitly with Noah and reaching fulfillment with the dawn of the new covenant with the death, burial, and resurrection of Jesus Christ.

The Covenant with Noah

While God announces his covenant with Noah and all creation prior to the flood (Gen. 6:18), he establishes it after the deluge subsides (Gen. 8:20–9:17). The first mention of this covenant simply highlights God's plan to preserve Noah and the others in the ark (Gen. 6:18). God's covenant with Noah reaffirms his original intent when he created the earth which the flood had "disrupted." So he solemnly promises that a suspension of the natural order will never again interrupt the fulfillment of humanity's mandate at creation (Gen 1:26–30; 9:1–7).

The Covenant with Abraham

The next covenant is the one God made with Abraham as recorded in Genesis 12:1–3. The essence of this divine promise is that God would bless Abraham in two ways: (1) God would make him into a great nation and so make his name great, and (2) through him God would bless all people on the earth.

The Covenant with Israel (the Mosaic Covenant)

God established his covenant with Moses just after a significant development anticipated in Genesis 15 had taken place: the emancipation of Abraham's descendants from oppression in a foreign land (Gen. 15:13–14; Exod. 19:4–6; 20:2). The focus at Sinai is less on what Abraham's descendants must do in order to inherit the land and more on how they must conduct themselves within the land as the unique nation that God intended them to be (Exod. 19:5–6). In order to be God's "treasured possession," "kingdom of priests," and "holy nation," Israel must keep God's covenant by submitting to its requirements.

The Covenant (Promise) with David

The covenant God made with David is really a promise from God which was conveyed to David by Nathan, the prophet, which basically continues the trajectory of both the covenants with Abraham and Moses (2 Sam. 7:8–11, 23–26).

The promise to David identifies more precisely the lineage of the "offspring" who will mediate international blessing: He will be a royal descendant of Abraham through David.

The New Covenant

Because of the persistent failure of the Israelites to live according to God's covenant requirements, consequences were necessary. This led to punishment for both the nation of Israel and its monarchy, culminating in judgment: the destroyed temple and Babylonian exile. The exile of the nation and the demise of the monarchy had to be overcome for God's creation plan to be realized. Covenant history thus continued through the prospect of a "new covenant."

The New Testament (covenant) declares that all God's covenant promises are realized in and through Jesus, the long-awaited royal offspring of David.

According to the New Testament gospels and letters, the new covenant was ratified through the sacrificial death of Jesus on the cross. Accordingly, the New Testament emphasizes the forgiveness of sins and reconciliation back to God, something only fully attainable under the new covenant. With the New Covenant, the Old Covenants are fulfilled. How mankind relates to God has been drastically changed.

Thus, according to both Paul and the writer of Hebrews, the new covenant is far superior to the old. Jesus came to fulfill the Old Covenant and begin the New Covenant. In 2 Corinthians 3:1–18, Paul explicitly contrasts the New and the Old covenants, highlighting the vast inferiority of the old compared with the surpassing glory and permanence of the new.

CHAPTER 4

Does God Exist? Compelling Reasons to Believe

And without faith it is impossible to please God, because
anyone who comes to him must believe that he exists
and that he rewards those who earnestly seek him.

—Hebrews 11:6

All Need to Build a Relationship with God

As we've seen in the previous chapter, an opportunity to have a relationship with God in the New Covenant is for all of mankind. This is truly amazing and compelling. Just think about this for a moment: the God of the universe, our Creator and Lord, the One who is omnipotent, omniscient, omnipresent, etc., wanting to know us personally and be in a meaningful relationship with us. Why would anyone want to reject this opportunity?

God has done the initiating. He is knocking on the door of our lives. It is now up to each one of us to respond individually. God in his love has given mankind the blessing of free will from which we can decide on our own if we want a relationship with him. He wants us to love him back. However, he won't force us to if we don't want to.

We all know there are people who choose not to pay much attention to God and things spiritual. There are those who don't see any value to having God in their lives. Then there are people who go as far as to say they are atheists. Atheists are those who have come to the conclusion in their minds that God does not even exist. How they can come to this conclusion begs many questions. Regardless, they are free to think and say what they want.

Yes, for many, establishing a relationship with God does not come easily. This is even true for those who are highly motivated to have a quality relationship with God. There are many reasons why it is difficult to have a relationship with God. It often takes persistence and much effort to work through the obstacles to coming to faith. This has been true since the days Jesus was walking on the earth.

In the gospel of John, we see how the Jewish people Jesus was teaching were having a hard time accepting what he was saying. There were many who had come to believe, and then there were many who began believing and then struggled with the words of Jesus. Many then turned their backs on him. This is recorded in John 6:60–66. And then Jesus asks his disciples an important question in verses 67–69:

> 67 "You do not want to leave too, do you?" Jesus asked the Twelve.
> 68 Simon Peter answered him, "Lord, to whom shall we go? You have the words of eternal life. 69 We have come to believe and to know that you are the Holy One of God."

Jesus alone is the one who has the words of eternal life. This is what He offers everyone who will believe.

We can ask, why do some people who've had faith decide to give up on their faith? As the disciples asked, where else can anyone go for finding God and finding the truth?

Some people have doubts that keep them from accepting Jesus. I believe many of these doubts persist because they are not used as motivation to investigate and study deeper to find the truth.

In reality we all have doubts at times. Philip Yancey in his book *Reaching for the Invisible God: God: What Can We Expect to Find?* says, "Doubt always exists with faith, for in the presence of certainty, who would need faith at all? We will always see too much to deny and too little to be sure."

Compelling Reasons Start with God's Existence

God has given all people the choice of whether to have a relationship with him or not. A relationship with God first begins with each of us coming to a decision on whether to believe that God does indeed exist and is worthy of us committing our lives to and giving him our complete love and devotion. Let's explore this.

One of the books I found to be very interesting and compelling is *I Don't Have Enough Faith to Be an Atheist* by Norman Geisler and Frank Turek. Both of these authors have doctorate degrees and have done extensive research and study in the topic of Christian apologetics. Christian apologetics is the branch of Christian theology which seeks to defend the faith and provide compelling evidence that supports the message of Christianity. It is a great help to those who are searching for reasons to believe in God.

This book begins by Geisler and Turek identifying what they believe are the five most consequential questions in life. The following is their list.

1. Origin—where did we come from?
2. Identity—who are we?
3. Meaning—why are we here?
4. Morality—how should we live?
5. Destiny—where are we going?

I'm going to briefly comment on each of these questions.

Origins

To begin, we are challenged to explain our origins. How did the heavens (space and the universe) and earth begin? The Bible is clear on this in the first verse in the first chapter of Genesis. God created the heavens and the earth.

The first chapter of Genesis describes in general terms all that God created, including human beings. However, Genesis chapter one does not get into specifics about how God created everything. This is to be expected as it is consistent with how the scriptures address scientific issues like this.

As we consider the idea of origins, we come face-to-face with the long-term debate about whether the heavens and earth were created by someone (God) or if they were created by natural causes (no one). Given all the study and research on the question of origins, there is still no proof, just theories. Therefore, one's position either way is a matter of faith.

In the literature on Christian apologetics we can find many discussions about origins. Many pose the question, "If there is no God, why is there something rather than nothing?" Based on what is known about the evidence, two primary options stand out: (1) either no one created something out of nothing or (2) someone created something out of nothing. Christian apologetics reveals there is a good amount of reasonable evidence to believe God is the one who created the heavens and the earth.

Given all the evidence, I understand there are many atheistic or unbelieving scientists who are now changing their minds and accepting there is a God or at least a higher power. According to a Pew Research Center survey done in 2009, just over half of scientists (51 percent) believe in some form of deity or higher power. Specifically, 33 percent of scientists say they believe in God while 18 percent believe in a universal spirit or higher power.

President Barack Obama nominated Christian geneticist Dr. Francis Collins to head the National Institutes of Health in 2009. By this time, Dr. Collins had written a book entitled *The Language of Love: A Scientist Presents Evidence for Belief.* Read this if you would like more information on this topic. There is an article involving Dr. Collins with the title *Evidence for Belief: An interview with Francis Collins*. This can be found at the following Pew Center Research link: https://www.pewforum.org/2008/04/17/the-evidence-for-belief-an-interview-with-francis-collins/.

Science does show evidence for God in the world he created. It points vividly to a designer. Consider the following as a glimpse into this evidence.

- *Consider the earth.* Its size is perfect and corresponds to enabling gravity. Earth is the right distance to the sun, and the rotation of earth around the sun at the speed of nearly 67,000 mph is perfect. The earth's rotation on its axis allows the entire surface of the earth to be properly warmed and cooled every day. The earth and the universe operate by uniform laws of nature.
- *Consider water.* Water is colorless and without taste. No living organism can survive without water. It is uniquely suited to life. Water is a universal solvent. Water is chemically neutral. Water freezes from the top down and floats, so fish can live in the water. We know 97 percent of the earth's water is in the oceans. On earth, there is a system designed which removes salt from the water throughout the globe.
- *Consider the human brain.* It is truly amazing. The human brain processes more than a million messages a second.
- *Consider the eye.* It is also amazing. It can distinguish among 7 million colors. It has automatic focusing and handles an astonishing 1.6 million messages.

As we all can imagine, the list of all the amazing items which reveal design would be very long. How many items would it take to be persuasive to you? Probability statistics of creation happening by mere chance would be extremely low, in fact, miniscule.

Identity

A case can be made for the tremendous impact God can have on one's identity. I address this more fully in the chapter entitled "Created in God's Image for a Special Relationship," as well as elsewhere in this book. This chapter focuses on the value of human life based upon the notion that we are all made in God's image. This reality emboldens our identity with purpose and God-given worth.

Meaning in Life

The question about why we are here relates both to meaning and purpose. It's obviously true that all people have struggled with the idea of what is the purpose of life. I wonder where most people look to find the answer to this question.

I propose it is God alone who can give people a sense of purpose. For those who have no belief in God, who or what can give them purpose in life? I can only surmise they have no sense of objective purpose. This is because purpose relates to design and authority. God is the only one who has the authority over all people to give purpose. The only one qualified to assign purpose and meaning to life is the creator—the one who designed us.

Another way to look at this is to question what gives life its significance. I think one of the most profound ways to understand significance is found in death. If there is no life after death, the purpose of life is extremely limited. In many ways, death is what gives life its significance. What comes after our lives on earth makes a big impact upon how we choose to live our lives on earth.

Without God, there is no ultimate purpose of life. Without God, life is pointless and meaningless. For Christians, we are all concerned about living our lives with purpose and in accordance with God's will. For more information on this, see the chapter "Does God Have a Specific Plan for our Lives" under the heading "God's Plan for Everyone."

Morality

When we think of morality, we must think of what is right and wrong and what is good and bad. For something to be defined as right and wrong or good and bad, there must be an all-encompassing moral standard which obligates all of us to follow it. For such a standard to exist, there must be someone who has the authority to establish and impose such a standard on all of mankind. Who can this be but God? God is our ultimate moral lawgiver. He qualifies for this as being our Creator and God.

We know secularly governed societies like the United States establish ways to govern themselves, which entails the right to establish laws and set consequences for breaking laws. This task is assigned to the legislatures—including federal, state, and local legislatures. They are responsible for establishing laws, and then assigning law enforcement authorities to enforce the laws. However, for state laws, these are only applicable and enforceable in the state in which one lives. For federal laws, these are only enforceable in our country.

Without God, any standards for right and wrong would have to be established by humans. However, how can a moral standard which obligates all peoples on earth to follow it be determined by a person or a group of people? What makes what one person thinks better and more compelling than another? Philosophically speaking, without God, any moral standard established by man has equal status and authority. No one's view has any more authority than anyone else's. So, without God, atheists have no basis to assert moral obligations.

Destiny

The idea of destiny is short and simple. What is to become of us after death? For Christians, our goal and destiny is to be in heaven with God for eternity. We sacrifice much on earth for the sake of Christ and to glorify God. We do this because we love God and find meaning and purpose in living life this way. We know the good works we do are not to earn our way to heaven. They flow from our new nature as Christians. Salvation is by God's grace through what

Jesus did on the cross. It's a free gift to those who are genuine in their faith and sincere in their relationship with God.

On the other hand, what is to become of those who do not believe in God? An atheistic belief system posits that life on earth is all there is. What is a person's destiny after life then? According to this belief system, there is no continued life after death. Where is the hope and joy in this destination? There is none. This destination only has sadness and regret.

For Christians, heaven is depicted as a beautiful place where there is joy, praise, worship, interactions, and no more pain and suffering. Heaven is for eternity. Why would anyone want to choose to reject God and forfeit the promise of a home in heaven like this?

In the Christian worldview, there is life after death for everyone. Some will go to heaven; and others, by their own choice, will be separated from God in what the Bible calls hell. I know of only these two destinations. As mortal created beings, we don't get to change how God has set things up.

Conclusion

Every human being is faced with answering the five most consequential questions in life:

1. Origin—where did we come from?
2. Identity—who are we?
3. Meaning—why are we here?
4. Morality—how should we live?
5. Destiny—where are we going?

As we know, many of our religious beliefs can be investigated, and their plausibility analyzed. Since all conclusions about these claims are based on probability rather than absolute certainty, they all, including atheistic claims, require some amount of faith. Based on the evidence I see, it takes a lot more faith to be a non-Christian than it does to be a Christian.

As I mention throughout this book, we all should put a premium on searching for the truth. There is no virtue or benefit for living life according to false beliefs.

Insights from Trip to Israel

My wife and I took a sightseeing trip to Israel in September of 2019. I came away with two notable insights from that trip (in addition to the many interesting places we saw).

One insight had to do with the historicity of Jesus. Many rightfully question whether Jesus did indeed walk the earth. Jesus Christ has been called many things by many people—including a great man, a great teacher, and a great prophet. From what I understand, unbiased sources would assert there is no legitimate scholar today who denies that Jesus is a historical figure who walked on this earth about two thousand years ago, that he did remarkable wonders and acts of charity, and that he died a horrible death on a Roman cross just outside Jerusalem. The evidence for Jesus walking the earth is in the history books and in the scriptures. I believe it is a reality everyone must deal with as they consider the truth of Jesus. This is just another confirmation that the Bible is indeed a real book about real people doing real things in real places.

So therefore, I believe we must make a choice between two options: either Jesus was who he said he was (the Messiah, our Savior, equal with God, the Christ, Lord of all, etc.) or he was delusional, a deceiver, a lunatic, and an imposter who was not the person he claimed to be. If this is the case, he would be the worst of all liars. These are the options we have as we deal with the reality that Jesus was indeed on the earth. This is the choice we will be held accountable to when we meet our maker face-to-face.

Another insight was how the timing was perfect for the coming of Jesus to the earth. The scriptures mention that Jesus came at the right time (Eph. 1:7–10, Rom. 6:6–8, and Gal. 4:4). There are many reasons for why this was the right timing. One has to do with the conditions of society back then, giving Jesus the ability to fulfill all prophesies mentioned about him in the Old Testament. This was possible only because he came to earth when he did. Coming today would not have worked out for this to occur! For instance, it was prophesied that Jesus would enter Jerusalem riding on a donkey (Zech. 9:9). Now could that happen today? No! Also, today the city of Bethlehem is controlled by the Palestinians, and Jewish people are not even welcome there. Jewish people cannot safely go there right now. It's certainly not an environment for the birth of Jesus.

Insights from Those Who Struggle with Faith

Bertrand Russell, a famous atheist, was asked what he would say if it turned out that he was wrong and God did exist. He said, "God, you gave us insufficient evidence." But you know, no one can truly say this unless they have explored all the evidence there is. Today, there is a lot more of this evidence than ever before. It's not hard to find.

It seems that many people just don't seem interested in spiritual matters, not necessarily because they don't believe but that they don't see the importance of an active faith.

We also know there are some people who don't believe simply because they are unwilling or don't want to make changes that belief entails. If you are one of these people, think about this. What if God told you that since you are not serious about him, he is not going to offer salvation to you? He rescinds the offer. How would you feel? Are you willing to bet your life on the belief that God does not exist? If not, everyone owes it to themselves to search for the truth.

We hear regularly about those who were Christians who have given up on their faith. When they list their reasons for this, it often relates to unanswered questions they have about a variety of issues. However, we all have questions. We must not forget that there are also, concurrently, many areas for which we don't have questions and have a lot of knowledge and evidence.

In reality, there are tons of reasons and evidence for faith which can't be dismissed easily. Many of the questions we have can be answered given time and effort. We need to find the right resources (experts and scholars) for the answers we seek and not just base conclusions on unsatisfactory answers given from those we know but who often don't give the best answers. We owe it to ourselves to put in the time and effort to get full and accurate answers.

One of the reasons why people decide to give up on their faith could be an unwillingness to believe. Insincere questions can be a good smoke screen to hide this fact.

Many of the questions skeptics ask can relate to topics for which we may not have a ready answer. That is okay! We don't have to respond right away with an answer. They can give us time to find an answer. Just because an answer may not be at hand does not mean it merits the denial of God. Only arrogance can take a person there that quickly. Also remember, asking questions does not always mean a person is really looking for answers.

Rice Broocks relates to this in his book *God's Not Dead: Evidence for God in Age of Uncertainty* when he talks about the endless kinds of questioning he receives from college students who appear to be open-minded but aren't really.

> I have been challenged repeatedly on university campuses; "You're going to have to prove to me that God exists and Christianity is true." My response? "If I do, will you believe in Him and follow Christ?" When they answer no I respond, "Your problem is not a lack of information. If you have all of your questions answered and still don't believe, then your real problem is spiritual, not intellectual."

Remember, in the early years of the Christian faith, there was no New Testament Bible, and yet many were able to come to faith under the harshest of conditions. Also today, many are able to come to faith without having answers to all the questions they are asking. Why is this so?

Who sets the standard for when there is enough evidence to believe in God? This threshold seems to vary from person to person. Why do some believe with less evidence than others? This might relate to a willingness to believe.

A wise man once said that "everything we decide to do should be viewed from God's perspective, against the backdrop of eternity." There are eternal consequences at stake.

Consider the Ramifications if There Was No God

The following summarize my thoughts if it were true there is no God.

1. There is no purpose of life. There is no "why" to life. Atheism is a philosophy of meaninglessness. Nothing has ultimate meaning.

2. There is no objective morality. There is no basis for morality, right or wrong. Evil can only be defined in light of what is good. Good can only be defined by what is right and moral based on a moral law giver. This moral law giver has to be someone beyond ourselves, one who commands the authority to establish what is right and wrong. Without God, nothing can be said to be good or evil. Autonomous, individual morality can give rise to anything.

3. There is no hope. Where there is no answer for death, hopelessness inevitably invades life.

4. This life is all you get. As some may say, eat, drink, and be merry. Self-centered living becomes a logical, acceptable, and expedient standard if this life is all there is. If so, then an ethical case can be made that it is the survival of the fittest.

5. There is no objective basis for forgiveness, mercy, justice, kindness, goodness, and self-sacrifice.

6. There is no objective accountability. We each have the final say about ourselves. No one is accountable to anyone else.

CHAPTER 5

Entering into a Relationship with God

I tell you, now is the time of God's favor,
now is the day of salvation.

—2 Corinthians 6:2

¹⁶ For God so loved the world that he gave his one and only
Son, that whoever believes in him shall not perish but have
eternal life. ¹⁷ For God did not send his Son into the world to
condemn the world, but to save the world through him.

—John 3:16–17

The way to enter into a personal relationship with God begins with
Jesus. All human beings are imperfect and unable to live a sinless life.
Sin separates us from God. God sent Jesus to earth to deal with this
issue and provide a way for us to come to him. We read in *John 14:6*
that Jesus is the only way to God:

Jesus answered, "I am the way and the truth
and the life. No one comes to the Father except
through me."

Dr. Harold Shank in his recent book, *Listen and Make Room*,
speaks about how God sent Jesus to earth to do the work necessary
to reconcile us back to him.

The cross was not purchased from a discount lumber store. Jesus didn't lead a ho-hum life. God did not send a low-ranking angel. We are not told, "Follow Moses; he's a good choice." God sent the best. God chose the excellent. The bloodshed at the cross was not donated by the Red Cross; it was divine plasma that cost God his life. God didn't send a sheep from his pasture, but the only son from his house.

As Dr. Shank clearly expresses, God sending Jesus to earth was no trivial or insignificant representative. What we got was God himself coming to earth. Jesus and God are one (John 1:1 and John 10:30). Jesus was our creator and now our redeemer. He had the utmost authority to change our status from sinner to saint.

The New Testament scriptures are filled with passages that clearly state that God wants all people to be saved. He wants to have this special relationship with everyone. He sent Jesus to earth to offer salvation to all people. It just takes a willing heart.

We receive the gift of salvation through faith in Jesus. This process includes being "born again" as Jesus mentions in *John 3:1–20*. This passage includes a discussion Jesus had with a Pharisee and a member of the Jewish ruling council named Nicodemus. Jesus told Nicodemus that no one can see the kingdom of God unless one is born again.

Jesus puts before Nicodemus a theological concept using fresh terminology. This is the first time the phrase "born again" is used. This was not a concept familiar to scholars of the Hebrew scriptures, such as Nicodemus.

Nicodemus was considered a brilliant theologian of his time and likely skilled in the art of debate. When Nicodemus heard Jesus say the new requirement of being born again, this is likely something Nicodemus had not expected.

Nicodemus questioned, "How can someone be born again when they are old?" This conveyed his confusion. Jesus was asking for something that was not humanly possible. He was making entrance into the kingdom contingent on something which could not be obtained through human effort.

To a Pharisee, keeping the law was considered the way to God. He believed that salvation came through his own merit. By calling Nicodemus to be born again, Jesus challenged this most religious Jew to admit his spiritual bankruptcy and abandon everything he was trusting in for salvation.

What It Means to be "Born Again"

Everyone who is born again belongs to God's kingdom. God accepts everyone who believes in his son, Jesus. So a person needs two births. The first one is the natural birth of the body. The second birth is a spiritual birth that comes through the water and the Spirit. It is a spiritual experience. This theme runs throughout the New Testament.

"Blessed be the God and Father of our Lord Jesus Christ, who according to His great mercy has caused us to be born again to a living hope through the resurrection of Jesus Christ from the dead" (1 Pet. 1:3).

Being born again is a spiritual concept, not a human, physical, earthy concept. The apostle John foreshadowed this concept in his prologue to his gospel:

> [12] Yet to all who did receive him, to those who believed in his name, he gave the right to become children of God—[13] children born not of natural descent, nor of human decision or a husband's will, but born of God. (John 1:12–13)

The Greek word for *again* in the phrase "born again" is *anóthen*, which can have several meanings, but the most common rendering is "from above." Born again=born from above.

To be born again, or born from above, means a transformation of a person so that he or she is able to enter another world and adapt to its conditions. To belong to the heavenly kingdom, one must be born into it. Jesus is saying that such a new birth requires a work of God's Spirit after the principle that all life reproduces after its kind.

As our physical birth is not something we can accomplish ourselves, so it is that our spiritual birth is not something we can accomplish on our own. We accept the gift of our salvation, our being born again, through faith. It is God who made the plan on how he would reconcile humans back into a relationship with him and he does the work of salvation. Jesus died and rose again through spiritual powers from above. We are also born again from above thanks to the spiritual work being done on our behalf.

This culminates in Jesus saying to Nicodemus the most famous verse in the Bible: "For God so loved the world that he gave his one and only Son, that whoever believes in him shall not perish but have eternal life" (John 3:16).

So having a personal relationship with God begins with us understanding who God is, examining the reasons for faith and making a decision to accept Jesus as our savior and thus going through the process of being born again. We repent of our sins and are baptized in water for the remission of sins and to receive the Holy Spirit (Acts 2:38). Baptism is a similar process to how the Jewish people under the Old Covenant went to get purified. They would regularly be baptized in a Mikveh when they needed purification. However, our baptism under the New Covenant is a onetime process for all time. (In our trip to Israel, we saw Mikvehs located in many places, very prevalent.)

Scripture teaches that our sins were imputed (charged/assigned) to Christ and he paid the full penalty for them by his death. Now Christ's own righteousness is imputed to us, and we receive the full merit of it. Without this reality, we could enjoy no relationship whatsoever with a holy God.

Eternal salvation comes to us now while we are living our lives here on earth. However, there is also the sense in which we have not received its fullness yet.

We are still living in a fallen world. We are awaiting the return of Christ and the final redemption, our home in heaven. *The best is yet to come!*

So based on all the above, each person has to individually come to terms with God. No one else's faith or walk with the Lord has any transference to us. Each person must establish their own personal, direct, one-of-a-kind relationship with their Creator. Each person will be separately held accountable for how they lived their lives and will face God at judgment day.

Judgment Day

The Bible declares that God "has set a day in which he purposes to judge the inhabited earth" (Acts 17:31).

This day of judgment, also known as the Final Judgment, is when Jesus, the Son of God, will judge "the living and the dead" before destroying the old heaven and earth, which are corrupted by sin.

Jesus Christ will act as the judge, as the Bible states in John 5:22: "Moreover, the Father judges no one, but has entrusted all judgment to the Son." Scripture declares that Jesus Christ will judge every person who has ever lived (Acts 10:42). Those who reject his offer of salvation face judgment.

And so at the final judgment, the destiny of the wicked and nonbelievers will be in the hands of Jesus who will assess everyone according to their soul's status.

Believers will also stand before Jesus, at which time they'll finally come to a full comprehension of his generous grace. Because of being in Jesus, we will be declared innocent and welcomed into the gates of heaven!

In 1 Corinthians 4:5, Paul says that Jesus will disclose the motives hidden in believers' hearts. Some people have gotten the misguided idea that all their sins will be displayed for everyone to see, but the Bible in no way supports that notion.

- "Therefore judge nothing before the appointed time; wait until the Lord comes. He will bring to light what is hidden in darkness and will expose the motives of the heart. At that time each will receive their praise from God" (1 Cor. 4:5).

- "For we must all appear before the judgment seat of Christ, that each one may receive the things done in the body, according to what he has done, whether good or bad" (2 Cor. 5:10).
- "But I tell you that everyone will have to give account on the Day of Judgment for every empty word they have spoken. For by your words you will be acquitted, and by your words you will be condemned" (Matt. 12:36–37).
- "In the presence of God and of Christ Jesus, who will judge the living and the dead, and in view of his appearing and his kingdom, I give you this charge" (2 Tim. 4:1).
- "Then I saw a great white throne and Him who sat on it, from whose face the earth and the heaven fled away. And there was found no place for them. And I saw the dead, small and great, standing before God and books were opened. And another book was opened, which is the Book of Life. And the dead were judged according to their works, by the things which were written in the books" (Rev. 20:11–15).

Authentic Faith

Faith is a journey. Faith builds and gets stronger over time as one nurtures one's faith. Faith can also be diminished if one does not nurture one's faith. How does one nurture faith? By being in regular fellowship with other Christians, by having meaningful times of worshipping God, by continual Bible study and by finding answers to the questions and doubts we have, never giving up. I believe finding answers to most reasonable questions is possible for the willing seeker.

Authentic faith is based on honesty, truth, humility, and openness. To be fair, it is not always easy to remain strong in the faith. Doubts can enter in from time to time, and this should be expected. We all need a safe place to express our doubts. We will all likely see faith ebb and flow in intensity over the years.

One of the common complaints we hear from skeptics is the hypocrisy they see among believers. I suppose there is a level of hypocrisy in all of us, believers and unbelievers. We are human. We make mistakes. We make misjudgments for many reasons. We must accept that it is difficult for everyone of faith to live up fully to the high standards we hear preached in our pulpits.

Humble faith that keeps appreciation for grace front and center reflects a more authentic relationship with God.

The Benefits of Being a Christian

The decision to become a Christian, a follower of Christ, is arguably the biggest decision anyone will make. Most if not all people will do a lot of thinking and investigation before taking this step. Most if not all people will hear the message much like presented in this book, that God created us to be in relationship with him and he made a way to make this possible through his Son. People then look at the evidence for faith and decide one way or the other.

Everyone knows that spiritual realities cannot be definitively proven. That is a standard too high to reach for matters of faith. Instead of proof, we must look for evidence, and there is plenty of it from many perspectives: history, science, cosmology, philosophy, scripturally, etc. How much evidence is enough depends on the person's open mind and willing heart.

Let's look at some relevant factors of what distinguishes people who choose faith from those who don't. We'll begin by asking a few questions.

What Sets a Believer Apart from a Nonbeliever, a Non-Christian?

A believer is one who has made the commitment to accept Jesus as their Lord and Savior. This person then maintains a spiritual focus to life on earth which gives the individual purpose, meaning, and direction. A Christian's citizenship is in heaven with one's "conversion." A Christian seeks to live a life reflecting Christian values, morals, and ethics. A Christian understands the Holy Spirit is in one's body and can rely on the Holy Spirit for strength and support. So this person would say there are many things that set them apart from nonbelievers.

The truth is, there are some people who profess to be a Christian who don't live like their faith makes much of a difference in their lives. What caused these people to want to initially become a Christian has since become blurred, and they are getting caught up into living lives like those who are unbelievers in their community. Therefore, there is not much that distinguishes them from the nonbeliever.

If a seeking young man came to you and asked how your life as a Christian differs from his as a moral non-Christian, what would you tell him?

The truth is many non-Christians live according to what many call Judeo-Christian values. These are people who treat others well, are kind, caring, and thoughtful. They can be considered good people. Some may even live better morally than those who profess to be Christian.

One of the main differences is that being good does not make one a Christian, neither does it make one eligible for a home in heaven with God after this life. The only way a person can be saved and have the promise of life after death with God is to become a Christian. That is through Jesus alone. Forgiven people are the ones who get to heaven.

As I mentioned above, we find in *John 14:6* where Jesus makes this clear: Jesus answered, "I am the way and the truth and the life. No one comes to the Father except through me."

The Christian understands the foundation for morality. God is the only being who can determine morality for all of mankind. Christians realize this and are accountable to this. Christians also realize that living a moral life is very important, but it is not the way to be accepted into heaven. We can't act good enough to get into heaven. So the big difference between a Christian and a moral non-Christian is that a Christian is saved by grace and has a home in heaven awaiting him/her.

What was your major motivation for choosing to accept Jesus as your Lord and Savior and becoming a born-again Christian?

It is my contention that most everyone who chooses to become a Christian does so to make one right with God so that they can have the hope of eternal life with God. We are humbled by our sin and ask for God's mercy and grace. We seek to be reconciled to God.

Can it be said that "no one is happier than a Christian"?

The reality is Christians have a joy that runs deep and is based on being right with God and the hope for a home in heaven. The scriptures often encourage Christians to be joyful. However, there is a sense in which joy is different than being happy. Happiness is based on one's circumstances. Joy looks beyond current circumstances. That's why the apostle Paul could be so joyful and sing songs while he was in prison and being tortured.

We don't choose to become Christians because we want an easy life which is filled with circumstances that always make us happy. There will be times of sacrifice, suffering, and difficulty because we are Christians.

Our Sales Pitch to Non-Christians

Evangelism is a spiritual likeness to sales. People in sales try to communicate the personal benefits of the product they are selling to attract others to buy it. For instance:

- The reasons you should hire me to do this work for you is... (how I can benefit you)
- The reasons you should buy this item is... (list the ways the person needs the item)

We come to faith first and foremost because of our recognizing God is real. Our sin separates us from God. God has made a way to reconcile us back into a relationship with him. The focus is on the spiritual side of the reasons.

I would think that most agree with me that we don't become Christians because:

- Life will become easier for us if we do.
- We will have less problems than non-Christians
- Bad things won't happen to us because God loves us and will protect us and our loved ones will not have car accidents, will get healed from diseases, won't have the health problems as other non-Christian humans have, etc.
- We'll be better off financially than non-Christians.
- We will have better marriages than non-Christians and won't get divorced.
- We will have more successful careers than non-Christians.
- We won't have adulterous affairs like non-Christians.
- We won't experience the problem of premarital sex as do non-Christians.
- We will get along better with each other.
- We will be able to handle psychological and psychiatric disorders better than non-Christians.
- Our teeth will be whiter than non-Christians.
- Overall, Christians will have a distinct advantage over non-Christians in about every area of life.

No, we don't become Christians because we want a better quality of life on earth as reflected in the above statements. That is not our sales pitch. Yes, we hope to have a more abundant and fulfilling life spiritually on earth than nonbelievers. But we should not compare ourselves to nonbelievers in things material. When we become Christians, we are told to set our hearts on things above, where Christ is seated at the right hand of God. Set your minds of things above, not on earthly things (Col. 3:1–2).

So if there were no advantages on the quality of physical life on earth to becoming a Christian, would that impact the number of people responding? Would that discourage people from believing?

We don't become Christians because we want to avoid the problems of life. In fact, Jesus clearly warns us that we will have troubles in life (John 16:33). The case can be made that life as a Christian is more difficult life to live because of the sacrifices we make, the service we give, the way we need to go out of our way to help people and get involved in the messiness of life. We don't just eat, drink, and be merry. We do things on earth because it has meaning beyond this life.

We don't become Christians because life will become easier. On the contrary, the Christian life will be more complicated where much is expected of us, including sacrificial giving of time and money, standing up for vulnerable people of all kinds, as well as confronting injustice, oppression, and promoting godly values while defending righteousness. We will have other priorities than unbelievers.

Again, our relationship with God is not based on deliverables we expect from God, i.e., blessings in this life. We are first and foremost drawn to God for what he can do for us for eternity, after this life.

On inaugural day on January 20, 1961, President John F. Kennedy made the profound statement for us to "Ask not what our country can do for us. Rather, ask what we can do for our country." Is the same sentiment true for us in our relationship with God? Should we be focusing more on what we can do for God?

In the gospels Matthew, Mark, Luke, and John, do we find that Jesus is asking us to focus on what God can do for us or the other way around?

In the story of Job in the Old Testament, Satan was making the point to God that Job is only faithful and righteous because of the good things he is getting out of his relationship with God. Satan basically said to take those good things away and watch Job lose his faith. Well, fortunately, this did not happen. Job maintaining his faith through all the trials was the point of the story.

What we can be assured of in our walk with God relates to the spiritual side of life. Christians will have:

- Forgiveness and reconciliation
- Peace with God
- The Holy Spirit in our lives and God being with us in every step of life

- Direct access to God through prayer
- A life of joy in knowing and loving God
- Hope and purpose in life and a spiritual destiny
- After we die, we will be in the presence of God in heaven. This will be our crown of life (James 1:12) and our crown of righteousness (2 Tim. 4:8).

When we become Christians, we join the family of God. This family is made up of other Christians as part of an adoptive family. There are many blessings in being a part of this family with so many other spiritual brothers and sisters. Developing a relationship with other believers can be a source of great encouragement and help through the challenges of life.

On the other hand, there are situations where Christians have differing views of how God works today and in the interpretation of scripture which can complicate these relationships. Sometimes, handling these disagreements is done without compassion, sensitivity, a desire to understand, and grace.

How Could We Maximize the Value of This Family to Our Lives?

- Get into a compatible and like-minded church family.
- Get deeply involved—establish relationships.
- Be committed to play a part in this family using one's spiritual gifts and personal talents.
- Have relationships where one can discuss the deeper issues of Christianity.

Why Doesn't Everyone Go to Church?

Becoming a born-again Christian automatically enlists one as a member of the family of God. The church is the family of God.

In English, the word *church* can have several meanings, including a building, a people, a denomination, etc. The Greek word for church is *ekklēsía* (pronounced ek-klay-see'-ah). It means a calling out (the called out), the whole body of Christians scattered through-out the earth. In Greek language, the church is the people and not a building.

Again, however, in English, we use the term *church* for several meanings. Most Christians meet together in what we call a church building, although some meet together in homes and not a desig-nated physical building. The church meets regularly to worship God, to encourage one another, and to reach out with the grace, mercy, and the love of God to a fallen world.

We are encouraged to remain connected to the church and Christian fellowship in the scriptures. We can be blessed and encour-aged by this, and we can also bless others and encourage them by this.

The apostle Paul speaks to this in *Hebrews 10:22–25*:

> ²² Let us draw near to God with a sincere heart and with the full assurance that faith brings, having our hearts sprinkled to cleanse us from a guilty conscience and having our bodies washed with pure water. ²³ Let us hold unswervingly to the hope we profess, for he who promised is faith-ful. ²⁴ And let us consider how we may spur one another on toward love and good deeds, ²⁵ not giving up meeting together, as some are in the habit of doing, but encouraging one another— and all the more as you see the Day approaching.

We know the church officially began after the resurrection of Jesus. This is when the work of Jesus was completed for why he came to earth. It was to pay the price for our sins in order to secure our forgiveness and the opportunity to be reconciled back into a saved relationship with God. *Andy Stanley* provides an interesting overview of this process in his book *Irresistible: Reclaiming the New that Jesus Unleashed for the World*, which is summarized here.

It was after the resurrection that Jesus' reengaged followers began to understand he had not come to simply add an additional chapter to the story of Israel. Jesus had not come to introduce a new version of Judaism. His movement was not regional. The Jesus movement was an all-skate. It was for all nations.

Jesus claimed to be the fulfillment of Judaism and a replacement for paganism.

Specifically, Jesus came to establish a new covenant, a new command, and a new movement. His new movement would be international. The new covenant would fulfill and replace the behavioral, sacrifice-based systems reflected in just about every religion of the ancient world.

We know the church was formed after the resurrection of Jesus. It began at Pentecost as recorded in Acts chapter 2. We also know from the scriptures and the history books how difficult life was for those in the early church. Those who followed Jesus during this time came under great persecution as it was the hope by their persecutors to extinguish them altogether. For almost three hundred years, they fended off pressure to integrate and incorporate the old ways. But with the conversion of Constantine the Great and the signing of the Edict of Milan, the church transitioned quickly from a persecuted minority to an encouraged and empowered majority.

It's hard to imagine if the church could have survived such cruel persecution without the support of each other. Being in fellowship then was critical for their very survival.

Fast forward to today and we see a different picture with vastly different conditions for those who live in America. The religious freedoms we have are significant. However, there are many places all over the world where there is not religious freedom but great religious persecution. This can be found in China and other communist countries.

It's a shame that today, many Christians don't see the value of being in close fellowship with other believers. Church involvement and attendance is diminishing year after year. What could be done to help more followers of Jesus to see the value of being in close relationship to one another?

As Americans, we live in a country where there is hardly any severe persecution. Maybe we would appreciate and need each other more if we were under persecution.

CHAPTER 6

—⁂—

The Challenges in a Relationship with Our Creator

For in him all things were created: things in heaven and on earth,
visible and invisible, whether thrones or powers or rulers or
authorities; all things have been created through him and for him.
—Colossians 1:16

Having a relationship with God is deeply personal. Although God is always the same, how God interacts with people can be different. Also, people are vastly different from each other based on many reasons, such as their family backgrounds, the experiences in life which shape them, their personalities, their intelligence, the personal issues they have, etc. The truth is, each person is a unique individual, and because of this, they will have a unique relationship with God. Therefore, it's typical that each person will have to work out their own relationship with God. The notion of *one size fits all* does not apply here.

Having a personal relationship with God refers to many spiritual aspirations, including the following:

- It reflects our efforts to do his will in our lives.
- It reflects a commitment to maintain a strong spiritual focus to life.
- It reflects a desire to come to know him deeper as time goes on.

- It reflects a desire for God to use us in service to him given our unique talents, abilities, and gifts.
- It indicates we understand how God relates to us, what we can expect from God along the way.
- It reflects an understanding of how we are to relate to God, fulfill our responsibilities, and do our part in our walk with God.
- The notion of "personal" refers to the idea that each person needs to work out one's own relationship with God.

So let's unpack what this all means and process how we understand this concept. Underneath each of those statements are questions which need to be answered and clarifications which need to be made as we understand how to build a personal relationship with God.

God's Immanence and Transcendence

First of all, it may be good to recognize that there are many Christians who have concerns with the terminology of having a "relationship with God." This concern comes from how it appears that we've "domesticated" God and that our phraseology of "relationship" can give false impressions and expectations.

We need to remember that Jesus's message was originally to a Jewish audience. In the Old Testament, the people came to God with an animal sacrifice and through a priest. God often spoke through prophets as well. There was also much ritual with obeying the law. One might say that much came *between* God and the people. *But in Christ, all this changed!* The book of Hebrews in the New Testament is particularly good at emphasizing this fact.

Jesus completed or finished the law and the Old Covenant. Jesus as the Lamb of God voluntarily went to the cross and died for us. He became the once and for all sacrifice for our sins. Jesus became the final high priest and mediator. No longer do animal sacrifices have to be made over and over again. The Old Testament way of a priestly mediator was gone. The people now had direct access to the Father through Christ. Many verses in Hebrews could be referenced to tell this story.

Hebrews 10:19–22 emphasizes the "new and living way" through Christ. Hebrews 4:14–16 states that God can now be approached with *confidence or boldness* through Jesus.

Through first-century Jewish eyes, all this would have been amazing! Barriers had been removed. Jesus has become "the way, the truth, and the life" and the only way to the Father (John 14:6; 1 Tim. 2:5). Not only could people now approach God directly through Jesus, but they could do so confidently and boldly.

The same applies to us today. We don't have to go through a priest or employ other procedures or rituals in relating to God.

Christianity has done a good job at emphasizing the immanent aspect of God. Immanence is how God is manifested in the world. God is present in the physical world and thus accessible to his creatures in various ways.

Jesus was the epitome of this as he came and walked among us. Now we have access to God through prayer. We have the Holy Spirit within us. So yes, God is personal and can be known by us. This is part of what it means to have a personal relationship with God.

However, there are issues which need to be considered with this concept. Some say we've emphasized God's immanence at the expense of God's transcendence. Transcendence is how God's nature and essence is exhibited beyond physical laws and is independent of the material universe. Some say in a desire to have a personal relationship with God, we lose a healthy reverence for God. We try to eliminate the mystery associated with who God is.

Many *fear we have brought God so far down to our level that we have almost created a false god of our own making.* God is personal like we are. But unlike us, God is great, majestic, and invisible! Many things about God are incomprehensible to our finite minds.

While we do believe we can have a personal relationship with God, the way we have neglected God's transcendence can give a false impression of what is meant by a relationship with God. We don't have a relationship with God in the exact way we have a relationship with our spouse, parent, or friend. God doesn't sit on the couch and have a two-way discussion with us.

Philip Yancey makes the following comments in his book *Reaching for the Invisible God: What Can We Expect to Find?:*

> Christianity claims a unique place among the world's religions. Our faith tells of a God before whom the strongest saints took off their shoes, bowed down, fell on their faces and repented in dust and ashes. At the same time it tells of a God who came to earth as a baby, who showed tender mercies to children and the weak, who taught us to call him "Abba," who loved and was loved. God is both transcendent and immanent. The theologians say God inspires at once awe and love, fear and friendship.

So what do we make of this? We would do well not to be cavalier and too casual by trying to remove healthy boundaries, bringing God down to our level.

Factors Which Complicate a Relationship with God

As we consider a relationship with God, we understand that this is a unique relationship. Indeed, a relationship with God is vastly different than a relationship we have with human beings.

There is just no other kind of relationship that can be fully compared to a relationship between humans and God.

We also know it is common to think of a relationship with God in terms and concepts which are similar to the relationship we have with other people. This can apply to some degree but necessarily falls short of describing our relationship with God. What we define as a healthy, functional, and intimate relationship with other people just does not fully translate to a relationship with God.

When we talk about a personal relationship with God, many speak in terms of a close and intimate relationship. The question is, "What kind of intimacy with God are we looking for in a relationship with him?"

Marital relationship experts say that true intimacy can only exist between equals. There are obvious ways we can see this being true with human relationships. And we can see how this cannot be true in a relationship with God.

This then creates a dilemma for us as we seek to have a close relationship with God.

This underscores there are many different dynamics involved in a relationship with God than we have with other humans. We'll discuss the idea of "intimacy with God" further down the road in this study. Right now, let's consider this notion of how a relationship with God is different than a relationship with humans.

Many of the differences in this relationship are based on the following variables:

1. God is too great for us to understand fully (Isa. 55:8–9 and Rom. 11:33).
2. God is a spirit (John 4:24), is invisible (Col. 1:15), and does not have physical characteristics.
3. We can't have a two-way conversation with God in the spoken word.
4. Much of the interacting with God is a one-way effort on our part. It is a relationship in which we must find comfort with being heard more than of hearing.
5. God has unimaginable power and splendor (Matt. 19:26; Eph. 1:19; Eph. 3:20).
6. God knows our thoughts (Matt. 9:4, 12:25; Luke 11:17) and can see into the future (1 John 3:20, Eph. 2:10; John 16:13). It's a relationship in which we are known more by God than we know God.
7. God is our Supreme Ruler, God, King, Judge, Lord who must be obeyed, worshipped, glorified, loved, and to whom we dedicate our lives.
8. Jesus calls us his friends in John 15:15 as a display of his immeasurable grace and tells us to obey him as a condition of our love for him (John 14:15). However, we should take

caution in treating God like a good buddy. This can easily be viewed as belittling, disrespectful, and irreverent to God.

9. God sets the terms of the relationship, not us. He has the last word. There are no compromises. He will do what he will do.

10. We are held accountable to God for how we live our lives (Heb. 4:13).

11. It's no use trying to change God like we try to do with our spouses!

12. It is difficult to know what to expect from God in this relationship. So many Christians have differing ideas and beliefs in this area. Some of this can lead to disappointment and alienation with God.

13. Any problems in the relationship are our fault, not God's.

14. The consequences of a failed relationship with God will be devastating to us.

15. The joy of a successful relationship and a home in heaven will be tremendous. This is a relationship where our greatest intimacy will be experienced in the future rather than the present. We will find ultimate fulfillment in our experience with Christ in the future which is yet to come.

16. Because of all the above, it is obvious we are not in an equal relationship with God, which makes intimacy with God a greater challenge for us.

Factors Which Facilitate a Relationship with God

Earlier, we looked at many scriptures which provide clear evidence that God created us to be in a loving and active relationship with him. As we consider this relationship further, we can be encouraged by the many ways this relationship can be facilitated, enriched, and strengthened even given the obstacles facing it.

Consider the following:

1. God has made us in his image, which makes it possible to relate to him. Because of this, we are the most unique of

the creatures God has created. No other creatures can have a personal relationship with God.

2. In coming to know Christ, we have put off our old self and put on the new self, which is created to be like God in true righteousness and holiness (Eph. 4:17–25).

3. God has given us the Bible, the scriptures, which provide us many insights into how God wants us to have a relationship with him. God speaks to us through the scriptures, which provide what we need to live godly lives, grow spiritually, have a deeper knowledge of him, and which will lead us to heaven for eternity with God.

4. God came to earth in the person of Jesus Christ. Jesus is the exact representation of God, and we can learn a lot about God from knowing Jesus.

5. God forgives us of our sins (1 John 1:9). We have a clean slate. Our past is not held against us. If we sin, Jesus also intercedes on our behalf continuously (Rom. 8:34). We are no longer separated from God but are reconciled back into a restored relationship with him (Rom. 5:10–11).

6. We know, as believers in Jesus Christ, we have the right to be called children of God (John 1:12). God is our loving heavenly father. This places us in a very special relationship with God.

7. No one and nothing can separate us from the love of Christ (Rom. 8:35–39).

8. Jesus as our Lord and Savior will lead us to our home in heaven. There is no condemnation for those who are in Christ Jesus (Rom. 8:1).

9. God is not a God of confusion (1 Cor. 14:33). He wants to be understood. He wants a relationship with mankind. The basis of this relationship is having the framework in place for being able to relate to God. One important piece of this framework is that God is a God of logic. We can relate to God because he is logical at all times.

10. God has made us partakers of his divine nature (1 Pet. 1:2–8; Gal. 5:22–23).

11. God gives us free will from which we can truly love him and interact with him. This is our choice and essential in order to have an authentic relationship with him. We are not robots or puppets but have an interactive and interdependent relationship with him.

12. God gives born-again Christians the Holy Spirit to reside within us (Acts 2:38; John 14:15–31; Rom. 5:5). If we live by the Spirit, we will not gratify the desires of the sinful nature (Gal. 5:16). We can be led by the Spirit (Gal. 5:18). The Holy Spirit guides us and helps us but does not control us.

13. When we do good works, we live as God intended us to live. We were created to do good works (Eph. 2:10).

14. God does not change. He can be depended on to keep his many promises (2 Pet. 3:9; Heb. 6:13–15; Heb. 10:23). We can therefore trust in his promises as the basis of our relationship with him.

15. God will be with us (Phil. 4:9). Included among God's promises is a commitment to be with us always (Matt. 28:20, Heb. 13:5).

16. God wants us to partner with him in living godly lives. We must use our gifts, talents, and abilities for his glory, and he will be with us through our journey as his children.

17. In the hustle and bustle of life, there are certainly many ways we can get off-track in our Christian walk with the Lord and depart from the special relationship we have with God. In these situations, an attitude of repentance, rededication, and spiritual renewal is needed. Fortunately, God loves us so much that he will accept us back into a relationship with him.

All of these considerations reveal how God wants to have a relationship with us and how he does what is necessary for this to happen. Nothing can stop us but ourselves.

We will explore many of the above items in more detail as we progress in this study.

God Is Great and Beyond Our Understanding

The fact that there are so many unique aspects of who God is reveals the extra challenge it is for us humans to relate to him.

First and foremost, we are talking about having a personal, intimate, close relationship with the God who is beyond our understanding. Again, there are no equals to God. He is unique. He is the one and only (Deut. 4:35). Isaiah 46:9 says, "Remember the former things, those of long ago, I am God, and there is no other; I am God, and there is none like me."

Scripture teaches that we can have a true and personal knowledge of God, but this does not mean we will ever understand him exhaustively. The Bible is clear that God is ultimately incomprehensible to us; that is, we can never fully comprehend his whole being. The following passages confirm this:

- "Great is the Lord, and greatly to be praised, and his greatness is unsearchable" (Ps. 145:3).
- "Behold, these are but the outskirts of his ways, and how small a whisper do we hear of him! But the thunder of his power who can understand?" (Job 26:14).
- "For my thoughts are not your thoughts, neither are your ways my ways, declares the Lord. For as the heavens are higher than the earth, so are my ways higher than your ways and my thoughts than your thoughts" (Isa. 55:8–9).
- "Oh the depth of the riches and wisdom and knowledge of God! How unsearchable are his judgments and how inscrutable his ways! 'For who has known the mind of the Lord, or who has been his counselor?'" (Rom. 11:33–34; Job 42:1–6; Ps. 139:6, 17–18; 147:5; Isa.57:15; 1 Cor. 2:10–11; 1 Tim. 6:13–16).

These verses teach that not only is God's whole being incomprehensible, but each of his attributes—his greatness, power, thoughts, ways and wisdom—are well beyond human ability to fathom fully. Not only can we never know everything there is to know about God, we can never know everything there is to know about even one aspect of God's character. But you know, this is really a positive reality! We would not want a God we could understand fully. That kind of God would not be great enough.

Because God can never be fully known, those who seek to know God should be deeply humbled in the process, realizing that they will always have more to learn. The appropriate response to God is a heart of wonder and awe in light of his incomprehensible greatness.

It is a real challenge to relate to an entity we don't fully understand. This is true in human relationships and in our relationship with God.

Having said all of this, a case can be made that we take this concept to an extreme. We use it as an excuse for when we have a difficult time explaining why things happen. Calvinist-oriented believers do this all the time in defending their perspective. This is especially true when they deal with their views on why God allows (causes) suffering, pain, and evil to hurt us. They often say we just can't explain this because we can't fully understand God. To me, their explanation is like a convenient evasion to distract from the deficiencies in their doctrine.

Roger Olson, PhD relates to this in his book *Against Calvinism: Rescuing God's Reputation from Radical Reformed Theology* states the following about this:

> Finally, I will argue that high Calvinism falls into contradictions: It cannot be made intelligible. By "intelligible" I do not mean philosophically rational; I mean capable of being understood. A sheer contradiction is a sure sign of error; even most Calvinists agree about that. The greatest contradiction is that God is confessed as perfectly good while at the same time described as the author of sin and evil.

I believe we have been given enough knowledge about God to be able to understand things much more than Calvinists would want to admit. To do this requires us to reject the Calvinist notions of God's extreme sovereignty and his pervasive providence. We may not be able to know everything there is to know about God and how he acts, but we can know enough to help us see him as always loving and present with us.

God Can Be Understood Enough By Us

For Christians, I believe God has revealed himself to us enough for us to be able to come to acceptable answers to the important questions we have in life. Now that statement may be disagreed with by many who expect God to explain things simply or by those who believe God is so complicated that we can't have explanations for many of our questions.

One of the arguments Calvinists make frequently to defend their doctrinal positions is to convey the notion that we should not expect to find answers for many of our tough questions. They seem to say this regularly in an attempt to cause us to be at peace with the apparent unknowable. They emphasize regularly that we must be willing to accept that we as humans will just not be able to understand as much as we'd like to about God in order to answer many of the tough questions we have as to why God does what he does.

I believe much of this is due to many of the mistaken views of the Calvinist doctrine. We often won't be able to understand the logic of how the doctrine of Calvinism makes sense because much of it doesn't make logical sense. As a diversion from this, many Calvinists appeal to the notion that we can't always understand God as the reason why we can't understand their doctrine.

Randy Pope, who recently retired after serving as the pastor of the Perimeter Church (Presbyterian affiliated) in Atlanta and a high Calvinist himself, used an illustration several years ago at the beginning of a series of sermons to explain reformed theology at his church. I listened carefully to these sermons and took many notes. He said that we only know a little when it comes to understanding God's ways. His illustration was to put a dot on a chalkboard and say that this dot represents the amount of the understanding we have in contrast to the large amount of other space on the chalkboard representing what we can't understand.

Most Calvinists I have encountered, and read from, try to make this similar case. They say we have to be comfortable with accepting the ubiquitous unknowns about God. It appears that Calvinists use this strategy so that we back down and not push too hard for more logical answers and explanations.

Isaiah 55:8–9 states:

> "For My thoughts are not your thoughts,
> Nor are your ways My ways," declares the LORD.
> "FOR *as* the heavens are higher than the earth,
> So are My ways higher than your ways
> And My thoughts than your thoughts."

In Isaiah 55, we see that God's thoughts and ways are high above those of mankind. However, the case can be made that the difference between man's thoughts and God's thoughts is largely one of degree. The fact that God is beyond our ability to fully understand is not because God is irrational or illogical but because he is much greater than us, much more complicated than us, and is in a spiritual realm unknown to us, which makes us not able to understand him fully. The only way we have information on who God is comes from how God chooses to reveal himself to us in the scriptures, not from our direct or firsthand knowledge derived from our earthly research or investigations outside the scriptures.

I propose that the scriptures do reveal enough about God for the purpose of us using our minds to comprehend him so that we can have a relationship with him and understand what is important to understand. God cannot be substantially hidden from us if we are to have a meaningful relationship with him.

It has been said that if what we believe is considered beyond the realm of rational thought, then its legitimacy does not have to depend upon meeting the rigors of the intellect. However, God wants us to be able to use our intellect to understand him to satisfy the principles of a healthy relationship. Again, if God's ways are irrational, illogical, too confusing, or ever changing, we can never come to understand God at all. Thankfully, they are not!

Christianity Needs to Offer More Explanations

It seems to me we need more satisfying explanations to the difficult happenings in life than to blame our confusion on our limited abilities as humans. Calvinists ask us to surrender to their overused excuse that we just have to accept we can't understand. They use this frequently. However, for us to be made in the image of God means we are designed to use our minds, to explore concepts, to look for answers to tough questions and rightly expect to find answers to be reasonable and credible.

Christians need to be able to have answers to the tough spiritual questions. These are often associated with the whys of evil, pain and suffering, unanswered prayers, etc. Otherwise, people frustrated by the tough questions will be unsatisfied with Christianity and may just give up on it. Or they may even look elsewhere for answers.

Roger Olson, PhD in his book *Against Calvinism: Rescuing God's Reputation from Radical Reformed Theology* relates to this idea:

> Someone has said that no theology is worth believing that cannot be preached standing in front of the gates of Auschwitz. I, for one, could not stand at those gates and preach a version of God's sovereignty that makes the extermination of six million Jews, including many children, a part of the will and plan of God such that God foreordained and rendered it certain.

One of the Calvinist doctrines impacting all this is their belief in the premise that God is in control of all that happens. Many believe God's providence means God will watch out for us and protect us and our loved ones from harm. Therefore, when tragedy hits, people who believe God is controlling everything look to God and ask, "Why did you allow this to happen?" An argument can be made that it is in fact this premise where the real problem is and from where misdirected blame gets placed on God. Because of this, the reputation of God can become blemished.

There are other theological perspectives which provide alternative premises and beliefs than what Calvinism offers. With free will believers, the premises would be different, leading to different conclusions. More explicit explanations can be offered for the tough questions largely based on the notion of free will.

Examples of Inadequate Calvinist Explanations

Extreme Calvinist Jerry Bridges has written a book called *Is God Really in Control?: Trusting God in a World of Hurt*. His book is written to affirm that yes, God is really in control of every little detail of our lives. Here are some excerpts from his book which illustrate what I've been criticizing about how Calvinists often mistakenly say we have to be comfortable with accepting the unknowns about God:

> The circumstances in which we must trust God often appear irrational and inexplicable... We are always coping with the unknown.
>
> Here's the important point: In order to trust God, we must always view our adverse circumstances through the eyes of faith, not of sense.
>
> God's sovereignty is also exercised in infinite wisdom, far beyond our ability to comprehend.
>
> God's plan and His ways of working out His plans are frequently beyond our ability to fathom and understand. We must learn to trust what we don't understand.
>
> Every day we live is determined by Him. Does He ever leave us to our own devices? Never! He constantly sustains, provides for and cares for us every moment of every day. Did your car break down when you could least afford the repairs? Did you miss an important meeting

because the plane you were to fly in developed mechanical problems? The God who controls the stars in their courses also controls nuts and bolts and everything on your car and on that plane you were to fly in.

For reasons known only to Himself, God permits people to act contrary to and in defiance of His revealed will in the Bible. However, He never permits them to act contrary to His sovereign will, which remains incomprehensible to us.

We admit that we are often unable to reconcile God's sovereignty and goodness in the face of widespread tragedy or personal adversity.

Our finite minds simply cannot comprehend an infinite being beyond what He has expressly revealed to us. Because of this, some things about God will forever remain a mystery to us. The relationship of the sovereign will of God to the freedom and moral responsibility of people is one of those mysteries.

I put these words of Jerry Bridges here to show how his thinking represents how Calvinists misunderstand God. I believe God wants to be understood by us to a large extent. Relying on the idea that there is so much we can't understand has to be argued by Calvinists because it helps distract from them having to make sense of their doctrine.

Calvinist John MacArthur provides a specific example of this regarding the Calvinist doctrine of the salvation process. John speaks often to the dilemma of understanding how God's sovereignty and man's responsibility fit together in the process of becoming a Christian. He basically says he can't explain it or understand it. It is just something we must accept. See below a sampling of what he teaches on this which summarizes the reformed church's position on soteriology (their doctrine of salvation). This comes from one of his sermons on John 3, which includes the most popular verse of scripture, John

3:16. This sermon can be found on the Internet at his church: "gty. org." Link is https://www.gty.org/library/sermons-library/43-17/ belief-judgment-and-eternal-life.

> "I want to tell you the truth. And the first truth I want you to understand is that salvation is a divine work that God does from heaven down, that doesn't depend on you." We saw that. It's absolutely crystal clear in verses 1 to 10.
>
> So you have then as clear a presentation of sovereign salvation in verses 1 to 10 as anywhere in Scripture, and right against it you have a clear presentation of human responsibility. And the question that if I don't answer today, you will be asking in every verse, is 'How do those two things fit together?' 'How can salvation be solely a work of God and me be held responsible for believing or not believing? How can those two go together?' Those are twin truths that run parallel.
>
> May I tell you? They will always run parallel. They will never come together. They will never intersect. They will never be diminished; legitimately, they are what they are. The fact that you don't understand how they go together only proves that you're less than you should be. It doesn't say anything about God. Your inability to harmonize those things is a reflection of your fallenness, my fallenness. People ask me all the time, "How do you harmonize those?" And my answer is, "I don't. I can't." They can't be harmonized in the human mind."

So again, John MacArthur tries to make the case that we must be at peace to accept what he says we can't understand on such an important topic. He tries to minimize the human brain's ability to understand such a basic spiritual truth, the salvation process. He appeals to the fallenness of the human condition as why we can't understand. It seems obvious to me that scripture is written with the intention it could be understood by us. Why else have the scriptures? Why is it that we can't understand this issue, especially as this is one of the most important topics of scripture? If it is intended for us not to understand this part of scripture, why don't the writers of those scriptures tell us this upfront when these concepts are presented?

As an alternative to the Calvinist notion of God being in control of everything including causing or having his hand in all evil, pain, and suffering, read the chapter on "Maintaining Faith in the Midst of Suffering" as another way of understanding this without needing to blame God for it.

CHAPTER 7

What Does an Intimate
Relationship with God Mean?

[19] Therefore, brothers and sisters, since we have confidence to enter the Most Holy Place by the blood of Jesus, [20] by a new and living way opened for us through the curtain, that is, his body, [21] and since we have a great priest over the house of God, [22] let us draw near to God with a sincere heart and with the full assurance that faith brings, having our hearts sprinkled to cleanse us from a guilty conscience and having our bodies washed with pure water.
—Hebrews 10:19–22

Jesus replied, "Anyone who loves me will obey my teaching. My Father will love them, and we will come to them and make our home with them."
—John 14:23

Come near to God and he will come near to you.
—James 4:8

As we have seen so far, Jesus has changed everything for us. It is because of his resurrection that the God story in the history of mankind comes to fruition. Jesus came to earth to set us all free from the power of sin and death and to offer everyone the opportunity for eternal life with God.

Becoming a believer and follower of Christ puts us on a path of great meaning and purpose in life filled with tremendous gratitude and joy. What in life matters any more than this?

Being able to have a relationship with God is an amazing opportunity! So let's explore the notion of having a close and intimate relationship with him.

The apostle Paul experienced a longing for God and expresses this in the following passage in Philippians 3:7–11:

> 7 But whatever were gains to me I now consider loss for the sake of Christ. 8 What is more, I consider everything a loss because of the surpassing worth of knowing Christ Jesus my Lord, for whose sake I have lost all things. I consider them garbage, that I may gain Christ 9 and be found in him, not having a righteousness of my own that comes from the law, but that which is through faith in Christ—the righteousness that comes from God on the basis of faith. 10 I want to know Christ—yes, to know the power of his resurrection and participation in his sufferings, becoming like him in his death, 11 and so, somehow, attaining to the resurrection from the dead.

Each person must work out their own relationship with God. I suspect that since each person is a unique individual, then the relationships we establish with God will be different in some respects. If, by definition, a person in a right relationship with God means one is in a saved relationship, then the differences in our right relationships with God are nothing to be concerned about. We should be content and thrilled with the love and acceptance God gives us and enjoy the many blessings we receive from our relationship with him. However, we all know that not everyone is in a right relationship with God.

Questions about Intimacy with God

As I often do in exploring topics, I like to generate thought-provoking questions to help us dig deeper into a topic. Here are a few for the idea of having an intimate relationship with God.

- Should everyone seek an intimate relationship with God? What does that even mean?
- How close to God should we strive to be? How do we even define this closeness?
- Can we criticize Christians who don't want to seek this kind of relationship?
- Does God treat everyone the same?
- What can we do to get closer to God?

When we talk about an ideal personal relationship with God, many like to set the bar high and speak in terms of having a close and intimate relationship with God. However, we know that the scriptures don't use this term in describing how we interact with God. One of the ways the scriptures relate to the extent of closeness we are to have with God is regarding love: we are to love God with all of our heart, soul, and mind (Matt. 22:37–38).

If we don't set the bar high and seek an intimate relationship with God, what does that say about our love for God and our zeal for God? How could anyone justify setting the bar lower? Is there a way to rationalize that all we need to have is a mediocre relationship with God?

The Case for Intimacy

If we are to love God with all our heart, soul, and mind, this requires that we give this pursuit our all, our very best. A case can be made that loving God this much is the most we can do. Loving God this much demands our full attention and our greatest commitment. It suggests having a deep love, the deepest of all kinds of love, with expending a huge amount of effort and focus to achieve it.

We know that intimacy is a vague concept. So what is intimacy, and how close is intimate?

The reality is intimacy cannot be quantified or defined by specific amounts. I believe this is a pattern in scripture when a level of commitment and dedication is required. God does not relate to quantity but quality in the scriptures. God does not set an exact amount for what he wants from us. I believe he wants us to pursue him by continually seeking more.

For example, the same vagueness is inferred when we are told to follow the Golden Rule as stated in Matthew 7:12: "So in everything, do to others what you would have them do to you, for this sums up the Law and the Prophets." There are no specific actions which can be identified to explicitly quantify how we are to show we are fulfilling this requirement. There are no limits set. We are not told how much to do for others and when what we do is enough.

We also see this with our charitable giving. The apostle Paul says in 2 Corinthians 9:7, "Each of you should give what you have decided in your heart to give, not reluctantly or under compulsion, for God loves a cheerful giver." Here we see that the amount is not specified. God wants giving to be a response of the heart. The heart refers to depth or extent of effort, but not in specific quantifiable terms. There are no limits set. We are not told how much to give and when the amount is enough.

So the question is, "What kind of intimacy with God are we looking for in a relationship with him?" What kind of intimacy is possible? What kind of intimacy do you want to have with God? When is it enough?

Closeness through Knowing God

Since there are no limits set, I think the point is that we need to have an insatiable appetite for coming to know God. The better we know and understand God, the deeper and stronger our relationship with him will be.

Intimacy with another person is in proportion to how well we know the other person. It comes from experiences we have with the other person. For intimacy to grow, the experiences must be positive in order to keep us pursuing the other person.

When we think of a relationship with God, can there be any negative experiences with him? Will God ever treat us poorly or in an unloving way? The answer has to be *no*! So this provides a tremendous basis for establishing an intimate relationship with God.

Intimacy in Terms of a Metaphor of Spatial Language

In human terms, intimacy is the deepest of relationships. It is what we call the experience of really knowing and being known by another person. It's not easy to come up with ways to describe intimacy. It's interesting to note that we frequently use spatial language when describing what intimacy is. For example, an intimate friend is someone we feel very *close* to. They know us at a *deep level*. As another example, if something happens that damages the intimacy with our friend, they feel *distant* from us. Or a person who doesn't know us intimately knows us at a *superficial level*.

We all know what it's like to be sitting right next to a person with whom we feel *distant* while we can feel *close* to a person who is three thousand miles away. It's not a physical measurement but an emotional one.

But of course, intimacy is not just understood in spatial terms. It's primarily considered in relational terms. With our most intimate friends, we characterize the relationship as being one where there is trust, sincere care for each other, good communication, someone we can depend on, etc.

Many Approach a Relationship with God Differently

Again, it is evident that people have all kinds of a relationship with God. It is probably true that each person has the exact kind of relationship they want with God at the time.

Some want a close, very personal, vulnerable, open, and intimate relationship with God. Some want a good relationship with God, but not to the extent just mentioned. Some see highly dedicated

Christians as radical or extreme in contrast to the kind of relationship they try to have with God. Some label these Christians as fanatical or Jesus freaks. Then there are other Christians who are more moderate, reserved, and conservative in their relationship with God. And then some have a marginal relationship with God.

I believe the personality and emotional makeup of people has an influence on the kind of relationship people seek with each other and with God. Some are more inclined to approach God and life more from the head and others more from the heart. Many are both!

Some people are what many call touchy-feely kind of people. They can be known to interpret things through their emotions, wear their emotions on their sleeves, and react more emotionally than others. They want to experience life emotionally. They are more emotionally expressive about most things. Because of this, some look to have more of an emotional relationship with God than others.

Some people are not as emotionally oriented and relate to people and God on a more cognitive and rational basis. Some of this difference may relate to those who are extroverts and those who are introverts. Because the more cognitive oriented person is not as emotionally reactive, they may sense that others more emotional in their orientation think they aren't experiencing life or God as passionately as they should. Some emotionally oriented people may assess the quality of a person's faith based on their emotional reactions or the lack thereof.

As mentioned earlier in this book, what we want in a relationship with God and expect to have with God often depends on our doctrinal beliefs and understanding of scriptures. Some look to hear God's voice and believe God is speaking to them regularly. Some believe God is in control of everything happening in their lives and spend a great deal of effort trying to figure out why God allowed something to happen to them. Some believe God's providence means that God will protect them from bad things happening to them. Some believe God has a specific and unique plan for their lives. And so when bad things happen, this throws their faith off-balance.

Because of all of this, the truth is, even though we all try to follow the same scriptures, we see things differently and expect different things from God.

I have a friend who is very emotionally oriented and comes from the view that God speaks to him regularly. Everything that happens is interpreted through the lens of God being involved in it by causing it to happen. He recently shared a video with me of a person using a metaphor to encourage others to trust God to handle our problems for us.

Video here: https://www.youtube.com/watch?v=Aj4Eg4QKKJs.

In the video, he said, "Give your worries, your cares, your problems to Christ and he'll take care of every need that we got. Give everything you got to God and let him handle it for you."

When I challenged his thinking, saying that I believe this video took the metaphor too far, he then questioned me, asking me then, "How do you lead people to Christ if you can't tell them to trust in Christ and give their burdens to him?"

I basically responded by saying something I mentioned earlier in this book about why we become Christians. It is based on dealing with our sins which separate us from God and reconciling us back to God for salvation and eternal life. Not because we want God to solve our problems in life for us. It also relates to my Christian worldview that affirms we are in a partnership relationship with God. This partnership concept is critical to my understanding of how God works with us in this life. We'll discuss this concept in the chapter entitled "Our Relationship with God—a Partnership."

That story about the discussion regarding the video is an example of how Christian people approach a relationship with God differently. Based on what we know about differing doctrines, such as Calvinism, differing denominations, and the ways each person is free to think whatever they want, we can understand why people in a relationship with God expect differing things from God.

As I've mentioned in the introduction and other places in this book, I believe that many are misinformed and misguided in how they approach a relationship with God.

Many may think of intimacy with Christ as some lofty level of mysterious, feelings-based communion with the Divine, as if it involved some knowledge of God that goes beyond what scripture has revealed. We must be cautious about this.

Enhancing Our Intimacy with God

I believe there are simple and obvious ways to understand how we can enhance our intimacy with God.

Love

One way relates to our love for God. We need to nurture this love and keep it growing. A deep love for God creates a desire for more closeness with him. Many would say we have barely experienced the depth of what loving God is really all about. When we obey God and love others, it's like an expression of love to God also.

God's Word

Another way is that we need to build our relationship with God based on the scriptures. Again, there are a lot of influences out there to encourage people to seek more from God and spirituality, which are not clearly stated in the scriptures. I relate to several of these in this book. I believe if something is important, it would be clearly and frequently stated in the scriptures. This underscores the need for us to be "in the scriptures." We need to have time for reading and studying the scriptures. We must not forget that knowledge is good and powerful, but so is obedience. One of Satan's most powerful tactics is planting weeds in the church—not literal weeds but false teachers who dilute the Word of God. False teachers are everywhere, and they can come from well-intentioned people. Be on guard.

Prayer

Prayer is an obvious way to stay close to God. Prayer is keeping company with God. Prayer involves us thinking of God frequently and telling God our most intimate and personal thoughts. As we open up to God regarding all of this, we make ourselves more vulnerable to God, which will demonstrate God's love and trustworthiness. I believe God is thrilled when his children are open and honest with him. After all, we do know that he knows our thoughts anyway. We really can't hide from him. So we should embrace this reality and tell God what's in our heart as a sincere effort to be transparent.

Service

One of the ways we get closer to God is in being active in our service to others in need. We are close to God when we do things that are close to his heart. What breaks God's heart should break our heart. Caring for the oppressed, poor, disadvantaged, and needy are ways we can please God. As Jesus said in Matthew 25, when we help others in need, it's like we are doing this to Jesus himself. Matthew 25:40 states, "The King will reply, 'Truly I tell you, whatever you did for one of the least of these brothers and sisters of mine, you did for me.'" I think when we spend time helping others, it's like spending time with God also.

Godliness

There are many scriptures encouraging us to live godly lives. This simply means living lives that are pleasing to God. Some of what is mentioned in these passages includes faith, knowledge of truth, doing good, having compassion, pursuing righteousness, and having endurance and perseverance. We can't go wrong by living according to the fruits of the Spirit in Galatians 5:22–23: love, joy, peace, patience, kindness, goodness, faithfulness, gentleness, and self-control. The apostle Paul said in 1 Timothy 4:8, "For physical training is of some value, but godliness has value for all things, holding promise for both the present life and the life to come."

Worship

True worship is a heartfelt expression of love, adoration, admiration, fascination, wonder, and celebration. It's something that happens in your heart and soul when you begin to praise God for who he is and thank him for what he has done. True worship is seeing afresh the tremendous worth of God and, in response, giving him the best of everything we have. Through true worship, we are somehow transformed. Our lives are renewed, energy is gained, hope is received, and love is offered and embraced. There is something divine about worship that is hard to define and difficult to grasp but there nonetheless. This can renew our spirit and keep us close to God. As we all can agree, some of our most intimate times with God are when we sing songs that touch our hearts.

Suffering

Suffering together with others brings people closer together. The same is true with God. Suffering teaches us a lot about life and enhances our relationship with God. Suffering clarifies what is truly valuable. Suffering sows the seed of compassion. Suffering makes us homesick (for heaven). Suffering teaches us how to pray. Suffering separates the superficial from the significant. Suffering can draw our interests toward God. One of the most rewarding reasons that suffering has value is experienced by those who can say with conviction, "I know how you feel. I've been in your shoes." Suffering prepares us to minister comfort to others who suffer (2 Cor. 1:4).

Our Relationship to Jesus as Lord

For whatever reason, many Americans have a distorted view of who Jesus is and how to respond to him. According to the Barna Group, less than half of American adults believe Jesus Christ lived a sinless life while he was on earth. Also, *only* two-thirds of those who do claim to be born again strongly believe Jesus was sinless. It is no surprise, then, that our culture has a hard time with the concept of Jesus as Lord.

The Jewish leaders at the time of Jesus did what they could to discredit Jesus by trying to convince the people that Jesus was a fraud, demonic, and a blasphemer. They did this because Jesus was a threat to their status, power, and authority. They threatened to kick people out of the synagogue if they believed in Jesus, which was a huge punishment back then. This largely worked. Today, those who reject Jesus as Lord do so not because of any threats of punishment if they would choose to accept Jesus as Savior and Lord but because of other factors, such as apathy and an unwillingness to believe.

When people respond to the gospel call and accept Jesus as their Lord and Savior, they are baptized by immersion according to the scriptures like Acts 2:38, Roman 6:1–11, Matthew 28:19–20, etc. in the salvation process. During this ceremony, many who do the baptizing ask for the person to confess their faith in Jesus as their Savior and, at the same time, ask the person if they will accept Jesus as the Lord of their life (Rom. 10:9–10). After all, even the demons believe in God and know Jesus as the Holy One (James 2:19; Matt. 8:28–29; Luke 4:31–37). All this underscores the importance of accepting Jesus and committing one's life to following and obeying Jesus. By giving our allegiance to Jesus, we submit to his Lordship as he leads us safely home to heaven.

When we accept Jesus Christ as our Savior, it involves recognition of his Lordship. We cannot and do not receive him as Savior only. We receive him as Lord and Savior.

Most Americans will admit that having a Lord is a foreign concept. In our secular culture, we would not use this term in our daily living. This is a spiritual concept, and therefore we must turn to the scriptures to understand what this means and how it works.

The term *Lord* is used in the New Testament to identify Jesus over six hundred times. The Greek word for *Lord* is *Kurios* (koo'-ree-os), which means "supreme in authority, master, owner." Jesus as Lord makes reference to his deity.

The following scriptures enlighten us as to what it means that Jesus is Lord.

Philippians 2:9–11:

Therefore God exalted him to the highest place and gave him the name that is above every name, [10] that at the name of Jesus every knee should bow, in heaven and on earth and under the earth, [11] and every tongue acknowledge that Jesus Christ is Lord, to the glory of God the Father.

Romans 14:8–9:

[8] If we live, we live for the Lord; and if we die, we die for the Lord. So, whether we live or die, we belong to the Lord. [9] For this very reason, Christ died and returned to life so that he might be the Lord of both the dead and the living.

Matthew 28:18:

[18] Then Jesus came to them and said, "All authority in heaven and on earth has been given to me.

Some will say that when we submit to Jesus as Lord, we give our lives to his authority and control. Why does "and control" need to be in that statement? We submit by seeking to give our lives to his authority. Jesus does not want to control us. He wants us to voluntarily respond to him out of our love for him. He wants to lead us but not control us. There's a big difference.

And so as we seek to live our lives as Christians, we must make a pledge of commitment that will seek to cultivate a life of submission to Christ. This is an ongoing process and not a onetime event.

Jesus as our Lord is not a tyrant. He does not force his way upon us. He wants us to choose to believe and follow him. He wants us to voluntarily submit to him.

CHAPTER 8

---- ❦ ----

Comparing Human Relationships
to One with God

How one actually sees God and one's relationship to
God is going to influence one's desires, one's
decisions, and the habit of one's life.

—Balint Nagy

We know a lot about relationships between people. Social scientists have studied this for decades, if not centuries. We know more about this now than we ever have. I believe we know the most about marital relationships, the most intimate of them all. We also know a lot about family relationships.

There is a sense in which what we know about relationships and why they are healthy and functional can apply to some degree to indicate how to have a healthy and functional relationship between a person and God. However, due to the uniqueness of the relationship between a human being and God, many indicators don't fully apply. Some don't apply at all. The simple reason is in how vastly different the two beings are.

Research studies can focus on human to human relationships. I don't know any that are focused on the relationship between a person and God involving input from both.

Obviously, the relationship between human beings lends itself to empirical examination. It can be observed through our senses and with feedback from the participants. All kinds of aspects of the relationship can be studied. Psychological and medical testing can be done. However, none of this can be used to understand the relationship between God and a person. In investigating this relationship, it is most often a one-way analysis.

Biblical Metaphors Regarding God's Relationship to Mankind

There are many metaphors God uses in scripture to explain our relationship with him.

- **We are the clay, and he is the potter.**

Jeremiah 18:1–6; Isaiah 64:8. This is a metaphor with many levels of meaning and application. Simply, this reflects God's creativity and care in making us. It reflects a vision for how God hopes we will turn out and of his purpose for our lives reflected by our design. Underneath all of this infers a special relationship God would like to have with us.

- **He is the Vine, We are the Branches.**

John 15:1–11. This metaphor relates to Jesus being the true and perfect vine through whom the life of God flows. We are told in verse 4, "Remain in me, as I also remain in you. No branch can bear fruit by itself; it must remain in the vine. Neither can you bear fruit unless you remain in me." There is a two-part process being referred to here: remaining in Jesus and Jesus remaining in us. This represents what we are to do and what Christ will do. We do the work of "remaining in Jesus, abiding in Jesus." Jesus does the work of remaining in us. It's a partnership relationship.

- **We are the sheep, and he is the shepherd.**

John 10:1–18. In this passage, God speaks as the chief shepherd of his people to the under-shepherds he has appointed to watch over his people for him. These shepherds are the religious leaders of Israel. They are denounced for being more concerned with feeding themselves than their sheep. Instead of caring for the sheep entrusted to them, they have neglected them. Jesus can easily make a distinction between himself as the good shepherd and the Pharisees and other religious leaders as the bad shepherds. He compares the bad shepherds to hired hands, non-owners whose connection to and protection of the flock has limits. The flock's best interests are not primary; their personal interests are. Good shepherds have to go the extra mile and put their own lives at risk. Bad shepherds would not do this. This sets Jesus apart from the religious leaders who supposedly shepherd the people of God. Whereas Jesus is selfless, they are selfish. Whereas he would lay down his life for the sheep, they would abandon all to save themselves. Whereas Jesus lived in complete obedience to the Father, they were obedient to their own personal interests and placed this above all else.

- **We are his children.**

Romans 8:17; Galatians 4:6. Here God uses the father-to-children metaphor in describing the relationship he has with us. He is our heavenly father. He is our adoptive father. The relationship we have with God is mostly as an adult-child-to-God our father relationship. This is a relationship begun through choice. It reflects the way God can show his love to us and vice versa. It relates to the inheritance in store for those who are God's children.

- **We are his friend.**

John 15:15. Jesus is giving his disciples a pep talk to inspire them to be strong as they are about to encounter troubles and challenges ahead. He has chosen these eleven people for a special reason

(Judas has already left by this time). Jesus brings up the idea that they are not slaves/servants. He wants them to know he regards them with high esteem. He wants to call them friends. Because they are friends, he has given them information to the extent that no one else has received. He stresses again that he wants them to bear fruit, to ask for anything in his name, and to obey his command to love each other.

- **We are the bride. He is the bridegroom.**

Matthew 9:15; Matthew 25:1–13; John 3:29. This is a marriage metaphor to relate to the kind of relationship we can have with God. This is a picture of God's interest in his people and his desire to bring us into his fellowship. *This relationship is about choice.* We must choose to love him. Again, not for what he does for us but for who he is. This is about God's pursuit and desire for us. Everything about a healthy marital union has been designed by God to be a reflection of the interaction that we are meant to have with God himself. We make the decision to enter into a relationship with God. He sets the terms for this relationship.

I propose the marital relationship between a man and woman is the closest one for use in comparison about how we can have an intimate relationship with God. The marital relationship is the deepest of all relationships. The parent-child relationship is a close second.

We understand much about what makes marriages work, what indicates they are healthy as well as what can cause them to break down and deteriorate. Unfortunately, even with this knowledge, the success rate of marriages shows people are not very good with them. With the divorce rate around 50 percent, we see it is difficult to develop and sustain a healthy, positive, and lasting marital relationship.

The reasons for this are found within the persons themselves. Humans have personal frailties, issues, problems, and weaknesses which negatively impact relationships. It is these same realities that are involved in a relationship between a person and God. So it could logically be expected that many humans might not be very good at a relationship with God either.

So let's look at what we know are characteristics of healthy, intimate marital relationships between a husband and a wife. At the same time, I'll reflect on how they relate to our relationship with God.

Marital Relationships Compared to our Relationship with God

The list of ways people characterize healthy marital relationships could be very long if we separated each quality out on its own. So I have grouped many items together under what I thought was the appropriate heading.

We would all do well if we each had all of these qualities with the relationship we have with our spouses. I think we can use these qualities to relate to a quality relationship we can have with God.

1. Unconditional Love

Love is the main motivator in the decision to get married. Love is much deeper than being attracted to each other. Love includes emotion, but it is deeper than emotion. A love that leads to a desire to commit to each other is ideally deep and wide. It is based on a connection to each other that desires more of each other. Love is based on a good understanding of who each other is and a commitment to be there for and with each other for the long haul. This kind of love is a combination of agape love (deep unconditional love), eros love (romantic love), philia love (friendship love), and storgē love (family love). This deep love creates a hunger to spend time with each other, to cherish each other, and to protect each other. In healthy relationships, love grows deeper over time.

Response: For most people, it is a challenge to love someone we don't know personally. It's a challenge to love someone we can't see. There is an inherent challenge in developing a love relationship with an invisible God. We can know a good amount about God and Jesus from the scriptures. The love we are to have for God is agape love. This comes more from our cognitions (our minds) than our emotions. Love for anybody is strengthened over time as we have an interaction with the person. Our interactions with God are largely on another plane than the physical. God has set the highest reaches for us in commanding us to love him with all our heart, soul, and mind (Matt. 22:37). We need to spend a lifetime reaching for this kind of love. We love God because he has first loved us (1 John 4:19).

2. Mutual Respect

Respect is holding each other up as very important to each other. Respect values who each person is and cherishes this. Respect is said to be one of the most important qualities to have in a marriage and a close relationship. Respecting each other means not having a score card of what one likes and does not like about the other. Respect offers unconditional acceptance. Respect needs to be treasured and cherished. Respect can be diminished, so it needs to be nourished. It is based on two people agreeing to value each other. How can one be in a healthy marital relationship without mutual respect?

Response: Our relationship with God is based on respect and much more: tremendous awe with a humble heart. God is not our equal, so we need to have this in mind at all times. The respect we have for God is like no other. It is based on God being our creator, king, Lord, and all that comes with him being a sovereign entity. God made us in his image reflecting that he has respect and love for us.

3. Unwavering Commitment

Making a commitment to each other is a critical decision made while taking a relationship to higher levels of intimacy. To decide to get married for a lifetime requires an unwavering commitment. Marriage is not for temporary commitments. A commitment places the relationship in the highest of priorities in one's life. A commitment is a promise. It is based on the reality that there will be ups and downs in a relationship, but that they can be worked through and the commitment preserved. A committed relationship is the only kind that offers one to feel secure in the relationship. Insecurity can eat at a relationship and destroy the bond between two people.

Response: God expects the highest level of dedication and commitment from us. The level of love he commands of us reflects the commitment needed. We are to seek first the kingdom of God (Matt. 6:33). Our relationship with God must be the highest priority in our lives. In human relationships, like a marriage, it is clearly evident that people are not the best in keeping their commitments. The result is often divorce. With God, not keeping our commitment has grave consequences. We must not take this commitment lightly. We see God's commitment reflected in the reason he created the heavens and the earth, for us to have a relationship with him. God also showed us his commitment by giving us his son to come to earth and die for us.

4. Effective Communication

It's been said, "As communication goes, so goes the relationship." Communication between two people is for sharing thoughts, feelings, and needs and to deal with questions, issues, and the sharing of all kinds of ideas. Communication is a process where there is a sender (speaker) and a receiver (listener). Communication can break down on either side. Some people may say, "Good communication is defined as when there is full and complete understanding between two people." However, I think we can all agree that there are times when we don't want to share every thought we have. We want some things to stay hidden and not expressed. So when you ask yourself, "What is good communication?" the answer would be "it depends." It depends on what is deemed as appropriate in the situation. Sometimes we just want to be superficial as when we are greeting people. Sometimes we don't want to get too deep. Sometimes we might want to mask what we're thinking to not offend someone. Sometimes we need to be very clear and need the other person to know exactly what we are trying to communicate. Good communication takes into consideration nonverbal aspects also. It's been said that "one cannot not communicate." That's because everything we do communicates something, even our silence. Healthy communication is vital for a healthy relationship.

Response: Human beings communicate all the time, every day. Much of this communication takes place in person while some is over the phone or through e-mails and texting. Communication is almost always a two-way process. Communication with God is on a different plane, away from the physical. It's likely that we communicate with God mostly through prayer. God communicates with us mostly through the Bible, his written word. We know the scriptures talk about the Holy Spirit communicating with our spirit (Rom. 8:16). We will be exploring later about the controversy of other ways God may communicate with us, i.e., "Does he talk to us through our minds a lot?" The kind of intimacy two people have is based on the deep and effective communication they have with each other. For us and God, the kind of communication is just different.

5.   Mutual Trust

Trust is the foundation of a good relationship. Without trust, a relationship is on thin ice and will not be healthy and likely will not last. Trust must be earned, and it happens over time. Words can be cheap. Deep trust comes when people have many experiences together and have shown themselves to be trustworthy. Trust is a fragile thing. Be very careful with it and protect it at all costs. If trust is broken, it can be repaired. However, it will take time and a willingness to go down that path. Once trust is broken, a crack will always remain. Trust is what makes a relationship secure.

Response: Trust with God is a different experience as we are dealing with the spiritual world. The scriptures say that God is trustworthy and God expresses through the scriptures that he wants human beings to trust him. The question is, "What does it mean to say we trust God?" What do we trust God for...for everything or for specific things? In the relationship we have with God, we have a perfect being who never makes a mistake combined with a human being who makes mistakes all the time. We trust God for what we are certain he will do. He will keep his promises and remain true to his godly nature.

6. Honesty and Transparency

How can there be a healthy relationship without honesty and transparency? Trust is based on truthfulness. Truth matters. Being open with each other and sharing true thoughts and feelings is the way to have a healthy interaction and relationship. Each one needs to be candid with their partners about their thoughts, feelings, desires, and needs. Each one needs to receive these with a heart for understanding and working through concerns. If people stop being open and transparent, walls between two people can develop. Strong relationships are when two people can be mutually vulnerable with each other.

Response: God by his very nature cannot be dishonest. God will reveal what he wants to reveal to us. We don't make any demands in this area. God expects us to be honest with him. Another difference between us and God is that God knows what we are thinking (Matt. 9:4). He can read minds. Humans think they can, but we really can't! We can't hide from God in any sense of the term.

7. Shared Values

Values reflect what is most important in a person's life. If these are different between two people, it would be hard to develop a strong, committed, and trusting relationship. A person's values are what guide one's life. If values are different, people are going in differing directions on what is most important to them in life. This will be a source of much disagreement and disappointment. Those with very different values should not enter into a marital relationship.

Response: In a relationship with God, he sets the standards for our values and morality. We must adopt his values as our own and live our lives by these values. We must do a lot of changing and adapting in the process of adopting God's values. We have the Holy Spirit to help us. We must strive to be perfect and holy…a never-ending pursuit. Being made in God's image reflects that we have similar attributes and abilities. These can help us to live as God wants us to live.

8. Meeting Each Other's Needs

Much has been learned in recent years about understanding the personalities of each other and the differing needs each one has. Spouses need to be open about all of this. They should come to know what the needs of each other are and commit to doing what they can to meet these needs. This reflects the level of love and commitment each one has to the relationship. This is one of the basic reasons why people enter into relationships.

Response: God's will for our lives relates to the needs he has. As we humbly live in obedience to God, he will be with us each step of the way. God meets all of our spiritual needs. Our physical and emotional needs are another story. Life is difficult for human beings. God confirms this in John 16:33. For a deeper look at this aspect of our relationship with God, read the upcoming chapter "Our Relationship with God—a Partnership."

9. Conflict Resolution and Problem Solving

It is inevitable that in a relationship between two people, there is going to be disappointment and conflict. This is not an indicator that a relationship is dysfunctional or unhealthy. In fact, conflict that gets resolved, especially in positive ways, is helpful to a relationship and indeed strengthens a relationship. Positive conflict resolution includes problem solving and the use of effective communication. It represents a desire to make the relationship better and can bring people to an improved understanding between each other and in how to prevent future issues. Unresolved conflict, which is so common, can be hurtful and can eat away at a relationship. Unresolved issues never go away. It is best to deal with issues as they occur when they are small. Waiting to deal with them can make it a more difficult process and makes them bigger. When agreement can't be reached, compromise becomes the next step. This should resolve the situation. When issues between people have caused deep hurt, it may take forgiveness in order to resolve the situation.

Response: It is inevitable that there will be problems between people based on the human nature of people. However, God has a godly nature. He makes no mistakes and does nothing wrong that needs to be resolved. The issues or problems between us and God will be caused by us. They will be our fault. Thankfully, God has deep love for us and offers us grace, mercy, and forgiveness. We must initiate the process of resolving our conflicts with God, beginning with a humble and repentant heart.

10. Equality and Balance of Power

Equality is a concept that can easily be misunderstood. No relationship is completely equal. It is not to be understood as literal equality. It is to be an approximate equality. Equality keeps relationships safe and fair. A marital relationship between people who are so different and unequal can be very difficult to be healthy. In fact, many marital problems emerge because of the unequal nature of a relationship. Inequality can lead to one person dominating another. For instance, in a boxing match, if one person is physically way superior in strength and skill, the unskilled person does not stand a chance. In a high school debate, if one person is way superior in knowledge of the subject, the other person does not have a chance. In a marriage, if one person has many more strengths combined with the other person being very weak, the relationship is not evenly matched. Those who are significantly more intelligent and skilled at debating can usually out argue and manipulate the other person. Those who have the power in the relationship can use that power to dominate the other person who likely is intimidated and afraid of the person.

If one holds most of the power, the other is often mistreated. So how does one get more power in a relationship? The saying "power concedes nothing without a demand" is relevant here. Improvement in self-esteem can be helpful. Learning communication and negotiation skills can be helpful. As an example and reminder, the apostle Paul encourages Christians not to be unequally yoked with unbelievers in 2 Corinthians 6:14.

Response: Here again, there is a vastly different relationship between God and humans versus the relationship between humans and humans in this area. God holds all the power. He has complete control of everything but chooses to give a significant amount of power to humans by way of free will. He voluntarily limits the amount of his sovereignty by giving this power to humans. This allows humans to make independent decisions which can result in humans doing things against God's will. This dynamic will be addressed in the chapter on "Is God in Control of Everything?"

11. Physical and Emotional Intimacy

In a marriage relationship, physical and emotional intimacy is vitally important. This is designed by God to be unique to the marital relationship. Meeting each other's needs for physical intimacy and being emotionally open to another are ways to be very close to each other.

Response: Obviously, we don't have a physical relationship with God. The emotional aspect of the relationship varies from person to person, partly because of the personality differences between people. God wants us to love him with all we've got…but that is not largely an emotionally oriented kind of love. It is agape love.

12. Spending Quality and Quantity Time Together

The purpose of establishing and pursuing a quality relationship with another person comes from a desire to spend a lot of time with that person, to share one's life with another. Unfortunately, over time, many relationships lose the special connection they've had with their partner. People's lives can drift apart for many reasons. There needs to be a commitment to remain present with each other. Quality time together is important as well as quantity of time together. Couples must stay interested in each other's lives, including their hobbies, careers, etc. Each person needs the support of the other.

Response: Since God is always with us, we are never apart from him. However, we can take our focus off him as well as spiritual matters easily. We are to set our minds on things above as Paul tells us in Colossians 3. We are to set our minds on things of the Spirit as Paul says in Romans 8. We spend time with God as we set our minds on God through reading scripture and other Christian materials, prayer, fellowshipping with other Christians, etc. When do we not spend time with God?

13. Taking Responsibility for Maintaining a Quality Relationship

As a rhetorical question, "Whose responsibility is it for the relationship to remain healthy and meaningful?" The answer obviously is each person. The problem is, often one or maybe even both lose interest over time. Each person should take responsibility to keep the relationship vibrant. If, indeed, one loses interest and the other does not, then there are ways to deal with this. Counseling may be necessary. The reality is, the one with the least interest has the most power.

Response: As born-again Christians, we are adopted into the family of God. In our relationship with God, he will never lose interest in us. His love for us will never wane or decline. Although there is nothing that can compare or compete with the value of knowing God and being reconciled back into a meaningful relationship with him, there are those who still make the choice to give up on their faith and reject this relationship. God won't reject us. We would have to be the one to break up the relationship. The apostle Paul and others warn us many times to keep our faith strong (2 Cor. 13:5; 1 Cor. 15:2; Col. 1:22–23; John 16:1; 2 Pet. 2:20–22; Heb. 2:1). We need to continually nurture this relationship as we discussed in the last chapter.

14. Our Interdependent Relationship with Each Other

Healthy relationships are between people who are interdependent upon each other. It's a two-way street with each one needing the other. We look for people who can complement us. This would be those who have strengths we don't have and who can offset our deficiencies and weaknesses.

Response: This relates exactly to the kind of relationship we have with God. It is an interdependent relationship where God relies on humans to do things and we rely on God to do things. See the chapter on "Our Relationship with God—a Partnership" where I go into much more detail about this.

CHAPTER 9

―――― ✲ ――――

Created in God's Image for a Special Relationship

[26] Then God said, "Let us make mankind in our image, in our likeness, so that they may rule over the fish in the sea and the birds in the sky, over the livestock and all the wild animals, and over all the creatures that move along the ground." [27] So God created mankind in his own image, in the image of God he created them; male and female he created them.

—Genesis 1:26–27

[1] This is the written account of Adam's family line. When God created mankind, he made them in the likeness of God. [2] He created them male and female and blessed them. And he named them "Mankind" when they were created. [3] When Adam had lived 130 years, he had a son in his own likeness, in his own image; and he named him Seth.

—Genesis 5:1–3

Whoever sheds human blood, by humans shall their blood be shed; for in the image of God has God made mankind.

—Genesis 9:6

Entering into a discussion of what it means for man to be made in the image of God is a challenging endeavor. From what I understand, there is a fair amount of debate and discrepancy among biblical scholars on what is meant by man being made in the image of God. Obviously, this makes it even more challenging for those of us who are not scholars who want to understand this concept.

Even so, I think there may be a renewal of appreciation emerging for how important the concept is of man being made in God's image. In Latin, the phrase is "imago Dei" (pronounced "emaugo day").

Most of us are familiar with this idea and have likely used this term in many differing contexts. However, I'm not sure how many of us have delved deeply into the ramifications of its significance. Even though we call "made in the image of God" a phrase, it's much more than that. It's a concept. Some now call this concept a doctrine because of the widespread and far reaching implications and applications of what it means. The term *doctrine* refers to a position, policy, or particular set of beliefs about a topic.

God Created Man Very Good

Genesis chapter 1 tells of God's creative work when he created the heavens and the earth. In verses 1 through 25, we are told of God creating everything except man up to that point. Periodically, after creating what he did in those twenty-five verses, the scripture says, "And God saw that it was good" on six occasions (in verses 4, 10, 12, 18, 21 and 25). On the sixth day, God then created man. We are then told in Genesis 1:31, "God saw all that He had made, and it was very good."

In that verse, God elevated the quality of what he made from "good" to "very good." The "very good" came after man was created. There has to be some significance in this narrative. The creation of man was more special than all God had created before that event. By saying this, we can understand that God deliberately elevated the value of man above all the other things he created by saying, in effect, man was made very good. I believe that is because man was made in God's image.

There are atheists who believe that there is no God and that man was made out of nothing by no one. If there is no God, there's no chance we were made in his image. If that is true, that would mean we are the result of an impersonal process like evolution. If there's no God, then we have no soul and are merely material objects.

The question is, "If humans are not endowed with value by God, then what determines human worth?"

Being in the image and likeness of God is applicable only to human beings. This distinction is not attributable to other created beings. It might be hard to fathom, but we are God's masterpiece. Mankind is the only being or thing in this world with inherent value. We're the only aspect of creation Jesus was willing to die for. We're the only aspect of creation in this world with whom God wants to have a relationship. We are special indeed!

What It Means to Be Created in God's Image

Every human being bears God's image and likeness. However, the scriptures do not provide an explanation for what this concept means, which makes discussing it more challenging. So we have to use our God-given minds to figure this out the best we can.

Since there is no explicit definition, we will have to make a case for what we best think it means and represents. And from this understanding, we can then make inferences and application. Because the scriptures don't give us explicit definitions, we must be cautious about our interpretations.

One of the areas of disagreement and discrepancy among biblical scholars is whether the image of God refers to man's bodily appearance and physical likeness. Some scholars would suggest that this should be included in the understanding of what it means for man to be made in the image of God. Others disagree.

Since we know that God is a spirit (John 4:24), a case can be made that it's not the material part of humanity which refers to the image of God. But from another point of view, the human body is incredibly complex and represents the majestic. Our bodies are perfect in many ways. This reflects God's nature. Can anyone even imagine a better way to make the human body?

The fact that God came to earth (Jesus) in the body of a human being says something about his acceptance of the human body being fit for him. This infers that the human body was an acceptable likeness of him. We all know the human body is truly amazing and therefore does reflect the glory of God. The human body is said to be the temple of the Holy Spirit (1 Cor. 6:19), which gives it added value!

Again, although scripture mentions being in the image of God in several places, it never gives us a precise definition of what this means. In fact, scripture does not even attempt to define this. The question is, "Why not?" If we think about this, it may be that trying to define this phrase would be like trying to define God.

We know we learn about God from the various passages of scripture regarding his character, nature, attributes, and other descriptions. These all point to various elements of who God is but do not provide a full and total explanation. In fact, scripture tells us that God is beyond our understanding (Isa. 55:8–9; Rom. 11:33–34; 1 Cor. 2:16). God is one of a kind. There is no other like him (Isa. 45:22). So there is no way we could put into words a description of who God is fully.

In reality, there is something very comforting about this. Most of us would admit that we want a God who is great, majestic, very complicated, powerful, and beyond the ability of our minds to fathom. This is the kind of God who is omniscient, omnipotent, and omnipresent who can create the heavens and the earth out of nothing. This is the kind of God who is worthy of our praise, admiration, dedication, and worship.

Definitions of "Image of God"

So we come back to the question, "What is meant by the 'image of God' in mankind?" Men and women are made in the likeness of God.

So how do we come up with a reasonable definition or idea of how to determine what it means for man to be made in the image of God? I found some interesting descriptions from searching online.

Definitions from Christianity.com:

> Imago Dei, or Image of God, means in likeness, or similarity, to God. Humans are created with a unique nature and set of abilities and qualities that mirror the divine nature of God.
>
> Image of God is defined as the metaphysical expression, associated uniquely to humans, which signifies the symbolical connection between God and humanity. The phrase has its origins in Genesis 1:27, wherein "God created man in his own image..." This biblical passage does not imply that God is in human form, but that humans are in the image of God in their moral, spiritual, and intellectual essence. Thus, humans reflect God's divine nature in their ability to achieve the unique characteristics with which they have been endowed. These unique qualities make humans different than all other creatures: rational understanding, creative liberty, the capacity for self-actualization, and the potential for self-transcendence.

Definition from Bible Dictionary:

> But what is meant by the terms "image" and "likeness"? Three approaches to this question are commonly found, and no doubt all three have some merit. Many have concluded that humans are image-bearers due to their superior intellectual structure. Others have stressed that God mandates that humans function as rulers and managers of the creation as they image him (Gen

1:26-28; Psalm 8:5–8). Yet another approach stresses the created relationships of humans; they image God as they relate to him, to each other, and to nature. Just as the Creator is a being in relationship, so are his creatures. Putting these views together, humans are like God in that they are uniquely gifted intellectually (and in many other ways) so that they may relate to God and to each other as they live as stewards of the world God has given them to manage.

When the Bible talks about God creating human beings in his image and likeness, this could be a way of saying we are a close replica of God himself. This image likely reflects wonderful qualities and abilities as those are the only kind God himself has. The term *likeness* confirms we are not an exact copy.

When the scriptures refer to us as being in the divine image, this does not mean that we're little gods. This is what those in the Word of Faith movement promote.

I encourage you to look at the Bible Project website for their video on the "Image of God" at the following link: https://bibleproject.com/explore/image-god/.

Being in the image of God distinguishes us from all other living creatures, which, by implication, are *not* made in the image of God. Genetically, we may be almost identical to our nearest animal relative, the chimpanzee, but spiritually we are poles apart.

I've put together a chart below that compares that attributes of God to the attributes of mankind and then a contrast to the attributes of animals. (We won't find much there even as we know many like to compare some people to animals!)

Attributes of God	Attributes of Mankind	Attributes of Animals
Sovereign *(Psalms 103:9;* *2 Chronicles 20:61)* Supreme Ruler, Lord of All in Heaven and Earth	• Mankind rules over the earth. • Mankind has a lot of power and ability. • Checkered history in submitting to God's authority. • Mankind consists largely of spiritual beings needing and wanting a God who is in ultimate control.	The animal world has no metaphysical qualities similar to mankind and God. The animal world has no relationship with God. The animal world functions according to the survival of the fittest.
Infinite *(Psalms 90:2;* *Revelation 10:6; 1* *Timothy 1:17)* Self-Existing, Eternal, Everlasting, Without Origin	• Mankind had a beginning, being created as mentioned in Genesis 1. • Mankind is a fragile mortal being. • Life after death for all—heaven or hell. • Eternal life through Jesus for the faithful.	The animal world has no life after death. The animal world cannot be compared as being similar to mankind in any significant way other than having physical attributes, such as a physical body, some kind of brain, and an animal nature.
Spirit *(John 4:24; 2* *Corinthians 3:17)* Invisible, Non-Physical	• Mankind has a physical body. • Mankind has a soul and a spirit. • Mankind's body is a temple for the Holy Spirit.	Animals have physical bodies but do not have a spirit.
Immutable *(Malachi 3:6;* *1 Samuel 15:29)* Never Changes	• Mankind can change in positive and negative ways with free will.	Animals are generally responsive to instinct and physical needs.

Omnipotent *(2 Corinthians 6:18; Luke 1:37; Ephesians 3:20)* All Powerful	• Mankind has great brain power with creative and innovative abilities. • Mankind has free will which gives us great power. • Mankind has power given from God. • Mankind's power is miniscule compared to God's.	Animals have brains with substantially less intellect than mankind and rely on instinct and perception of their environment to survive.
Omniscient *(Hebrews 4:13; Isaiah 46:9–10; Romans 11:33; Matthew 6:8; Matthew 9:4)* All Knowing, Unlimited Intelligence, Knows What We Think and Need	• Man has intelligence, but within limitations.	See above.
Omnipresent *(Jeremiah 23:23–24; Psalm 137)* Everywhere	• Mankind is only physically present in one place at a time. • Through technology, mankind can be present in many places. • Nothing compares to God's ability.	
All Wise *(Romans 11:33; Ephesians 3:10; Jeremiah 10:12)* Perfect Unchanging Wisdom	• Mankind can be very wise through age and experience. • Mankind can receive wisdom as a gift from God at times. • Mankind has little brain power compared to God.	

Rational *(Isaiah 1:18; James 3:17; Ephesians 4:17–28; 1 Corinthians 14:33)* Thinks and Acts Logically, He is not a God of confusion.	• Mankind is a rational being just like God. • Logic is needed to interact with others. • Mankind has differing abilities to be logical. • Mankind's brain power is not as great as God's.	
Relational *(2 Corinthians 1:3–5; John 16:23; Luke 6:36)* Wants to Share Love and Care for Others, Social Being	• Humans are social beings in need of meaningful relationships. • Need to share and receive love.	
Holy *(1 Peter 1:16; Matthew 5:48; Revelation 4:8)* Pure and Perfect, Righteous	• Mankind has ability to pursue holiness but is limited in power. • Mankind gets help from God. • Mankind is nowhere near perfect.	
Just *(Deuteronomy 32:4; Amos 5:24; Micah 6:8; Isaiah 61:8; Psalm 89:14)* Justice for All, God Wants Justice from Everyone	• Mankind wants justice, but coupled with mercy due to tendency to make mistakes and bad choices. • Life with humans is not fair. • Checkered history with justice.	
Faithful *(Lamentations 3:22–23; 1 John 1:9; Psalms 145:17)* True and Trustworthy	• Checkered history with being faithful to other humans, i.e., marriage, other agreements. • Checkered history with being faithful to God.	

Love *(1 John 3:1;* *1 John 4:7–8)* Loves Everyone	• Mankind has great capacity to give and receive love. • Extremely important to most. • Many people can be unloving, indifferent and hateful.	
Good *(Psalms 34:8;* *Psalms 145:9;* *Mark 10:8)* Nature, Essence and Motivation Is Good, Full of Goodwill	• Mankind has both a good and evil nature—human nature • Some choose goodness mostly over evil and bad while others choose the opposite. • Morality is becoming less godly oriented in many societies.	
Gracious *(Psalms 145:8;* *Ephesians 1:7; Joel 2:13)* Compassion in Giving What Don't Deserve, Forgiving	• Most humans are gracious while others can be very coldhearted. • Humans have a selfish nature.	
Merciful *(Isaiah 30:18;* *Luke 6:27–38; Psalms* *86:15; Ephesians 2:4–5)* Compassion in Not Giving What Do Deserve, Forgiving	• Most humans are merciful while others can be very coldhearted. • Humans have a selfish nature.	
Glorious *(Isaiah 43:7;* *Psalms 72:19;* *Exodus 32–34)* Splendor, Importance, Greatness	• Mankind is an incredible being capable of positive behavior and great accomplishments. • Mankind is capable of the opposite of the above.	

Based on the above analysis, mankind has many qualities which are similar to God although different in amount, frequency, duration, and consistency of application. We are earthly beings with physical bodies but also have the promise of spiritual bodies in the afterlife (1 Cor. 15:42–44).

Some of the qualities of mankind vary greatly between people. There is a wide contrast. Some humans choose to treat others in loving, kind, gracious, and merciful ways. Then there are others who choose to be very uncaring, hateful, vicious, and evil. Some turn to God and seek to have a quality relationship with him while others reject God and live a self-centered existence. Because of free will, we know it is up to each person to choose how they want to treat others.

Based on scripture, we know that any amount of sin separates us from God. Thankfully, God has made a way to restore our relationship with him. This is made possible through the sacrifice of Jesus who went to the cross to pay the price for our forgiveness and reconciliation. No one else could do this.

Sin has corrupted, broken, marred, and damaged our relationship with God, but it does not diminish or change the image of God within us. It is the fact of this image, combined with the love and purposes of God, that we have inherent worth. This worth is in all human beings. For those who respond to the gospel call and dedicate their lives to the Lord, there is eternal meaning and purpose to life with the hope of being with God in heaven after this life.

The Essence of Humans Does Not Change

We are the same beings now as Adam and Eve were when God created them. Let's explore one physiological attribute of human beings, which shows that the essence of a human being does not evolve or change over time. We are the same as Adam and Eve in every way. Being in God's image did not change with Adam's sin.

One of the ways we can be described as a non-changing human being is through science. One area to look at is our DNA.

DNA of Humans

Each person's genome is made of a chemical called deoxyribonucleic acid or DNA. Genome is an organism's complete set of genetic instructions. Each genome contains all the information needed to build that organism and allow it to grow and develop.

DNA or deoxyribonucleic acid is a long molecule that contains our unique genetic code. Like a recipe book, it holds the instructions for making all the proteins in our bodies. It is the hereditary material in humans and almost all other organisms.

Nearly every cell in a person's body has the same DNA. Most DNA is located in the cell nucleus (where it is called nuclear DNA), but a small amount of DNA can also be found in the mitochondria (where it is called mitochondrial DNA or mtDNA). Mitochondria are structures within cells that convert the energy from food into a form that cells can use.

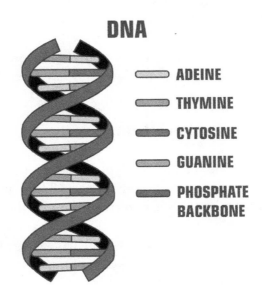

The information in DNA is stored as a code made up of four chemical building blocks or bases: adenine (A), guanine (G), cytosine (C), and thymine (T). Human DNA, our genome, consists of approximately three billion (3,000,000,000) bases pairs and is packed into twenty-three pairs of chromosomes. More than 99 percent of those bases are the same in all people. The order, or sequence, of these bases determines the information available for building and maintaining an organism, similar to the way in which letters of the alphabet appear in a certain order to form words and sentences.

DNA bases pair up with each other, A with T and C with G, to form units called base pairs. Each base is also attached to a sugar molecule and a phosphate molecule. Together, a base, sugar, and phosphate are called a nucleotide. Nucleotides are arranged in two long strands that form a spiral called a double helix. The structure of the double helix is somewhat like a ladder, with the base pairs forming the ladder's rungs and the sugar and phosphate molecules forming the vertical sidepieces of the ladder.

An important property of DNA is that it can replicate or make copies of itself. Each strand of DNA in the double helix can serve as a pattern for duplicating the sequence of bases. This is critical when cells divide because each new cell needs to have an exact copy of the DNA present in the old cell.

The point of all this is to show that humans have a unique DNA that no other creature has, and this has never changed since Adam and Eve.

The Image of God in Us Is Permanent

Can we ever not be the image of God? Can the image of God be diminished in us or taken away from us? There are some scholarly people who mistakenly try to make the case that this happens because of the sin of Adam and Eve. This is what they call the fall. Here they try to make the case that the fall has damaged and changed mankind. This is especially true of some of those who are Calvinists or of the Reformed Theology perspective.

Not all agree. Some Calvinists believe that the image of God is not damaged, marred, lost, or affected in any way because of the sin of Adam and Eve. Some have said that since being made in the image of God was mentioned in Genesis 9:6 after the fall, this implies there was no indication that man lost the image because of the fall. This suggests that the image of God did not change and does not change based on circumstances.

I believe the image of God, the imago Dei, has to be based on premises which do not change. If it can change, then we become less than the image of God. This image stays with all of us for life. We can never cease to be in the image of God. We reflect this image at all times. The big premise associated with man being made in the image of God is that this image has to be permanent. It is permanently built into who we are when God created us just like our DNA. It cannot be changed or altered.

Mankind's God-Given Worth

Another area to consider about being in God's image is our God-given value and worth. This is a very important distinction of what it means to be made in God's image.

Being made in God's image is the transcendent and all-encompassing basis for the self-worth of all human beings. All humans have worth given to us by God. Man does not have the authority to determine our worth. Man does not decide which human being has worth and which human being does not have worth.

If a human being's worth can be assigned by another human, then humans can determine to diminish and dehumanize anyone they choose. If so, it could be based on any criteria. Maybe this would be based on how useful and productive a human could be.

If that could be the case, the value of the lives of those who are impaired in some way can then be reduced. The life of a child with Down syndrome can be diminished. A child born with physical disabilities, mental disabilities, or with medical issues can be diminished. In addition, those who are poor, disadvantaged, illiterate, uneducated, or lower functioning for whatever reason could be diminished. None of this is acceptable to God. It should be rejected by us also. Man has no basis to ascribe gradations of worth to other humans.

It is because of the image of God that man attains his worth. This is something we can't change. There is no way this can be altered if it comes from God. This reality provides no exceptions. Since it comes from God, it can't be denied or refused.

Our concept of the image of God has to encompass the notion that all humans have inherent God-given value. *Inherent* refers to existing in something or someone as a permanent element, quality, or attribute. We also believe that a person's value does not diminish or change based on the person's behavior, abilities, or anything. The worth of human beings comes from the concept of the sanctity of human life. "Sanctity" refers to the quality of being holy and sacred.

So therefore, a definition of being in the image of God must fit the criteria of being permanent, inherent, and applying to all humans under any condition for all time.

We can never improve upon God's image in us. The imago Dei is complete, done, and finished. There is nothing to add. God could not have made us any better than he did. He was very pleased with how he made man.

Many Misapply the Concept of Being Made in God's Image

Having done a fair amount of research into what others say about the image of God and what this means, it is quite evident to me that there are many views on how this is understood. Based on my understanding, I believe many Christians are misapplying the meaning of this concept.

It appears that many like to focus on the sin of Adam and Eve and try to make the point that this event impacted the image of God in them, and subsequently, in all of mankind. Many adjectives are used to describe this effect, including the image of God was distorted, marred, broken, corrupted, dimmed, hidden, and shattered because of their sin. This is the case made by Mike Cosper in his book *Imago Dei: God's Image, God's People, God's Mission.* However, this notion is contrary to my understanding that the image of God is permanent and cannot be changed or diminished by one's behavior.

What changed because of the decision by Adam and Eve to disobey God relates to their spirituality and relationship with God. Their sin did not change their humanity. It just revealed it.

Adam and Eve were created as humans. As humans, we all have the propensity to sin. We all have independent free will that allows us to make decisions which are contrary to God's will. Adam and Eve's sin changed things for them, but not the image of God in them. What changed was the status of their relationship with God just like this happens to humans today.

The remedy for this culminated in Jesus coming to earth and going to the cross as a propitiatory sacrifice for all people. His death, burial, and resurrection provided the way for us to get back into a restored relationship with God. Jesus doesn't restore our humanity. What Jesus does is not related to the image of God in us. Jesus restores the relationship we can have with our Creator in ways never seen before. It is the final remedy by God. Nothing else needs to be done. We are offered this reconciliation and promise of life eternal with God.

So the impact of sin and the process of reconciliation have nothing to do with our being made in God's image. Our image is intact. What sin has done has everything to do with our standing and relationship with God. Becoming a Christian, being in a restored relationship with God, is how we build upon the foundation of our being in God's image.

Once people are covered by the redemptive work of Jesus, we grow spiritually every day. As we pursue living godly lives instead of living for our own selfish motives, we become more like Jesus. When the scriptures talk about us becoming new creations (2 Cor. 5:17) and being transformed (Rom. 12:1–2), it is referring to our spirituality, not our physicality or human essence. It is because of being in God's image and likeness that God relates to us in this way. God does not do this for any other of the creatures of his creation. Being born again, transformed and made new, are spiritual concepts for human beings.

The spiritual activity is what bears upon our standing with God. It also brings us into the opportunity to have relationships with other believers, God's spiritual children. This aspect is very important to our lives and walk with God. Having a spiritual family is important to our continual growth and encourages us to persevere to the end (when we pass from this life to the next).

As saved Christians, our lives reflect Jesus to the world. We are then in alignment with the purpose for God in creating us in his image.

A person's worth is not based on what a person accomplishes in life, how a person behaves, and what a person believes. Imago Dei does not depend on our mental capacity, moral capacity, or social capacity. It doesn't depend on one's spirituality. Again, everyone has God-given value and worth because of being made in God's image. It's permanent, inherent, and applicable to all human beings.

Paul Copan, PhD in his book *Is God a Moral Monster: Making Sense of the Old Testament God?* Speaks to what it means to be made in God's image. He says the following:

> When God created human beings, he uniquely equipped them for two roles, as the early chapters of Genesis suggest. The first is our *kingly* role: God endowed us to share in ruling the creation with him. The second is our *priestly* role of relating to ("walking with") God and orienting our lives around him. Being made in God's image as priest-kings brings with it the ability to relate to God, to think rationally, to make moral decisions, to express creativity, and (with God) to care for and wisely harness creation. This is a privilege, not bondage!

We read in Genesis chapter 1 where God gave Adam and Eve the charge to rule over the earth. This is a charge that is applicable to all people. Dr. Copan refers to this process as man sharing with God the role of ruling over creation. This relates to the idea of the partnership we have with God. Dr. Copan refers to the image of God being what makes it possible for humans to be in a relationship with

God due to having godly qualities—including thinking rationally, having free choice to make decisions, having creative abilities, and, with God's help, the ability to harness our lives to conform to God's will. Dr. Copan goes on to say,

> Our being made in God's image is simply God's "spreading the wealth." God's rich goodness overflows to his creation, which lives, moves and has its being in him. Though God created freely and without constraint, God is bursting with joy and love to share his goodness with his creatures. He allows us, his image-bearers, to share (in a very limited way) in his characteristics. God enables us to participate in the life of the divine community, the Trinity—a life that fills him with great joy and pleasure (see 2 Peter 1:4). God bestows on us the great compliment of endowing us with a privileged position and with important capacities—ones that reflect God's own wonderful nature.

Dr. Copan bolsters the points I have made earlier in this chapter about how God made humans to possess great qualities and strengths which are a reflection of his majestic image. I believe Dr. Copan affirms we share elements of God's divine nature by how he created us. Humans were given a lot of *wealth*. Embedded within our human nature are many positive godlike qualities, as well as our proclivity to sin, which comes with the free will we have which can be used for good or bad. Again, these are qualities of our nature which are inherent and permanent.

Image of God Related to a Relationship with God

All of God's creation work and the plans he has for mankind are based on God's desire to have a special relationship with human beings. The "image of God" concept includes the idea that God calls humans into a relationship with him. Being in the same likeness of God is the basis for this relationship. Humans are the only created beings with whom God seeks to have a personal relationship, a relationship with similar beings.

There is no "created kind" that speaks equally to mankind other than other human beings. Given how we were made, in God's image, we are the only beings able to relate to God. God sent his son to earth only for human beings. Being in a righteous relationship with God enables so much interaction between us and God. This is based on his promise that he will always be with us.

CHAPTER 10

Our Relationship with God—a Partnership

For we are God's handiwork, created in Christ Jesus to do
good works, which God prepared in advance for us to do.
—Ephesians 2:10

²³ Whatever you do, work at it with all your heart, as
working for the Lord, not for human masters, ²⁴ since you
know that you will receive an inheritance from the Lord
as a reward. It is the Lord Christ you are serving.
—Colossians 3:23–24

A man had transformed an overgrown plot of ground into a beautiful garden and was showing a friend what he had accomplished. Pointing to a bed of flowers, he said, "Look at what I did here." His companion corrected him, "You mean, 'Look at what God and I did here.'" The gardener replied, "I guess you're right. But you should have seen the shape this plot was in when He was taking care of it by Himself."

We chuckle at the man's reply, but I think it comes close to expressing two weighty spiritual truths—we are coworkers in a partnership with God, and we have tremendous abilities thanks to how God created us.

This story reminds me of some of the stories Jesus told. One is about the wise man who built his house upon the rock (Matt. 7:24–27). This reveals that people do have a lot of wisdom they can use for doing good. In the Parable of the Weeds, Jesus explains that the one who received the seed that fell on good soil is the man who hears the word and understands it. He produces a crop, yielding a hundred, sixty, or thirty times what was sown (Matt. 13:23). Here we see that a person's God-given abilities enables him to use his mind to accomplish great things.

These passages can help us see that God in his sovereignty has chosen from the very beginning to partner with man in the execution of his will. It all started with God tasking Adam and Eve to do many things with the earth, including having dominion over it. Adam and Eve tended the garden. They were gardeners. From there on, we see how man did great things in partnership with God.

Working Together with God

Working together with God is a common theme throughout the Bible. As we explored in the previous chapter, we are made in the likeness of God. That implies God made us with great skills and abilities. God has elected to work through us and in partnership with us. God needs us as we need God. I call this an interdependent relationship. This partnership is predicated on the reality that we have a close and trusting relationship with God.

C. S. Lewis once wrote concerning this partnership with God in his book *The World's Last Night and Other Essays*:

> For He seems to do nothing of Himself which He can possibly delegate to His creatures. He commands us to do slowly and blunderingly what He could do perfectly and in the twinkling of an eye.

This helps to explain why God formed and chose the nation of Israel to partner with him in his plan of world redemption. We looked earlier at the Covenants God established with the nation of Israel. This culminated with the final agreement, the New Covenant, which God established with everyone.

The church was then birthed and commissioned to go to all the peoples of the world to deliver the good news of this great redemption that had been bought on everyone's behalf (Matt. 28:19–20). What a privilege to be part of this magnificent plan. We are all now invited to participate in a profound partnership with God to bring about the world as God wills it to be.

Philip Yancey speaks to this idea of God working with us and through us in a partnership relationship. In his book *Reaching for the Invisible God: What Can We Expect to Find?*, he refers to this idea in reference to Romans 8:28:

> Things happen, some of them good, some of them bad, many of them beyond our control. In all these things, I have felt the reliable constant of a God willing to work with me and through me to produce something good.

Many successful companies—including Apple, eBay, and Twitter—were built by multiple leaders whose productive relationships and combined skill sets were a recipe for success. There is often a common trend in these corporate partnerships. It includes the pairings of well-rounded people recognized for their strengths as well as their individual limitations. Combined together, they represent a powerful team because of what they collectively bring to the partnership, complementary skills, and strengths that are harmonized together.

In a similar way, God gives us the incredible privilege of partnering with him in his kingdom work. As we've noted earlier, it begins with the initiation of a relationship with him.

Reading further in Philip Yancey's book cited above, he counters the idea as some think that God just wants to do all things through us by getting us out of the way with the following understanding instead.

Far more impressive is the miracle of God's condescension, his humble willingness to share power and offer us full partnership in this mission of transforming the world.

He goes on to say:

I used to feel spiritually inferior because I had not experienced the more spectacular manifestations of the Spirit and could not point to any bona fide "miracles" in my life. Increasingly though, I have come to see that what I value may differ from what God values. Jesus, often reluctant to perform miracles, considered it progress when he departed earth and entrusted the mission to his flawed disciples. Like a proud parent, God seems to take more delight as a spectator of the bumbling achievements of his stripling children than in any self-display of omnipotence.

Philip Yancey relates to the partnership we have with God when inferring that it seems God takes more delight as a spectator. This correlates to the joy God has in his relationship with mankind. For God, who wants to interact with mankind, there would be no joy if he were controlling people and forcing them to do what he wanted. We must understand that God takes delight in our accomplishments! God receives more glory when we do good things in loving ways from our hearts than if he was always the one controlling us. Philip goes on to say,

From God's perspective, if I may speculate, the great advance in human history may be what happened at Pentecost, which restored the direct correspondence of spirit to Spirit that had been lost in Eden. I want God to act in direct, impressive, irrefutable ways. He wants to "share power" with the likes of me, accomplishing his work through people, not despite of them.

"Take me seriously! Treat me like an adult, not a child!" is the cry of every teenager. God honors that request. He makes me a partner for his work in and through me. He grants me freedom in full knowledge that I will abuse it. He abdicates power to such an extent that he pleads with me not to "grieve" or "quench" his Spirit. God does all this because he wants a mature lover as a partner, not a puppy-love adolescent.

Here Philip Yancey speaks of Pentecost as a turning point in history. He perceives that what began happening is a reflection of how God now wants to share his power with people in a partnership relationship. He sees God understanding how humans will mess up along the way but also how God knows people can mature over time and appropriately use the freedom and power he gives them.

God Wants Us to Use Our Skills and Abilities

The partnership we have with God reflects how God entrusts us to do things using our intellectual and physical abilities, personalities, strengths, interests, and talents as well as our experiences, training, and education and background. We use these to partner with him to provide for our needs and to accomplish his purposes. The careers we pursue are often based on our personalities, interests, and talents. God has created us to have great abilities. He wants us to use these as we journey together with him through life.

As I've mentioned before, I've had a clinical license in social work for over thirty years. I first obtained my master's of science in social work degree, and then after a few years, I underwent supervision while doing psychotherapy. I then passed the state exam for the clinical license. I've also participated in a great many hours of continuing education through the years of my career. I became very skilled at doing the work I was doing.

I remember the time I spoke to a counseling colleague who was also a Christian. He told me that he prayed before each session asking God to get him out of the way so that God would lead the counseling session. This is a prime example of what I disagree with, even as well-meaning Christians seek to be as spiritual as they can be.

As a partner with God, I don't believe God uses me by stripping away all my skills, abilities, and experience to replace me, so to speak, by stepping in to take over in the counseling sessions. I believe God wants me to use my skills, abilities, training, and experience to help people. I believe that God will be with me in the sessions and provide help through the Holy Spirit to complement my abilities.

I just believe its shortsighted for Christian people to talk like my counselor friend did and think one is being very spiritual by asking God to take over one's life and ignore what we bring to the challenge. God uses our personalities and abilities to make a difference in the world.

Applying this concept in other settings might make it a little more obvious to us. Should we expect a skilled brain surgeon who is a Christian to pray before going into surgery that God take over for him or her? Should we expect a pilot of a 747 airliner to pray the same?

I recently read where someone posted the following saying on Facebook: "Jesus + nothing = everything." There were many people who commented to that posting, saying things like "Amen" and "This is very true." However, we can't even be certain what this means without an explanation. On the face of it, it appears to say that Jesus alone can meet our physical and emotional needs and will take care of all our problems... He does not need anyone helping him to accomplish things. If so, to me, this is erroneous and misguided theology. I think it should be stated this way, "Jesus + me [Godly person] = everything."

I think of the apostle Paul and his personality and abilities. Paul briefly lists the reasons he can have confidence in the flesh in Philippians 3:4–7. Paul had demonstrated great strength of character and leadership qualities, although misguided, as he went about defending his Jewish faith by persecuting Christians who the

High Priest saw as heretical. This occurred before his conversion as explained in Acts chapter 9. I believe God chose Paul precisely because he was such a strong, accomplished, and zealous person.

God did not want to strip those positive qualities away from Paul. He wanted to use those abilities for his purposes. Yes, we read where Paul does say that God had given him the gift of his grace through the working of his power to do the things God wanted him to do (Eph. 3:7). God knew that he was the right person at the right time for the ministry God had in store for him.

God put Paul in the position he did to be able to use Paul's personal qualities for accomplishing the work. God did not look for an insecure, emotionally damaged, weak person for the ministry he had in store for Paul. Similarly, I firmly believe God does not want to erase our personalities, strengths, and life experiences just for him to come into our lives and take over for us.

Paul describes the concept of partnership several times in his writings. He speaks to how it is helpful to be in partnership with others to accomplish great things. In Philippians 1:3–5, the apostle Paul wrote to the church at Philippi and said, "Every time I think of you, I give thanks to my God. Whenever I pray, I make my requests for all of you with joy, for you have been my partners in spreading the Good News about Christ from the time you first heard it until now."

The church at Philippi and Paul enjoyed a partnership between them in spreading the gospel. The purpose of their partnership was to accomplish something that neither of them could do alone.

Paul knew he could not spread the gospel alone and neither could the Philippians. It took both of them together to accomplish this task.

This passage is an example of the partnership humans have with God. Without the planting and watering that humans did, it would not have grown.

1 Corinthians 1:9:

"God is faithful, who has called you into fellowship with his Son, Jesus Christ our Lord."

The word in the above scripture which is important in connection with Jesus Christ is *fellowship*. The Greek word used for "fellowship" is *koinonia*, and it is used by Paul again and again. It can mean a partnership, and I believe that is the way it is used here in this verse. This is one of the greatest privileges given to us. If we are in Christ, if we have come to him and accepted him as our Lord and Savior, then we enter into a partnership with him. He is willing to be our partner. I believe this is how God often works in our world today. God works in partnership with people to accomplish his will to change the world.

I have come across some Christians who have expressed that they dislike the term *partnership* in describing an aspect of our relationship with God. This is partly because they believe the term implies a relationship between equals. The term *partnership* can be defined as persons (or entities) joined together to accomplish common objectives. However, this does not have to imply that each partner is equal in every way. This underscores the value of a complementary relationship where one partner has strengths the other one does not and vice versa. One of our strengths with God could be that we are physically present in the world to do work for God. Also, again, I don't want to underestimate the good things we bring to God's work based on whom each of us are.

When we are born again and give our lives to serve and glorify God, we enter into an agreement or partnership at that time. God gives us the Holy Spirit and adopts us into his family as we see stated in *Galatians 4:3–7*.

When we were newborn Christians, God sent his spirit into our hearts. The Holy Spirit is to be a helper to us. See the chapter "Our Relationship with the Holy Spirit" for more information on this.

Our Partnership in Godliness

The apostle Peter lays a lot of responsibility upon us as we try to live a godly life. We find this clearly stated in 2 Peter 1:3–9:

> ³ His divine power has given us everything
> we need for a godly life through our knowledge
> of him who called us by his own glory and good-

ness. [4] Through these he has given us his very great and precious promises, so that through them you may *participate* in the divine nature, having escaped the corruption in the world caused by evil desires. [5] For this very reason, *make every effort* to add to your faith goodness; and to goodness, knowledge; [6] and to knowledge, self-control; and to self-control, perseverance; and to perseverance, godliness; [7] and to godliness, mutual affection; and to mutual affection, love. [8] For *if you possess* these qualities in increasing measure, they will keep you from being ineffective and unproductive in your knowledge of our Lord Jesus Christ. [9] But whoever does not have them is nearsighted and blind, forgetting that they have been cleansed from their past sins.

Godliness is about being like God. It's about being like Jesus Christ. It's about what we all should strive to be as Christians. It's the essence of the Christian life. I believe the principles of godliness are largely about the partnership we have with God in being godly.

The Greek word for godliness is *Eusebeia* (εὐσέβεια), which has the connotation of awe, devotion, piety (loyalty, dutiful conduct) toward God. Devotion signifies a life given or dedicated to God. A godly person is one who has a godly lifestyle, where God is at the center of one's thoughts.

Therefore, godliness can be defined as devotion to God which results in a life that is pleasing to God. It is lived out by those who have a pervasive sense of God's presence, a correct concept of God's character, and a constant awareness of our obligation to God. Godliness is also the avoidance of things which we know don't please God. These are often mentioned in the scriptures as the "what not to dos," often mentioned before the listings of what we should be doing.

In sum, godliness is the cultivation of a quality relationship with God. Godliness is about having a hunger and thirst for God.

Godliness represents dedication and dependability. This all relates to the idea of having an intimate relationship with God.

An Interpersonal Relationship with God

To me, the context of how we relate to God is like an interpersonal relationship. Yes, God in his sovereignty and greatness gets to set the rules and boundaries. We are the created ones; he is the creator. He created us to be in relationship with him. As we know, how this relationship has functioned with God and man has changed over the years.

When Jesus came into the world, God was among us as a human being. With his death, burial, and resurrection, we have the New Covenant in our relationship with God. The Old Testament system of external, ceremonial, symbolic worship is over. There are no more temples, no more priesthood, no more altars, no more sacrifices, and no more specific allocated places of worship where God is to be sought and found. We have access directly to God through Jesus. Our bodies are temples of the Holy Spirit which is in us (1 Cor. 6:19).

We have the New Testament to show us how to interact with him under this New Covenant. Again, we find that our relationship becomes a partnership kind of relationship where we have responsibilities and God has responsibilities. We are in a cooperative relationship with God.

Paul Copan relates to this idea in his book *Is God a Moral Monster: Making Sense of the Old Testament God*. He states the following:

> God's relationship with us isn't a commander-commandee arrangement (similar to the "divine cop in the sky" notion). In that kind of relationship, God's will merely coerces, overriding the choices of human agents. Rather, God seeks the interpersonal intimacy with us in the context of covenant-making. Critics typically paint the picture of two false alternatives: sovereign coer-

cion or total human autonomy. However, if we see God's activity and human nature as harmonious rather than in conflict, a new perspective dawns on us. When God's intentions for us are realized and when we're alert to the divinely given boundaries built into our nature and the world around us, we human beings flourish—that is, we enjoy loving, trusting relationships with God and one another because we're living out the design-plan.

People have all kinds of views about God. Some believe God is one who demands perfection and is quick to take vengeance. Thus, he is out to catch them doing wrong. Others believe God is a God of unending tolerance and grace and they can do just about anything and God will forgive them and accept them. Yes, these are two extreme distortions. However, not all distortions are this extreme.

Dr. Copan refers to two false alternatives, or distortions, which interfere with a clear picture of the interpersonal intimacy God wants with people. He alerts us to the extreme notion of God's sovereignty which seeks to control people and what many see as the opposite of this being total human autonomy or free will without any boundaries.

Let's look very briefly at these two options. First, God does not want to control people but persuade them. How can one have a healthy relationship if one is being controlled? Control requires coercion most of the time, and that is not God's way. Instead of God controlling everything, he self-limits his control by giving to man great power through free will.

This brings us to the other false assumption Dr. Copan references. God did not design us to use our free will totally autonomously where we do everything without God. Although an option, this would be disastrous as we have seen throughout human history. God knows humans must have free will but within the context of boundaries. These boundaries relate to both the strengths and limits of human nature—how God made us. Being made in the image of God, we have many innate positive qualities and strengths. There are also many huge differences between us and God which impact how we play out our relationship with God. We establish boundaries by harnessing our free will and using it to help us conform to the will of God.

All of the above relates to the relationship God wants to have with us—an interpersonal relationship, a partnership relationship. This relationship is one where, based on our loving motivation and innate abilities, God expects us to do many good things while also holding God's hand along the way. This is how we embrace the help we can receive from the Holy Spirit. As Dr. Copan mentions, we must be alert to the divinely given boundaries built within our nature. The idea of total human autonomy is contrary to this.

Again, the partnership relationship is based on the concept that mankind has independent free will. Without having free will, we would then be unable to use our skills, abilities, and strengths. If free will is taken away, how can we have control over anything in our lives? If we don't have free will, how could God hold us accountable for anything?

Now I realize that there are many Christians who like the notion of God being in control of everything and embrace it wholeheartedly. To me, it just does not make sense. I speak further about my views on this in an upcoming chapter, "Is God in Control of Everything."

An Example of the Partnership Relationship

Jerry Bridges, in his book *The Pursuit of Holiness*, speaks to the partnership we have with God. As a strong Calvinist, Jerry is one of their most ardent apologists. Part of the Calvinist doctrine is to accept the notion of free will but only in the context that it is not autonomous free will. To Calvinists, this means free will is with God-imposed boundaries and not independent of God's control.

The idea of a partnership with God incorporates humans' independent free will into the nature of the relationship man has with God. It's a relationship where people choose to obey his will. It is contrary to the notion of God controlling everything and forcing man to obey God's will. So even though Jerry is a strong Calvinist, it seems he does see some of the contradictions in that doctrine. This is what Jerry says:

> God puts responsibility for living a holy life squarely on us. We are to do something. We are not to "stop trying and start trusting;" we are to put to death the misdeeds of the body. Over and over again in the epistles—not only Paul's, but the other apostle's as well—we are commanded to assume our responsibility for a holy walk. Paul exhorted, "Put to death, therefore, whatever belongs to your earthly natures" (Colossians 3:5). This is something we are told to do.
>
> Peter said, "Make every effort to be found spotless, blameless and at peace with him" (2 Peter 3:14). The clause *make every effort* addresses itself to our wills. It is something we must decide to do.
>
> During a certain period in my Christian life, I thought that any effort on my part to live a holy life was "of the flesh" and that "the flesh profits for nothing." I thought God would not bless any effort on my part to live the Christian life, just as He would not bless any effort on my part to become a Christian by good works. Just as I received Christ Jesus by faith, so I was to seek a holy life by faith. Any effort on my part was just getting in God's way. I misapplied the statement, "You will not have to fight this battle. Take up your positions; stand firm and see the deliverance the Lord will give you" (2 Chronicles 20:17) to mean that I was just to turn it all over to the Lord and He would fight the sin in my life. In fact, in the margin of the Bible I was using during that period, I wrote alongside the verse these words: "Illustration on walking in the Spirit."

> How foolish I was. I misconstrued depen-
> dence on the Holy Spirit to mean I was to make
> no effort, that I had no responsibility. I mistak-
> enly thought if I turned it all over to the Lord,
> He would make my choices for me and would
> choose obedience over disobedience. All I needed
> was to look to Him for holiness. But this is not
> God's way. He makes provision for our holiness,
> but He gives us the responsibility of using those
> provisions.

For those who have studied Calvinism, this is a somewhat sur-
prising admission by Jerry Bridges. Jerry is one who has written several books promoting and defending the Calvinist doctrine, including the extreme notion of the sovereignty of God and how God is in
control of everything. It is really encouraging to hear this from him.
It appears he is admitting the truth about the personal responsibilities we have in our walk with God.

In the passage above, Jerry is making the same argument I have
been trying to make in this book regarding the partnership relationship we have with God. Jerry's argument also challenges those who
believe we should just "let go and let God handle things." Regarding
this, Jerry talks about how he misconstrued dependence upon the
Holy Spirit when he said he thought it meant "I was to make no
effort..." He then gives further indication of what "God is in control" means. He said, "I mistakenly thought if I turned it all over to
the Lord, he would make my choices for me..." Question, "How is
it that God could take control and make people's choices for them?"
(My answer is, I don't believe he does.)

I speak about the role of the Holy Spirit upcoming in chapter 12. Unfortunately, there are many varying beliefs about how the
Holy Spirit works in our lives as believers. It is quite confusing. I will
humbly share an alternative viewpoint in an effort to clarify this.

In Jerry's statements above, he relates to several scriptures which
point out the responsibilities we have in our walk with God. I provide a review of an additional twelve scriptures with an analysis of

each one in the next section below. These scriptures highlight God's way for us to pursue holiness and enjoy an appropriate relationship with him.

A relevant scriptural reference for this is Philippians 2:12–13:

> [12] Therefore, my dear friends, as you have always obeyed—not only in my presence, but now much more in my absence—continue to work out your salvation with fear and trembling, [13] for it is God who works in you to will and to act in order to fulfill his good purpose.

That scripture relates to the partnership we have with God. We are to work out our salvation on the one hand, and God is also working in us to fulfill his purpose for our lives on the other hand.

Scriptures Pointing to Man's Partnership with God

I've selected ten passages of scripture to review which point to man's responsibilities in living godly lives. They celebrate the partnership we have with God. Instead of just quoting these scriptures, I thought it best to provide some commentary to them to help us see the connection of how they relate to the concept of our partnership with God.

- John 14:5: *"I am the vine; you are the branches. If you remain in me and I in you, you will bear much fruit; apart from me you can do nothing."*

Saying "apart from me you can do nothing" does not mean we are unable to function. We can do many things without a dependence on Christ. We can raise a family without him. We can run a business without him. We can be very active, even as a non-Christian. We can fill our days with tremendous activity and busyness. However, without the right level of connection with him, we will not become Christlike as we should be.

What we can't do without being "in him" and connected to the Holy Spirit (Jesus) are the things we receive from the Holy Spirit. They are spiritual in focus.

Here we find an example of the wonderful balance of the Christian life. It's not a total dependence on God for everything. It's an interdependent relationship. It's a partnership.

- Colossians 3:2 "¹ Since, then, you have been raised with Christ, set your hearts on things above, where Christ is, seated at the right hand of God. ² Set your minds on things above, not on earthly things. ³ For you died, and your life is now hidden with Christ in God. ⁴ When Christ, who is your life, appears, then you also will appear with him in glory."

God does not control our hearts, and he does not control our minds. He needs us to use our mind, will, and emotions in the right way. We are to focus our minds on things of the Spirit, the spiritual world, because we have given our lives to God in his service and for his glory. If we focus on "things above," we will have in mind what God wants and our decisions and actions will reflect the outcomes of this focus.

- Colossians 3:5: "⁵ Put to death, therefore, whatever belongs to your earthly nature: sexual immorality, impurity, lust, evil desires and greed, which is idolatry. ⁶ Because of these, the wrath of God is coming. ⁷ You used to walk in these ways, in the life you once lived. ⁸ But now you must also rid yourselves of all such things as these: anger, rage, malice, slander, and filthy language from your lips. ⁹ Do not lie to each other, since you have taken off your old self with its practices ¹⁰ and have put on the new self, which is being renewed in knowledge in the image of its Creator."

By putting to death, we are tasked with the requirement to use self-control to live by godly values and standards. We are told to rid ourselves of behaviors and attitudes which are unbecoming a child of God and follower of Christ. We need to take responsibility for this and realize that the new self we put on depends on our willingness to live differently than the ways of the world. Fortunately, we have God's help as evidenced by the fruit of the Spirit (Gal. 5:22–23) and in other ways due to the Holy Spirit in us.

- Colossians 3:12–14: "[12] Therefore, as God's chosen people, holy and dearly loved, clothe yourselves with compassion, kindness, humility, gentleness and patience. [13] Bear with each other and forgive one another if any of you has a grievance against someone. Forgive as the Lord forgave you. [14] And over all these virtues put on love, which binds them all together in perfect unity."

Here the apostle Paul gives us specific instructions on how we are to act because we are Christians. Our faith and dedication to Christ has to mean something. We can't be authentic followers of Christ and yet not try to live godly lives. Paul is telling us the qualities we are to have and is asking us to do them. Some of these will be harder to do for some people than others. We must remember, we have the Holy Spirit to help us in our weaknesses. We should be humble enough to know we need help and then in prayer to God, ask for help as we need it. Forgiving those who hurt us can be a very challenging task.

- Galatians 6:9–10: "[9] Let us not become weary in doing good, for at the proper time we will reap a harvest if we do not give up. [10] Therefore, as we have opportunity, let us do good to all people, especially to those who belong to the family of believers."

We are asked, encouraged, and admonished to do good deeds to others throughout the New Testament. This logically flows from our lives which are devoted to live for God. We have the capacity to do much good as we are made in the image of God. We must use our minds to harness our thinking to act in ways that help others and glorify God. We have the Holy Spirit to help us…reflecting our partnership with God.

- Ephesians 4:17–24: "17 So I tell you this, and insist on it in the Lord, that you must no longer live as the Gentiles do, in the futility of their thinking. 18 They are darkened in their understanding and separated from the life of God because of the ignorance that is in them due to the hardening of their hearts. 19 Having lost all sensitivity, they have given themselves over to sensuality so as to indulge in every kind of impurity, and they are full of greed.

  "20 That, however, is not the way of life you learned 21 when you heard about Christ and were taught in him in accordance with the truth that is in Jesus. 22 You were taught, with regard to your former way of life, to put off your old self, which is being corrupted by its deceitful desires; 23 to be made new in the attitude of your minds; 24 and to put on the new self, created to be like God in true righteousness and holiness."

The reality is, our thinking can become futile and work against us. There is a real battle for us to focus our minds in the right way, especially to focus our minds so we can put on the new self we have in Christ Jesus. Many fail because they don't fight this mind battle effectively.

- Ephesians 5:15–17: "15 Be very careful, then, how you live—not as unwise but as wise, 16 making the most of every opportunity, because the days are evil. 17 Therefore do not be foolish, but understand what the Lord's will is."

Here the apostle Paul encourages us to use our self-control and minds to live effectively and not lose out on opportunities which come before us. We should be able to see that so many of the scriptures written by a variety of authors have words of encouragement, instruction, and admonition to help us live more effectively for the Lord. These scriptures are asking us to do many things. Again, we have the Holy Spirit to help us.

- James 1:22–25: "²²Do not merely listen to the word, and so deceive yourselves. Do what it says. ²³Anyone who listens to the word but does not do what it says is like someone who looks at his face in a mirror ²⁴and, after looking at himself, goes away and immediately forgets what he looks like. ²⁵But whoever looks intently into the perfect law that gives freedom, and continues in it—not forgetting what they have heard, but doing it—they will be blessed in what they do."

Here, James, the half brother of Jesus, gives us very practical advice. He places responsibility on us to behave according to our beliefs. This requires self-control and making right decisions. It involves meditating and remembering what we've been taught and applying the teaching to our lives. Again, we have the Holy Spirit to help us.

- 1 Timothy 4:7: "Have nothing to do with godless myths and old wives' tales; rather, train yourself to be godly."

The apostle Paul gave this instruction to Timothy, and it applies to us also. Training ourselves means using our minds to equip us for living godly lives. So what would be an effective training regimen?

One analogy for training could be in terms of athletic training for participating in competitive sporting events. The kind of training depends on the kind of events one is planning to participate in. To play out this analogy, the following could be applied:

1. What is the level of competition one is striving for? What is the goal for the training?
   a) Do you want to train for a highly competitive event, such as the decathlon in the Olympics or a less lofty event such as a one-mile fun run?

    b)   Do you want to train to win, or be in the top three positions, or just to get a certificate of participation?

2.   What does training involve?

    a)   From what physical ability are you starting? Are you a natural athlete or someone with no skills or conditioning who needs extensive training?

    b)   Do you need a coach or trainer?

    c)   Training should be planned to equip you to reach your goal.

    d)   You will need to practice, practice, practice.

3.   When does training end?

    a)   Are you just planning to compete in one event or in many over the years?

    b)   Do you know when you will accomplish all you want to accomplish?

What this analogy about training reveals is that if we want to grow spiritually, it would be nice to have goals in mind, such as wanting to teach Sunday morning Bible classes at a church or wanting to lead a small group. The goals we have provide guidance for the kind of training we need to do.

- Titus 2:11–14: [11] For the grace of God has appeared that offers salvation to all people. [12] It teaches us to say "No" to ungodliness and worldly passions, and to live self-controlled, upright and godly lives in this present age, [13] while we wait for the blessed hope—the appearing of the glory of our great God and Savior, Jesus Christ, [14] who gave himself for us to redeem us from all wickedness and to purify for himself a people that are his very own, eager to do what is good.

The apostle Paul's encouragement to Titus relates to the things he should do to pursue godly and upright living. This applies to us today also. Here we are to choose to live godly lives free from worldly passions. This relates to the ability and responsibility God has given people to exercise free choice. We are to use our minds to be self-controlled and be eager to do what is good to others. This is an example of partnership as we have the Holy Spirit to help us also.

There are many other scriptures reflecting similar messaging, such as the following:

- *1 Timothy 6:11:* Flee from all this (bad stuff) and pursue righteousness, godliness.
- *Titus 2:2*: Teach the older men to be temperate, worthy of respect, self-controlled.
- *James 4:7–10*: Come near to God and He will come near to you.
- *Matthew 5:3–12*: The beatitudes…taught to mourn, be meek, hunger, and thirst for righteousness, be merciful, be peacemakers, etc.…great is your reward in heaven.
- *2 Corinthians 9:7*: Give what you have decided in your heart to give.
- *Hebrews 12:14*: Make every effort to live in peace with all men and to be holy.

CHAPTER 11

———— ⟨∽⟩ ————

Ways We Can Learn about God

Then they asked him, "Where is your father?"
"You do not know me or my Father," Jesus replied. "If
you knew me, you would know my Father also."
—John 8:19

We understand from the scriptures that there are several ways for us to learn about God. I think of at least five ways. One way is how God is revealed in creation. Another way is how God reveals himself in the scriptures. Another way is how God is revealed by looking at mankind who is made in the image of God. Another way is the miracle of Christian people having the Holy Spirit in them to comfort, teach, and provide spiritual guidance. The last way, and possibly the best and most clear, is how God is revealed through Jesus who walked the earth.

How God Is Revealed in Creation

From creation, we can understand about God's invisible qualities, such as his awesome power and divine nature. We see the beauty of the earth and the vast amount of space. We see evidence of intelligent design everywhere we look. Science has much to say about this and how probability statistics underscore the intricacy and the miracle of design.

The apostle Paul refers to this in *Romans 1:18–20*:

> [18] The wrath of God is being revealed from heaven against all the godlessness and wickedness of people, who suppress the truth by their wickedness, [19] since what may be known about God is plain to them, because God has made it plain to them. [20] For since the creation of the world God's invisible qualities—his eternal power and divine nature—have been clearly seen, being understood from what has been made, so that people are without excuse.

Looking at creation communicates so much about God in a language all can understand. There is no language barrier to seeing the majesty of creation. There is no way a person could not be amazed by all of this and not wonder about how this all came about. We can't even fathom how God could create all of this from nothing. How could anyone not think about this from time to time? Maybe thinking about this relates to a way to trigger the spiritual wonder, which is one part of our nature as human beings.

The earth we live on provides for all our physical needs, i.e., rain for water, plants, fish, and animals for food, air to breathe, people to have relationships with, human bodies which are complex and magnificent in many ways, night and day for rest, activity and keeping time, etc. This creation shouts of intelligent design and a designer who cares about people. Everyone can see it if they are willing to see it.

Many will say that if they want to feel close to God, they go into nature. They take walks in the woods, hear the brooks and the birds, see a variety of trees with the sun shining through them, and may come to a beautiful waterfall. Many like to find a spot to sit and just listen, watch, meditate, and pray. Some love to sit under the cover of a front or back porch outside a house while it is raining and meditate and pray. Some travel to our national parks and see some spectacular sights. Some go to places outside the city at night to look at all the objects in space. Some take cruises on the ocean and marvel at the vast expanse of the ocean waters and love to sit at night and see the moon reflect off the water.

In the early 1970s, I was a camp counselor for a Christian camp in Maine during a couple of summers. The camp was located a good distance from any cities. When looking at the sky at nighttime, one could see a tremendous number of stars. This was astonishing and a great way to hold devotionals outside!

For those whose intellectual curiosity wants more, there is much to study on the intelligent design theory. This will explore many amazing features of design in creation pointing to God as the creator.

How God Is Revealed in the Scriptures

We all know that the Bible is God's revelation to mankind. It is one of the ways God chose to reveal himself to us. We find occasions in the Old Testament where God is recorded speaking directly to mankind. We find many places in the Old Testament of God speaking to mankind through his prophets. We have many stories in the Old Testament of how God directly intervened in the affairs of the Israelites.

We looked at some of this already when we reviewed the Covenants that God established with the Israelites and then culminating with the New Covenant based on the work of Jesus on earth to reconcile us back to God. We know of some of the great men and women of faith and how they taught us about relating to God. We know that God greatly manifested himself among the Israelites in order to show the world whom he is.

In the New Testament, we have God on earth through Jesus interacting with mankind as recorded in the gospels and affirmed in the rest of the New Testament writings. We are taught of so much about what God expects of us for how we are to live our lives under the New Covenant in the New Testament scriptures.

How God Is Revealed through Mankind

Since God created mankind in his image, we can learn a lot about God by looking at human beings and how magnificently we are made. From one perspective, this is similar to how we learn about God through nature. The tremendous mind and creativity of God is seen in how amazing the human body is and how incredible are human abilities.

We see great things that humans can accomplish. Just look at the amazing architecture of many buildings. The systems mankind has put together for societies to function, the incredible advancement in medicine and technology, etc. We see many nonprofit organizations formed and sustained because of the love, generosity, and compassion of caring people. We see how we function to sustain life.

We also see how amazing the human body is. We see the complexity of the eyes, the ears, the ability to recreate, and the ability of the body to heal itself from many physical problems, such as broken bones and cuts on our arms. We see the many systems in the body, such as the circulatory system, digestive system, nervous system, respiratory system, skeletal system, and more which function incredibly together.

The only other option for all of this, if not God, then is chance. How can anyone really believe that all of this happens by chance? Mathematically and based on probability statistics, this is a fat chance!

How God Is Revealed through the Holy Spirit

One of the promises we have from God in the New Testament scriptures is the receiving of the Holy Spirit when we become Christians. We know from the scriptures that God has three parts to his being: (1) God the father, (2) God the son (Jesus), and (3) God the Holy Spirit. This is known as the Trinity. All of this means that we have God in us all the time, everywhere we are. Anywhere God is can be a way to gain evidence of who he is so that we can understand him better.

As I've mentioned in the first chapter, there are a great amount of differing views on how God works in people's lives today, especially in how the Holy Spirit works in us. This can be very confusing. What we must rely on is what we can learn about the Holy Spirit from the scriptures and from other Christians.

Because this is an important concept to understand, I have discussed this further in an upcoming chapter on "Our Relationship with the Holy Spirit." We know this is a big subject, and many books are written about this. It is obvious that more study will be necessary for people who want to understand this better.

How God Is Revealed through Jesus

When we consider Jesus, we see that God chose to come to earth, taking the body of a human. How incredible it is that God would send his son to earth with such love and humility. He sent his son with a purpose and a plan which centered around the goal of reconciling mankind back to God for all time. This is reflected in what the apostle Paul said in Philippians 2:5–11:

> [5] In your relationships with one another, have the
>   same mindset as Christ Jesus:
> [6] Who, being in very nature God,
> did not consider equality with God something
> to be used to his own advantage;[7] rather, he made
>   himself nothing
> by taking the very nature of a servant,
> being made in human likeness.
> [8] And being found in appearance as a man,
> he humbled himself
> by becoming obedient to death—
> even death on a cross!
> [9] Therefore God exalted him to the highest place
> and gave him the name that is above every name,
> [10] that at the name of Jesus every knee should
>   bow,

in heaven and on earth and under the earth,
¹¹ and every tongue acknowledge that Jesus Christ
   is Lord,
to the glory of God the Father.

Jesus is the long-anticipated Messiah whose coming was prophesied in many passages in the Old Testament. *Messiah* comes from the Hebrew word *Mashiach*, meaning "the anointed one," or "the chosen one." *Christos* (Christ) is the Greek equivalent of the Hebrew term *Messiah* (John 1:41).

John the Baptist was the first prophet to come to Israel since the prophet Malachi 430 years earlier. John the Baptist had been chosen by God, even before his conception, to be the prophesied forerunner of the Messiah. This was prophesied in Isaiah 40:3–5. John the Baptist served as the bridge from the Old Testament to the New Testament. He was the last in the long line of prophets who predicted Christ's coming.

Jesus had a public ministry for three years in which he traveled all over Israel (especially in the Galilee area and around Judea/Jerusalem), preaching and doing miracles. We learn of his heart for the downtrodden, oppressed, and the vulnerable. In Matthew 25, we learn about how he was concerned about those he labeled as the "least of these."

Jesus showed us who God is by what he said and what he did. He astonished everyone. Comments were made by people that they were amazed at Jesus as they had never heard anyone speak like him (John 7:46). He demonstrated the heart for serving others by washing his disciples' feet, telling them they will be blessed if they do this. He told of the story of the Good Samaritan to show us to care for our neighbors and have mercy on everyone, including those we may not like.

Jesus was God who walked our planet. He possessed miraculous powers as he could predict the future, know about people's backgrounds he just met, and know about events to come. As we saw in the scripture passage in Philippians, he was humble even though he is deity. He would get on his knees and wash the feet of his disciples.

He showcased his power by calming the winds and the waves. He could walk on water. He was so approachable that children could climb into his arms. Jesus was God exhibiting himself in language all could understand.

Jesus shows us what God the Father is like. He shows us the Father's love, his compassion and mercy, his righteousness, humility, authority, words, work and truth—even his glory. In Jesus Christ, the Father is made visible so that we can know him. We worship a Father who is just like his Son.

Given all of this, it can be puzzling why there are so many who just don't want to embrace a relationship with God.

CHAPTER 12

Our Relationship with the Holy Spirit

Peter said to them, "Repent, and each of you be baptized
in the name of Jesus Christ for the forgiveness of your
sins; and you will receive the gift of the Holy Spirit.
—Acts 2:38

I'd like to look at what we can learn about how the Holy Spirit works in our lives from the scriptures. Now this is not going to be an exhaustive or comprehensive examination of this as there are tons of scriptures on the Holy Spirit.

I begin under the premise which seems very clear that human beings can only understand so much about God and the spirit world. We must accept and be at peace with the reality that we will not have everything figured out.

When it comes to understanding spiritual matters, we must rely on the revelations in the scriptures which are an essential foundation in our spiritual journey. We follow the scriptures as best we can as we accept that this is God's word for us and how we are to live. When it comes to the Holy Spirit, there are many challenging passages to make us really think.

We know it is quite evident many Christian people have differing ideas about how the Holy Spirit works in our lives today. There are a wide range of beliefs on this.

We also know that the Bible is not a systematic treatise, dissertation, or a policy and procedures manual providing step-by-step guidance as we approach how to live as God wants us to live. We must search the scriptures for what we can learn about the role of the Holy Spirit.

Again, as I do research on topics, one of the things I like to do is write down questions that come to my mind. Here are some of the ones that surfaced regarding the Holy Spirit.

Questions about the Holy Spirit

1. Does limiting or encouraging the work of the Holy Spirit have anything to do with our salvation? Is it a salvation issue?

2. Are we controlled by the Holy Spirit? If so, does this control override our free will?

3. Does being led by the Holy Spirit mean that the Holy Spirit is in control of us?

4. Is life in the Spirit an unexplainable mystery and to what extent?

5. Does the Holy Spirit do anything without our permission?

6. Does the Holy Spirit work in our lives in ways we are not aware of and have not asked him to work?

7. Can we be experiencing the power of the Holy Spirit and not even know it?

8. Can we do any good works and deeds apart from the Holy Spirit?

9. What does "being filled with the Holy Spirit" mean? Does being "filled with the Holy Spirit" mean we empty ourselves to make room for the Holy Spirit?

10. When we get the Holy Spirit at baptism, do we get all of the Holy Spirit? Is there more of the Holy Spirit yet to come?

11. If the Holy Spirit will guide us into all truth (John 16:13), why then are there so many denominations and major theological differences among believers?

12. Are *all* of the workings of the Holy Spirit in New Testament times occurring today?

What We Learn from the Scriptures

The Bible certainly has much to say about the work of the Holy Spirit. The scriptures speak to how God works in the lives of believers and those who are unbelievers.

We know that the Holy Spirit is not an it. The Holy Spirit is the third person in the Godhead: God the Father, Jesus the Son, and the Holy Spirit. The Holy Spirit, therefore, is to be understood in the context of how we understand God and Jesus. The Holy Spirit has the attributes of God and Jesus, which means the Holy Spirit cannot be fully understood, controlled, or manipulated.

Given this, we must accept that since we can't fully understand God, we also can't fully understand the workings of the Holy Spirit. The Spirit works in ways which are beyond our understanding.

As part of the Godhead, some have called the Holy Spirit the "executor" of the Trinity—the being who carries out God's work in our world. It is safe to say that the work of the Holy Spirit is always in accordance with the purposes of God. Therefore, when we come across the Holy Spirit in the Bible, we find "God in action."

Although Jesus alluded to the Holy Spirit a few times previously in the Gospel of John (John 7:37–39), Jesus first introduces the Holy Spirit to his disciples nearing the time of his crucifixion in John 14:15–17:

> [15]If you love me, keep my commands. [16] And I will ask the Father, and he will give you another advocate to help you and be with you forever—[17] the Spirit of truth. The world cannot accept him, because it neither sees him nor knows him. But you know him, for he lives with you and will be in you.

The Greek word for *advocate* in the above scripture is *Parakletos* (pronounced par-ak'-lay-tos). The definition of this word encompasses the following descriptions: advocate, intercessor, comforter, and helper. The image here is of a legal advocate who makes the right judgment calls because the person understands the situation well. It's like advice that stands up in court.

Jesus spoke of the work of the Holy Spirit in John 16:7–15:

> ⁷But very truly I tell you, it is for your good that I am going away. Unless I go away, the Advocate will not come to you; but if I go, I will send him to you. ⁸When he comes, he will convict the world of guilt regarding sin and righteousness and judgment: ⁹in regard to sin, because people do not believe in me; ¹⁰in regard to righteousness, because I am going to the Father, where you can see me no longer; ¹¹and in regard to judgment, because the prince of this world now stands condemned.
>
> ¹²I have much more to say to you, more than you can now bear. ¹³But when he, the Spirit of truth, comes, he will guide you into all the truth. He will not speak on his own; he will speak only what he hears, and he will tell you what is yet to come. ¹⁴He will glorify me because it is from me that he will receive what he will make known to you. ¹⁵All that belongs to the Father is mine. That is why I said the Spirit will receive from me what he will make known to you.

Here Jesus calls the Holy Spirit "the advocate." Other translations say "the helper" or "counselor."

Jesus talks about the impact the Spirit will have on the world, what we could refer to as unbelievers. The Holy Spirit works in the lives of unbelievers by convicting them of their sin and showing them their need for a Savior (John 16:8). Some say that this is the only work that the Holy Spirit does in the life of the unbeliever.

Jesus then says that the Spirit will guide us (believers) into all the truth (John 16:13). It is certainly incredibly significant to have the Spirit, something to celebrate! I think it is worth pointing out that these terms don't seem to indicate that the Holy Spirit controls us. (Again, this is what many Calvinist-oriented people think.)

The scriptures tell us that the Holy Spirit is given as a deposit or guarantee that God will save us from our sins. Ephesians 1:13–14 states:

> [13] And you also were included in Christ when you heard the message of truth, the gospel of your salvation. When you believed, you were marked in him with a seal, the promised Holy Spirit, [14] who is a deposit guaranteeing our inheritance until the redemption of those who are God's possession—to the praise of his glory.

As God's children, we are given the Holy Spirit as a deposit ensuring our inheritance. Some make the case here that a guarantee is something that must happen.

Paul talks about our inheritance further in Romans 8:16–17:

> [16] The Spirit himself testifies with our spirit that we are God's children. [17] Now if we are children, then we are heirs—heirs of God and co-heirs with Christ, if indeed we share in his sufferings in order that we may also share in his glory.

We are coheirs with Jesus Christ. It's the idea that what belongs to Christ also belongs to us.

The truth is, every Christian believer has the Holy Spirit. He is given to us at our baptism according to Acts 2:38.

> [38] Peter replied, "Repent and be baptized, every one of you, in the name of Jesus Christ for the forgiveness of your sins. And you will receive the gift of the Holy Spirit."

We read in *1 Corinthians 12*, where Paul discusses the gifts of the Holy Spirit, that we all are not given the same gifts. In *verse 7*, Paul says, "Now to each one the manifestation of the Spirit is given for the common good."

Paul says in 1 Corinthians 12:3 that we can't even say "Jesus is Lord" except by the Holy Spirit.

Paul goes on in 1 Corinthians 12:11 to say that God determines the way the Holy Spirit will work in people's lives.

All these are the work of one and the same Spirit, and he distributes them to each one, just as he determines.

Being Filled with the Holy Spirit

We read in the scriptures where we are to be "filled with the Spirit." However, I don't think it is ever explained in the scriptures what being filled with the Spirit means.

> Ephesians 5:18 states, "Do not get drunk on wine, which leads to debauchery. Instead, be filled with the Spirit."

The Greek word for *filled* is pléroó (pronounced play-ro'-o) means "being made full, complete, full in quantity." From the passages in which the phrase "filled with the Holy Spirit" is used, we may get some idea what this means based on what is said in association with the phrase.

We read another passage of scripture about being filled with the Spirit in Acts 4:31:

> After they prayed, the place where they were meeting was shaken. And they were all filled with the Holy Spirit and spoke the word of God boldly.

So they spoke the Word of God boldly after being filled with the Holy Spirit. We can consider that this is how the Holy Spirit manifests himself when we are filled with the Holy Spirit.

There are many times in the scriptures when people are described as being filled with the Holy Spirit (Barnabas, Acts 11:24; seven men, Acts 6:3–7; Stephen, Acts 7:5; John the Baptist, Luke 1:15; Paul, Acts 9:17, Acts 13:9; etc.).

We read in the scriptures about the great power at work within us. In Acts 1:8, before Jesus ascended into heaven, he tells his disciples the following:

> But you will receive power when the Holy Spirit comes on you; and you will be my witnesses in Jerusalem, and in all Judea and Samaria, and to the ends of the earth.

Here Jesus tells them that the power of the Holy Spirit will enable them to testify to the world about Christ.

Paul talks about the power we receive in Ephesians 3:14–21:

> [14] For this reason I kneel before the Father, [15] from whom every family in heaven and on earth derives its name. [16] I pray that out of his glorious riches he may strengthen you with power through his Spirit in your inner being, [17] so that Christ may dwell in your hearts through faith. And I pray that you, being rooted and established in love, [18] may have power, together with all the Lord's holy people, to grasp how wide and long and high and deep is the love of Christ, [19] and to know this love that surpasses knowledge—that you may be filled to the measure of all the fullness of God.
>
> [20] Now to him who is able to do immeasurably more than all we ask or imagine, according to his power that is at work within us, [21] to him be glory in the church and in Christ Jesus throughout all generations, forever and ever! Amen.

How is the power of the Holy Spirit manifested in us? Consider the following ways.

- By us understanding God's love.
- Knowing God more personally and deeply.
- The good deeds we do.
- Bringing people to our minds who need our help and prayers.
- The fruit of the Spirit we exhibit.
- The courage and boldness we have.
- The comfort we receive in times of loss.
- Encouraging insights that come to our minds.
- Confidence and boldness in presenting the gospel to others.

In Romans 8:26, we are told by Paul, "In the same way, the Spirit helps us in our weakness. We do not know what we ought to pray for, but the Spirit himself intercedes for us with groans that words cannot express."

I would think that we don't know when this happens. We just believe it does.

Not Always Outward Evidence

There are many references in the scriptures of people receiving the Spirit without a record of any outward evidence being displayed as a result of them receiving the Holy Spirit in the book of Acts. When people became Christians, the Holy Spirit did come into their lives, but we do not find these same people exhibiting supernatural signs to confirm this.

The evidence of the Holy Spirit is not so much an outward sign but a changed life.

Paul says in 2 Corinthians 5:17, "Therefore, if anyone is in Christ, the new creation has come: The old has gone, the new is here!"

We are told in the scriptures to:

- Be led by the Holy Spirit (Romans 8:11–14; Galatians 5:18)
- Walk by the Holy Spirit (Galatians 5:16, 25)
- The Spirit guides us into all the truth (John 16:13)
- The Spirit is described as an advocate, helper, counselor (John 16:7)

One of the most popular scriptures about the work of the Holy Spirit is found in Romans 8. Here Paul tells us to set our minds on the Spirit. Is this how we embrace the power of the Spirit?

> ⁵ Those who live according to the flesh have their minds set on what the flesh desires; but those who live in accordance with the Spirit have their minds set on what the Spirit desires. ⁶ The mind governed by the flesh is death, but the mind governed by the Spirit is life and peace. ⁷ The mind governed by the flesh is hostile to God; it does not submit to God's law, nor can it do so. ⁸ Those who are in the realm of the flesh cannot please God. (Romans 8:5–8)

In an older version of the NIV in verse 6, it says, "The mind of the sinful man is death, but the mind *controlled* by the Spirit is life." However, as mentioned earlier, the word *controlled* does not fit with the Greek rendering of what is being said here. Other versions do not use the word *controlled*. The NASB version states: "For the mind set on the flesh is death, but the mind set on the Spirit is life and peace."

Things We Hear Today about the Holy Spirit

Today, we hear all kinds of teachings and comments on the Holy Spirit and how God works in our lives. We hear about the encouragement to "listen to the voice of God" (Charles Stanley). Rick Warren, pastor of the Saddleback Church in Southern California, said that "the Holy Spirit is my best friend. I know him well."

We hear teachings that tell us the following:

- The Spirit speaks to us by putting thoughts and ideas in our minds to do things.
- The Holy Spirit will help us say the right things, in the right time, in the right way.
- The Holy Spirit helps us resist things we can't normally resist.
- I am most likely to hear the Holy Spirit when I'm relaxed.
- The Holy Spirit guides us by our circumstances, dreams, revealing what God said in the Bible.
- The Holy Spirit gives us answers through nudges and impressions.
- Calvinist-oriented people believe that the Holy Spirit controls us.

So we can see from the above again that there are many differing ideas on how the Holy Spirit works in our lives today. This is confusing. The best anyone can say is to validate by the scriptures what others are saying. Many want to go beyond the scriptures, and some say that new revelations from the Spirit replace what the scriptures say. Be very wary and suspicious of those people!

There are also many Christian groups who hold the view that the miraculous manifestations of the Holy Spirit (miracles such as healing, prophesying, speaking in tongues, etc.) have ceased (1 Cor. 13), and we are encouraged to focus on loving one another, because the greatest of these is love.

I think that no matter what others say, we would do well to be guided by our experience and worldview. Going beyond this can put one in dangerous territory. It's okay not to be certain about everything. There is so much we just don't understand, and that just needs to be acceptable. No one should pressure us to go beyond what we understand. If someone tries, get them to defend what they are saying by what can be clearly understood from the scriptures.

This relates to another important consideration. As Christians, many of us are at differing levels of knowledge, understanding, and maturity. Those young in the faith need to be comfortable with accepting that they are not expected to know a tremendous amount. Don't let anyone make you feel inferior or second rate. It's okay to tell someone that we aren't sure what to think about a subject or issue at the time.

God Uses Us Based on Who We Are

Again, there are many Christians who believe all kinds of things when it comes to how the Holy Spirit works today. Some Christians believe we are to get ourselves out of the way so that the Holy Spirit can be free to work through us.

There are Christian leaders today who say that God likes to choose people without the background, skills, training, and proven abilities to do big, audacious things for him. Mark Batterson has clearly tried to make this case in his bestselling book *The Circle Maker: Praying Circles Around Your Biggest Dreams and Fears*. This is troubling to me in two ways. One is in what he is teaching. Another is in the large number of people who have read this book and have been influenced by his teaching on this.

As I mentioned in an earlier chapter, I heard a counselor friend of mine once say that he prayed before each session and asked God to take him out of the way so that God could work in that session. What kind of worldview thinks this way?

However, I believe God wants people to use their talents, skills, and training to help others. Why else do we do all the work to get the proper training? I believe God uses our personality, strengths, talents, abilities, background, experiences, etc. to accomplish his will. It is not that God wants to take all of those away and just let him operate in us, controlling all we do and say.

I think of the Giants of the Faith and what they brought to the table for God. For one, I think of the apostle Paul.

As I also mentioned in another chapter, the apostle Paul was a strong person, an assertive and courageous person, a dedicated and determined person, someone with a lot of personal strengths. I believe these are the reasons God chose him to be such a leader in the faith. It is very clear that God did not look for the wimpiest person who did not have strengths to be a leader.

General Overview

There are many scriptures relating to the Holy Spirit and how the Holy Spirit works in man. Again, we receive the Holy Spirit when we become Christians (Acts 2:38). We have gifts and abilities that come from the Holy Spirit (1 Cor. 12). We have fruits of the Holy Spirit which influence our lives (Gal. 5:22–23).

However, are there any scriptures which speak to the Holy Spirit controlling us? No, there are not. The Holy Spirit does not operate in us without our permission and participation. The Holy Spirit does not force us to surrender our will or abilities to make free choices in order to follow the Holy Spirit's guidance. The Holy Spirit instructs but does not enforce. The Holy Spirit teaches but does not take over our minds. The Holy Spirit empowers but does not overpower us.

All Christians know that if we want to hear from the Holy Spirit, the first place we turn to are the scriptures. We must examine and judge all spiritual matters based on the scriptures. However, we also know the Holy Spirit resides in all believers. We want to listen to and follow what the Holy Spirit is communicating to us. This process does not include hearing a voice speaking loudly, clearly, and definitively to us.

Even though listening to the voice of God is often emphasized regularly by some popular pastors across the nation today, I believe this can easily be misunderstood and create questions and doubts in people of faith. If we were to expect this to happen as a condition of being a believer, many will then question if indeed they believe enough or believe rightly because they don't hear this voice. Many may then question if they are even a Christian. See the chapter on "How God Speaks to us Today" to read more about this topic.

Seasoned Christians can sense at times when their heart is being tugged by the Holy Spirit. Mature Christians can sense at times when their minds are focused on something they believe is from the Holy

Spirit. All of this is hard to explain, especially to the nonbeliever. And it appears that this is overstated by some Christians who seem to confidently attribute many, if not most, thoughts to the Holy Spirit talking to them, as if this happens frequently. We hear some say, "God is telling me this or that" regularly. The challenge with this is that it is so subjective. There is no way to objectively verify any of this. So therefore, how helpful is it to share this with others? The truth is, if God wants us to know something important, we will find it in the scriptures.

Many Christians have experienced, or know others who have shared their experiences, where the Holy Spirit has put something on their hearts and minds so heavily, specifically and clearly which culminated in them doing something which has then proven to be helpful and important to someone. This usually occurs shortly after the strong impressions they've had. These stories are always encouraging.

In a general sense, it seems to me that our relationship with the Holy Spirit is a collaborative experience. It's a partnership relationship. It is our effort at listening, being focused properly, praying, etc., and the Holy Spirit communicating with our spirit (Rom. 8:16).

As we focus our minds on the Spirit and what the Spirit wants (Rom. 8:5–6), we experience those blessings that come with living our lives for Christ. We are to make every effort to live godly lives (2 Pet. 1:5), fight the good fight (1 Tim. 1:18), and do what the word says (1 Tim. 1:18–25). We must be careful to be wise and not foolish (Eph. 5:15–17) and make every effort to live in peace with men and God (Heb. 12:14). These scriptures allude to the way God and the Holy Spirit collaborate with our efforts.

Responding to Questions Posed in This Chapter

Many of the questions asked at the onset of this chapter have been answered in the body of the chapter. Some may not be so clearly addressed.

1. Does limiting or encouraging the work of the Holy Spirit have anything to do with our salvation? Is it a salvation issue?

Response: As we looked at earlier in chapter 5, we are saved by being born again. It is at this point that we receive the Holy Spirit. How the Holy Spirit works in our lives after our conversion is based on a number of factors, including how we submit to the Spirit, are led by the Spirit, manifest any gifts of the Spirit, and how we exhibit the fruit of the Spirit. This should be comforting to all of us. If we don't see manifestations of the Spirit as others do, that has nothing to do with whether we will have eternal life with Jesus after this life. The idea of us limiting the work of the Holy Spirit is often stated by people, but I believe there are only two scriptures describing an inappropriate relationship with the Holy Spirit. One is the warning not to grieve the Holy Spirit found in Ephesians 4:30. To grieve comes with the notion of causing sorrow, sadness, distress, and pain. If we strive to live godly lives pleasing to God, we will unlikely grieve the Holy Spirit. Another is that blasphemy of the Holy Spirit is an unforgivable sin as found in Mark 3:28–30. Although Jesus does not specifically define this sin, the context reveals this transgression as the persistent, knowing, verbal attribution of the work of God to Satan.

2. Are we controlled by the Holy Spirit? Does this control override our free will? Does being led by the Holy Spirit mean that the Holy Spirit is in control of us?

Response: As I've stated in the chapter, I don't see anywhere in scriptures where we are told that the Holy Spirit controls us in any way. Being led by the Spirit as we find in scripture (Gal. 5:18) is not control. The Greek word for *led* in this passage is *agó* which means to lead, bring, carry…not control.

3. Is life in the Spirit an unexplainable mystery, and to what extent?

Response: The spiritual side of life is a mystery to us except for how it is explained to us in the scriptures. We need to base our understanding of this in the scriptures. Now there are some who may try to convince us to listen to them because of their experiences. However, can those experiences be verified and validated?

4. Does the Holy Spirit do anything without our permission?

Response: The answer has to be no. If it is true, then that would mean that the Holy Spirit would be controlling us.

5. Does the Holy Spirit work in our lives in ways we are not aware of and have not asked him to work?

Response: I believe so. I don't think the Holy Spirit alerts us to what the Holy Spirit is doing. I think our position is trying to figure out what the Spirit is doing and how the Spirit is leading us so we can follow. Praying has a lot to do with this. We can often sense how the Holy Spirit has operated in our lives by looking back at situations for evidence of this.

6. Can we be experiencing the power of the Holy Spirit and not even know it?

Response: I would say absolutely yes! The Holy Spirit does not control us. I can also say confidently that we don't control the Holy Spirit! That would be like us trying to control God.

7. Can we do any good works and deeds apart from the Holy Spirit?

Response: Absolutely yes. The world is filled with non-Christians who don't have the Holy Spirit who are doing many good deeds.

8. What does "being filled with the Holy Spirit" mean? Does being "filled with the Holy Spirit" mean we empty ourselves to make room for the Holy Spirit?

Response: Unfortunately, we are never explicitly told what being filled with the Holy Spirit means. It is never defined for us. However, many talk as if they know exactly what this means. I've heard many differing kinds of explanations. What other people try to say about this is only conjecture. They may be right, but we must treat this with caution.

9. When we get the Holy Spirit at baptism, do we get all of the Holy Spirit? Is there more of the Holy Spirit yet to come?

Response: I've heard many speak about wanting more of the Holy Spirit. However, this to me does not make sense. The Holy Spirit is one being. Not various elements of that one being. I don't see how we can conceive of receiving gradations of the Holy Spirit. How is it that we can have the Holy Spirit and not all of the Holy Spirit? Maybe what people mean is that they want the Spirit more active in their lives.

10. If the Holy Spirit will guide us into all truth (John 16:13), why then are there so many denominations and major theological differences among believers?

Response: This has been a troubling question of mine for a long time. It is really troublesome to see how many people interpret the scriptures differently. This has been happening since the beginning of Christianity. Does the Holy Spirit have a part in this diversity of ideas? I don't see how. I do know that man is fallible and can make many mistakes.

11. Are *all* of the workings of the Holy Spirit in New Testament times occurring today?

Response: As I alluded to above, I don't know how anyone can speak to things they don't understand or have not experienced. However, it appears to happen all the time. Obviously, there is great disagreement in this area.

CHAPTER 13

God Is with Us All the Time

Jesus replied, "Anyone who loves me will obey my
teaching. My Father will love them, and we will come
to them and make our home with them."

—John 14:23

Christian psychiatrist M. Scott Peck, MD wrote a book entitled *The
Road Less Traveled: A New Psychology of Love, Traditional Values and
Spiritual Growth* in 1978. It sold over six million copies. The book
starts out in chapter 1, first sentence with three words: "Life is difficult." These three words communicate a big message. Probably all of
us can identify with that sentiment. Unfortunately for many people,
this is an understatement.

We know that just because life is hard does not mean that life
is not also filled with happy and meaningful experiences. Most of
us are glad we were born and we seek to make the most out of life
we can.

We know parenting is often very hard. Children can create great
heartache at times. However, that does not mean we regret having
children or that our children don't give us great joy and fulfillment.

One of the major reasons life is worth living and meaningful
is because of the people in our lives with whom we have close emotional and intimate relationships. Even for those who have been dis-

appointed with the relationships they have with their families and loved ones, there is always the drive to find meaningful relationships.

We are blessed to know about God our creator and how he made us to be in a close and meaningful relationship with him. We know about the creation story beginning in Genesis 1, which led to Adam and Eve being created. We know how they disappointed God, which changed the earthly conditions for everyone. We have been living in a fallen world ever since as a consequence of their sin.

Because of this, we face many challenges. Our world is a chaotic and uncertain place. We endure many hardships, tragedies, and devastating situations.

There are some Christians who struggle with their faith as a result of this. There are many who ask tough questions as to why awful things happen to them, wondering where God is in all of it. There are many who feel as though God is too hidden and too silent and would like more outward and clear manifestations of his presence. People long for something more convincing, something along the lines of a burning bush or the parting of the Red Sea. We know of the miracles Jesus performed and wish we could see more of this in our day and age.

There can be a lot of confusion for us because things happen that don't appear to make any sense. What many expect from God is not what they see. We wish God's presence would be more recognizable and understandable.

Powerful Examples from Earthly Relationships

We are told throughout both the Old Testament and the New Testament that God is with us. This can be a major source of comfort, encouragement, and peace when we are confronted with life's challenges.

We know from a human perspective how huge it is to have loved ones around us with whom we can share experiences, especially for the special and momentous occasions. We all have a basic and universal need for love, acceptance, and belonging. Big and small accomplishments are only meaningful when we have loved ones to

GOING DEEPER WITH GOD

share them with. We also need loved ones to be with us and encourage us through the sad and sorrowful events of life. Happiness and sorrow need the company of loved ones. For this to be missing, it can create trauma in people's lives of all ages.

This reminds me of a cute story. It's about a seven-year-old girl who had gone to bed. In the middle of the night, a thunderstorm came. Lightning was striking, and thunder was clapping very loudly. Once it started to occur, the girl went into her parents' bedroom and asked to lay in bed with them. Her father said that she would be fine. God would be with her. She said, "I know that, but right now I need someone with skin on!"

It's not only close family members who meet our needs. In other important settings and contexts of life, we need the company of others we admire, respect. and trust…those we can depend on. We see this especially during challenging times. We need leaders who are competent and capable of seeing us through difficult times—leaders whose presence encourages and empowers us.

As an example of this, I remember the scene in the 2001 movie *Pearl Harbor* when Colonel Doolittle was speaking to volunteer pilots in a briefing room who were about to take off in B25 bombers on the aircraft carrier USS *Hornet* with the mission to bomb Tokyo. This occurred four months after Japan bombed Pearl Harbor.

In the scene, Colonel Doolittle mentions how the brass in Washington did not want him to go with them on this mission. They feared for his safety. However, Colonel Doolittle said that he decided to go anyway. The scene then shifted to the faces of the pilots who looked very pleased and encouraged knowing he would be with them. He was admired and respected as their leader. Here they had a decorated expert flyer going with them into battle to lead them through this dangerous mission. This was an incredible morale boost for the pilots.

This example can help us understand the value of having God with us as we experience the challenges of life. To benefit from this reality, we must be mindful of God's presence.

It Is Very Special to Have God with Us

One of the clear promises of scripture for Christians is that God will be with us. We know, as believers in Jesus Christ, we have the right to be called children of God (John 1:12). This places us in a very special relationship with God.

Knowing God is with us has a special meaning to those of us who have accepted Jesus as our Lord and Savior. God has given all Christians the Holy Spirit to reside in us. This is how God is with us in a very personal and intimate way. The God of all creation lives within us. He comforts us in challenging times. He teaches us his ways. He enables us to serve him. When you think about it carefully, we can have no greater privilege than to have God with us.

There is a lot of debate nowadays as to just how involved God is with us. Hopefully, no believers seriously question if God takes an active interest in his creation. Based on his promises, we have confidence he does what he says he is going to do. The debate going on is more in terms of how much God is involved with us in our daily lives.

In the opening pages of the Bible, we find God walking with Adam and Eve in the garden. In the Old Testament/Covenant, we find God interacting with his chosen people to lead them, teach them important lessons, and discipline them. He is not a passive observer of the creation and all that takes place within it. He is an active participant in its affairs, guiding and directing according to his divine purpose.

God's presence with Israel was obvious during the wilderness wanderings after the Exodus. However, God did get very disappointed with his chosen people at times. At Mount Sinai, after the incident with the golden calf, God told Moses that he would not go with the people on their journey to Canaan because they were "a stiff-necked people" (Exod. 33:3–4). But Moses pleaded with God to accompany them on the journey and God relented (Exod. 33:12–17). And so, God was with Israel, leading them with a pillar of fire by night and a pillar of smoke by day. Where that pillar went, they went.

For Israel during the Exodus, "God is with us" meant two things: (1) that God was pleased with them (Exod. 33:16) and (2) that he was providing them with direction (Exod. 40:36–38). This would continue to be true in the remainder of the Old Testament. It would also be true in the New Testament/Covenant, but in different ways.

In the New Testament, we see God's presence in an even more intimate fashion. When God reassures Joseph concerning Mary's pregnancy, he tells him that the one to be born of Mary would be called Immanuel or "God with us" (Matt. 1:23). Jesus was Immanuel. He was God in human form, living and moving among us.

Those who followed Jesus for the three years of his earthly ministry experienced the presence of God with them in a very intimate and personal fashion. During Jesus's last night with his disciples, one of his apostles, Philip, asked him to show them the Father (John 14:8). Jesus responded to him saying that by seeing him, they had seen the Father.

In Matthew 18:20, Jesus tells us that where two or three of us gather in his name, he will be with us. While we don't see his physical presence among us when we gather, we can be assured that he is with us. As the church, we are his body. Wherever we are, he is as well. This is God's promise to us.

In the New Testament gospels, Jesus's followers experienced the presence of God with them in the person of Jesus. He was God in human form, walking, talking, and eating with them.

But the reality is, we have an even more intimate relationship with God now after Jesus physically left the earth. While Jesus walked side by side with the disciples, we have the Holy Spirit living within us. For those who believe in Jesus, God is with us every moment of every day.

In John 14:16–17, Jesus said, "I will ask the Father, and he will give you another advocate to help you and be with you forever—the Spirit of truth." Jesus promised that the Father would give us another advocate, the Holy Spirit. The Holy Spirit is God in us.

Jesus said that this advocate would be with us forever. The Holy Spirit will be our constant companion.

Jesus also said that this advocate would help us. The Holy Spirit helps us to live holy and godly lives. He teaches us the things of God.

He empowers us for service in the world around us. Although it may be hard to see what the Holy Spirit is doing at all times, we can trust he is working in our lives as this is a promise of God.

Yes, God is at work within his creation. He is not the god of deism, a god who creates a universe and then leaves it to itself. Instead, God has a plan for his creation, and he is working it out. It means that nothing will stop God from fulfilling his ultimate purpose. He is working through us to accomplish this.

Promises of God

The scriptures are full of tremendous promises we have from God. So what is a promise? A promise is a covenant or declaration that one will do exactly what one says or something will happen just as one has pledged. When God makes a promise to his people, it will come to pass.

The promises of God are about the present and the future. They are a guarantee by God. They are something we can rely upon. God's promises are never-ending. None of God's promises will ever fail. Nothing can stand against a promise of God to prevent it from happening. God does not hold back anything he promises. The promises of God must be met by a simple response of "thank you."

The promises of God are also ways to gauge that God is working in our lives. We can stand on God's promises and act on them. God not only gives promises, he helps to bring them about in our lives. So when we see a promise fulfilled, we see how God is present with us. When we see a promise about what can happen in the future, we will see God at work again.

Scriptural References

The notion that God is with us is profoundly underscored in the Bible. The following are some of the scriptures which speak to this promise:

- Matthew 28:20: "And teaching them to obey everything I have commanded you. And surely I am with you always, to the very end of the age."
- Romans 8:38–39: "[38] For I am convinced that neither death nor life, neither angels nor demons, neither the present nor the future, nor any powers, [39] neither height nor depth, nor anything else in all creation, will be able to separate us from the love of God that is in Christ Jesus our Lord."
- John 14:16–20: "[16] And I will ask the Father, and he will give you another advocate to help you and be with you forever—[17] the Spirit of truth. The world cannot accept him, because it neither sees him nor knows him. But you know him, for he lives with you and will be in you. [18] I will not leave you as orphans; I will come to you. [19] Before long, the world will not see me anymore, but you will see me. Because I live, you also will live. [20] On that day you will realize that I am in my Father, and you are in me, and I am in you."
- John 14:23: "Jesus replied, "Anyone who loves me will obey my teaching. My Father will love them, and we will come to them and make our home with them."
- 1 Corinthians 13:16: "Do you not know that you are a temple of God and that the Spirit of God dwells in you?"
- Hebrews 13:5: "Make sure that your character is free from the love of money, being content with what you have; for He Himself has said, *I will never desert you, nor will I ever forsake you.*"

Recognizing God's Presence with Us

The apostle John tells us in 1 John 4:13, "This is how we know that we live in Him and He in us: He has given us of his Spirit." This passage sure sounds like we are being told that we should be able to recognize the Holy Spirit's presence in our lives. Hopefully, most of us can see how this is true. Even so, I would also expect that most of us would ask, "How can we see this more?" How can we sense God's presence with us?

We have to ask ourselves, what kind of manifestation are we really looking for from God? There is the possibility that we are many times blinded from seeing God's presence because of the expectations we have. We fail to see God working because we are often looking in the wrong places.

This reminds me of an experience I had over thirty years ago. One evening, I had a longtime friend from Texas come to our house for dinner while he was on a business trip. He had flown into Kansas City and came to see us in a rented car. When he arrived, he asked me if I could find out how to roll down the windows in the car. He couldn't figure it out. So I got in the front seat looking for where the button was to work the windows. I looked all over the side of the door, in the compartment between the seats and on the dashboard. After about ten minutes or so, I finally found it. I was looking for a button to work an electric window. What this car had was the old-fashioned window winder lever. Because we were looking for something else, we just could not see it even though it was right in front of us. We expected to find an electric-operated window button!

I think it is very possible for many of us to miss seeing how God is working in our lives and in our world because we are looking in the wrong places and for the wrong things. We are expecting to find him in other ways. By looking somewhere else for what God is doing, we can miss seeing what he is doing in our lives. For example, maybe we are looking for some big manifestation of God's presence, like a miracle or clear word from God.

Instead of something big, it's very possible God is trying to get our attention in smaller ways. We need to be attuned to urgings the Holy Spirit puts upon our hearts. This could be about helping someone in need we've become aware about or showing simple kindness to someone. It could relate to taking advantage of an opportunity God puts before us that we could fail to see if we are focused on something else (especially when we are focused on our selfish desires).

In addition to what I've already mentioned, let's further explore the question "How can we sense God's presence with us?" Let's consider the many ways we can see that God is with us.

Yes, we have many promises from God about this, but so much of this is based on subjective evidence. So instead of trying to prove something, I am going to share what we could call indicators of God's presence with us. We'll look at many pieces of evidence from which to make our conclusions.

The following is a list that came to my mind as I contemplated this:

1. Coming to a saving faith and maintaining that faith. God has touched our hearts. We receive encouragement, and we mature as Christians. We grow stronger in our faith. God has his hand in all of this.

2. We study God's Word. We gain greater knowledge of the truth. We meditate on God's Word. We gain greater insights. We have thoughts that spring up in our minds and ask, "Where did this come from?" We read Christian books to expand our knowledge on topics. We search for the truth. God's Holy Spirit in us is involved in all of this.

3. We all need to find quality time for prayer (1 Thess. 5:17), reading scripture and meditating on scripture. Too often, we keep too busy and don't make time for this. We often sense God's presence when we are talking to him and making requests of him. We find God speaking to us through the scriptures. We find the Holy Spirit bringing thoughts to our minds as we meditate on the scriptures. Through all this, we can sense God's presence with us.

4. Based on Romans 8:26–27, we learn that the Holy Spirit helps us in our times of weakness. The Holy Spirit searches our hearts and intercedes for us directly to God himself. We can know this to be true even if we can't understand it. God is with us and in us to help us in our weaknesses.

5. Most of us can attest to the inspiration we can get when we worship God both in a congregate setting and by ourselves.

God speaks to our hearts through song, through preaching, and through fellowship and interaction with fellow Christians. Music especially, whether in a church service or another private setting, can be very inspiring and emotional for us. We often sense God's presence while we worship. What God wants from us is authentic worship. God wants us to live godly lives and worship him with the right heart. God does not like or accept counterfeit worship or lip service (Matt. 15:8, Isa. 29:13). God is with us when we worship him (Matt. 18:20).

6. Many times God uses the experiences in our lives as ministry opportunities for us. The experiences we have teach us much about life and give us insights in how to relate to others facing similar situations. God works through people to help other people. See the following for examples of this.

   a) Those who have had loved ones who have died can be a source of comfort and support for others through their loss and grief work.

   b) Those who have a child with Down syndrome can be a source of support for other new parents of children with Down syndrome.

   c) Those who have been divorced can help others in a similar situation.

   d) Those who are cancer survivors can help cancer patients.

7. God is with us when we display the fruit of the Spirit in Galatians 5:22–23: love, joy, peace, patience, kindness, goodness, faithfulness, gentleness, and self-control. The Holy Spirit is helping us develop these qualities. It's a concurrent effort with us and God working to develop these qualities together. Again, if we have them, we can see God at work in us.

8. We see God working when we put our faith into action (James 2:17) and our love into action (1 John 3:18). God created us to do good works (Eph. 2:10). When we help

those in need, God is there with us and empowering us with his Spirit.

9. When we speak of God with boldness, power, and courage, we have the Holy Spirit helping us (Acts 4:24–31).

10. God's power enables us to pursue godliness (2 Pet. 1:3–9). All our efforts will be met by his power in us to help us. This is the idea of concurrence: God working and we are concurrently working to achieve his will. We can do great things and bear much fruit as we abide in Jesus (John 15:1–8). If we see evidence of this, we will see God working in our lives.

11. Each of us has God-given skills, abilities, talents, and gifts. Some of these include gifts of the Holy Spirit (1 Cor. 12). Using these is where we will find evidence of God working extraordinarily in our lives.

12. We will have all kinds of troubles and trials in our lives. It is often in these times when God is helping us the most although we may not see it as we are going through these trials. Part of this can be the Holy Spirit working through other people to help us. We can often see evidence of this when we look back after the situation is over. We can also see how God has used the situation to strengthen and help us, having some good come from it (Rom. 8:28). I speak on this more in the upcoming chapter on "Maintaining Faith in the Midst of Suffering."

13. We see God working through the efforts of our mind. We are to be transformed by the renewing of our minds (Rom. 12:2). As we keep our minds focused on the Holy Spirit, we can be led by the Holy Spirit (Rom. 8:1–14). This relates to the idea of concurrence also, we and God working together.

14. Many Christians can speak about urges they have sensed in their mind to take some action. This is usually about a specific task. When the task is done, we find out how it met an important need for someone and how it was God

working to pull this off. These stories are always encouraging to hear.

15. In a similar way, there will inevitably be times when we feel that something is just not right and we have no sense of peace. If we feel like something is off or have an overall feeling of uneasiness, maybe it's the Holy Spirit trying to get our attention to do something. Feelings are not a guide, but they can be like an early warning system alerting us that something needs to be addressed. (Don't confuse this with not feeling at peace about making a good decision. Some right decisions are just difficult to make at times.)

16. As we've alluded to earlier, as we stand on God's promises, we will see evidence of them coming to pass. Test it out. Just make sure it is a legitimate promise from God clearly expressed in the scriptures. This is God with us.

17. Have you noticed how we can feel closer to God when we are in nature, away from the hustle and bustle of city life? We can sense God's presence when we are with him in the beauty and magnificence of the world he created.

18. The miracle of forgiveness is another example. Forgiveness is God's invention and God's way to handle the hurts and mistreatments in our lives. When we forgive others, we will find healing…if we handle this right. God knew we couldn't have relationships with others without forgiveness. This works and is evidence of God with us as these issues are worked through.

19. We can find evidence of God being with us when we step out in faith and get engaged in ministry, evangelistic efforts, other volunteer efforts, and find ourselves standing up for God to others. These are times we need to ask for strength from God. I believe the Lord puts many opportunities in front of us where we are needed to help someone. So often, it's easy just to stay in our personal comfort zones to protect us from situations that can challenge us. We will experience more of God's power in our lives when we stretch ourselves to do things we don't normally do.

By all of the above and more, we can see how we experience the promise that God is with us and for us.

Recognizing God's presence helps us in many ways. As we try to be fully attentive to him, we are able to see more clearly how he is present in our lives. This can be incredibly encouraging and emboldening. It strengthens our faith. It helps us to step out in faith more and to work jointly with him more. It enables us to give thanks more and enhances the meaningfulness of our worship.

I'm sure there are other items we could add to the above list. If we wonder if God's presence is knowable or question if God is hidden or too silent, we have much to think about. Maybe the answer is in being more engaged in godly activities. For some, maybe there is the need to reengage with God.

Times We May Not See God with Us

And so we ask ourselves, "What is the difference between times when we sense God's presence and those times we don't?"

The likely reason why we may not sense God's presence with us is because of us. It's not God's fault. He is constant and remains true to his promises.

Some of the reasons why we may not see clearly how God is with us are when we put God and spiritual matters on the back burner in our lives. We can become too busy at work and with other activities to the point of being distracted from that which is really important to us. God may be lower in our priorities. We can squelch and stifle our Christian focus and spiritual ways of living. We can become self-centered, uncaring, unkind, insensitive, harsh, and indifferent. Maybe we turn our backs on God and rebel against our values and reject our past beliefs.

There are certainly many other ways we can get off-track in our Christian walk with God and depart from the special relationship we have with him. In these situations, an attitude of repentance, rededication, and spiritual renewal is needed. Fortunately, God loves us so much that he will accept us back into a relationship with him.

Our promise that God is with us does not mean that God will necessarily keep us safe from harm, hardship, suffering, and heartache. His promise is to be with us through these difficult times. We are never alone. God is never absent if we remain faithful.

God can't be any closer to us than he is with the Holy Spirit being within us. God knows what we are going through. It is through the Holy Spirit where we get his help, comfort, and strength. God is in us, God is for us, and God is with us. God can help us through our times of trouble, sorrow, crisis, and joy. God will lead us home to heaven. Isn't that what really matters?

A Final Message of Encouragement

Again, what I believe Christians have as a clear promise from God is that God is with us to help us through any situation. Not necessarily to keep us safe or protect us from harm but to walk with us through our circumstances, whatever they are. God is not absent or far away from us. He has not left us on our own. He also wants us to stay connected to him and his family, our spiritual brothers and sisters, whom he can use to help us.

Now there are some who feel like God is not near and not accepting of them because of their shortcomings, weaknesses, and sins. It can feel hard or uncomfortable to pray to God and approach God when we have been doing sinful things, not honoring God, and not keeping God at the center of our thinking and lives. God knows this about us humans. We need to understand and appreciate the deep meaning of God's grace.

If we think we can only approach God when we've been good or when we've been as spiritual as we would like, then we are saying that God's acceptance of us is based on our works. That is not scripturally true. We can never be good enough. God's grace covers us when we are Christians, no matter if we are in a spiritually downer time or a spiritually high time. God's grace covers us when we sin. Jesus only had to be sacrificed for our sins one time for all time (Heb. 10). There is now no condemnation for those who are in Christ Jesus (Rom. 8:1).

CHAPTER 14

—

How God Speaks to Us Today

All Scripture is God-breathed and is useful for teaching, rebuking, correcting and training in righteousness, [17] so that the servant of God may be thoroughly equipped for every good work.

—2 Timothy 3:16

For the word of God is alive and active. Sharper than any double-edged sword, it penetrates even to dividing soul and spirit, joints and marrow; it judges the thoughts and attitudes of the heart.

—Hebrews 4:12

[18] I warn everyone who hears the words of the prophecy of this scroll: If anyone adds anything to them, God will add to that person the plagues described in this scroll. [19] And if anyone takes words away from this scroll of prophecy, God will take away from that person any share in the tree of life and in the Holy City, which are described in this scroll.

—Revelation 22:18–19

There has been a growing movement that has been picking up steam over the last ten years or so (could be longer) about the need to listen for the voice of God speaking to us in our minds. There are many contemporary Christian leaders speaking to the need for every day common Christians to be looking for God to speak to them outside of the Bible. Charles Stanley and Rick Warren are two prominent ones I know of who are doing this. The message from them is that Christians should be hearing God speaking to them regularly.

Rick Warren's Perspective on This

Rick Warren is the pastor of the Saddleback Church in Lake Forest, California, and has several sermons which can be easily found on YouTube on this topic. One is on "Understanding How to Recognize God's Voice" found at the following link: https://www.youtube.com/watch?v=-827QmRDjUA. In that sermon, Rick makes the following comments:

> You can't have a relationship with God if you don't hear from God. If you don't hear God speak to you, then that would be a one-way relationship. If a person doesn't talk back to us, we don't have a relationship with the person.
>
> Nothing is more important in life than hearing God's voice. The reason we can't hear God speak to us on a regular basis is because we aren't tuned in.
>
> Hearing from God verifies we are a Christian and have a relationship with God. It proves we are a child of God.

He refers to John chapter 10 about the metaphor of Jesus being the good shepherd and saying that the sheep listen to his voice.

Rick then goes on to give seven tests to know if one is hearing the voice of God. He said if what you heard from God passes all seven tests, you can be absolutely certain that you have heard from God. Rick said that if one of the seven tests is not met, then that means it is not from God. The seven tests are what Rick has formulated himself.

The seven tests are the following:

1. Does it agree with the Bible?
2. Does it make me more like Christ?
3. Does my church family confirm it?
4. Is it consistent with how God has shaped me?
5. Does it concern my responsibility?
6. Is it convicting rather than condemning?
7. Do I sense God's peace about it?

The problem with the above is that there is no direct and explicit scriptural support for numbers 2–7. Rick said that if one of the seven tests is not met, then that means it is absolutely for certain not from God (and vice versa). This assertion is a way of elevating his statements to being equal to the importance and authority of scripture. That is a dangerous place to be. I think it would be wise to caution anyone from speaking like this. That is because we can't be absolutely certain of anything but what is affirmed in scripture.

Charles Stanley's View on This

Charles Stanley is the founder of In Touch Ministries and is pastor of the First Baptist Church in Atlanta, Georgia. He is famous for emphasizing the need to listen to the voice of God. He mentions this regularly in his sermons which are on the radio and TV. I've heard him say this many times, and each time I've heard him he never explains what he means by it. Recently, I found a five-minute video on YouTube where he discussed what he meant by "listening to the voice of God."

This is found at the following link: https://www.youtube. com/watch?v=V4ocm31RJ7g. In this message, Charles states the following:

> Does God speak to us today? He's always speaking to believers, but we must be attuned to hear His voice. It is a matter of listening

and waiting, of humility and meditation upon
God's word and learning to recognize how God
communicates.

He mentioned an email he received which summed up questions people have about this. The lady in the email said: "I have prayed for God to speak to me, but I don't hear Him. My faith is strong and I know He will do for me what the Bible promises. But I've never heard Him say, 'Go buy this gallon of milk, don't buy this car, wait for what I have for you.' Am I not listening in the right way? Or is He guiding my everyday decisions, but I don't realize He's speaking? How do I hear God's voice?"

Charles then told a story of a time one Thanksgiving when he wanted to buy a turkey, but only had a short period to do that. So he prayed to God to show him what to do. Charles stated, "God said to me to go to this particular store and buy the turkey now. Did God tell me to go? Yes He did!"

Charles said one has to be spiritually tuned in to God's Spirit. The problem is with us, not God. Charles Stanley continues to say, we need to be in the Word of God. God primarily speaks to us through his word, but not always. When he speaks, He will make it clear. The question is, "Are you listening with a yielded heart?" If you come to God with a surrendered life, yielded to his Spirit with a clean heart, you can bet your life on this. God is willing to demonstrate his awesome power and love to grant your petition.

Contrary Viewpoints

On the other hand, there are also other pastors of national prominence and many scholarly people from a variety of religious orientations who speak against such expectations and this movement. They make the point that the scriptures are all sufficient and all we need for God to speak to us.

We've all heard stories of people saying God told them to do something which related to a horrible incident. I remember years ago when I was in Atlanta and hearing of a mother who abandoned her preschool son by leaving him on a street corner alone saying that God told her to do that. We hear of others doing terrible things saying God told them to do that. There are those who manipulate others by using this technique, saying God is telling them whatever it is they want to happen.

Now these are extreme, and no one would believe them. However, this speaks to the potential of abuse with this process. It also speaks to the apparent right anyone has to say that God has told them something in their mind. No matter who it is, how can we verify or validate what they are saying is from God talking to them? All of this is so subjective.

I have a friend who loves the Lord with all her heart and strives to be godly in everything she does. She likes to say that God is talking to her all the time. She regularly says that God has told her this or that. The question is "How can we know what to do with that?" There is no way we can verify if that is authentic. So I wonder, "Should others even share with another person what they think God is saying to them in their minds?" What is the benefit to us in hearing this?

Given all of this, it does appear there are differences in the ways Christians experience receiving messages from God. Many express receiving urges, nudgings, thoughts, promptings, and impressions they attribute to God or the Holy Spirit. I have sensed this at times. A recent case in point would be in the process of writing this book. However, since this is all so subjective, it's difficult to talk about.

Contrary to what Rick Warren has asserted, I believe there should be no question on whether God speaking to a person in the mind like this has any bearing on whether or not a person is a Christian. Hearing God's voice in our minds is not a requirement for salvation. For one thing, a requirement of hearing God's voice is not mentioned as part of the salvation process. Also, nowhere in the scriptures do we find it tells us that hearing the voice of God in our minds is a determining sign of whether one is a Christian or not. Therefore, no one can assert it is a sign that a person has an authentic relationship with God as Rick has asserted.

Questions about God Speaking to Us Directly

Several questions arise after thinking about all of this. These questions reflect the doubts and difficult time I have for accepting as truth what Rick Warren and Charles Stanley are saying.

1. If this is so important, where do the scriptures speak about God talking to common people directly in their minds, especially New Testament scriptures? What is the scriptural support for this concept? Shouldn't this be identified and used to support assertions made?

2. Why would God need or want to talk to us like this so frequently?

3. Most proponents of this say that we don't hear God because we are not "tuned in to God." What is the scriptural basis for this point? Where do the scriptures tell us about how to be tuned in to God so we can hear him speak to us directly in our minds? If this is so important, wouldn't we find it prominently in the scriptures?

4. Why do we need God to speak to us if we have to cross reference everything we believe we hear God telling us with what is already in the scriptures?

5. Are the scriptures insufficient for telling us everything important we need to know about how to live, get along with others, and relate to God?

6. Why is the Bible not sufficient enough for us versus us needing God to give us more by speaking directly to us today in our minds?

7. How do we distinguish between whether it is God speaking to us in our minds versus other thoughts we have in our minds that are not from God?

8. Do we need God to tell us more in our minds than what is in the scriptures to help make us to become more like Christ?

9. When people say God is telling them this or that, how can we verify the truth of whether this is actually God speaking

to them? If we can't verify it, then what do we do with this information?

10. Do we really need God to tell us when and where to buy a turkey for Thanksgiving or which car to buy?

We may often think about trying to listen to what God is trying to tell us when we pray and ask for God's guidance and help. There is a big emphasis on being able to know when God answers our prayers and what he is saying. I wonder if that is overemphasized. Maybe we just can't know.

Do We Need More Than the Bible?

As I've emphasized many times so far, the scriptures are what we can rely on for God's word to mankind. God speaks to each of us through the scriptures. The point can be made that those who want God to speak directly to them outside of the scriptures are implying that the scriptures are not enough for us today. Are the scriptures sufficient? What we have inside the Bible are dependable and enduring messages. We have the totality of the revelation that God meant to communicate, and it is speaking to us every time we read the scriptures.

Many biblical scholars would say it would seem foolish for people to crave for God to speak to them outside of the Bible since the Bible has everything we need to know from God. In response, some may try to make the case that since we pray to God asking him to help us with decisions and direction for our lives, what is wrong with God speaking to us directly about those items? Yes, we have the Holy Spirit (God in us) to help us. To be congruent, we must accept that this happens. I'm not saying that the Holy Spirit speaks to us with words. I believe the Holy Spirit can influence our thinking and nudge us along. Some may try to make the case that the Holy Spirit is more assertive in how he speaks to us.

However, many who ask God to speak to them are often looking for something different and more than answers to prayers.

Jesus warned against those who seek a sign (Matt. 12:38–39). So here he is. He is standing there in front of the Pharisees and scribes speaking, and they say, "Give us a sign." What does that mean? It means that the voice of Jesus Christ the Son of God wasn't adequate. They needed something more. They needed to feel more, touch more, and see more. They wanted more. And Jesus wouldn't give it to them. With the Bible, we have the wholeness of the revelation that God meant to communicate, and it is speaking to us every time we read it.

The only way in the New Covenant era to be certain God is speaking to us in an objective and verifiable way is through the scriptures. Yes, we know God spoke to people in the Old Testament through the prophets, dreams, and visions, as well as directly to people in other ways. But in the New Testament, things have changed. Listen to what the Hebrew writer says about this in Hebrews 1:1–3:

> In the past God spoke to our ancestors through the prophets at many times and in various ways, but in these last days he has spoken to us by his Son, whom he appointed heir of all things, and through whom also he made the universe. The Son is the radiance of God's glory and the exact representation of his being, sustaining all things by his powerful word. After he had provided purification for sins, he sat down at the right hand of the Majesty in heaven.

The New Testament scriptures are all about the difference Jesus has made for us all. The New Testament is all about what this means for us today.

When we read the Scriptures, we are not just reading a record of what God has said in the past. God actively speaks to us in the here and now through the words of this amazing book. We hear the voice of God when we read and study the scriptures.

The only way we objectively and reliably hear from Jesus is through the scriptures. Here we can point to the book, the chapter, and the verse. We can be certain we know from the New Testament scriptures all we need to know about how to be saved and be welcomed into the family of God. The New Testament scriptures give us all we need to know about how to live our lives in ways that are pleasing to God. For all this, nothing has been left out. Nothing needs to be added. No teachings or admonitions outside the scriptures have the authority of the scriptures.

This is not to say that the Holy Spirit "speaking" to us is not valid or helpful. Christians are given the Holy Spirit when we are born again. See chapter 12 for more information on the Holy Spirit.

It seems today that many want something more, something different from just the scriptures. We can hear about some of this through the teachings of the Word of Faith movement, as well as other teachings which seem to embellish how the mighty power of God is demonstrated today. Conflicting messages about all this can be very confusing to the seeking person and the new Christian.

Again, we need to point people back to the scriptures. Are there any instances in the New Testament scriptures in which common people describe a sense of God speaking to them through an inner voice in their daily lives? I don't think I can identify any.

We know today there are Christian people who train others on how to hear the voice of God. They often say that God's voice in your head often sounds like a flow of spontaneous thoughts. However, we can ask again, "Where in the scriptures are we instructed to seek after or expect to hear God speak to us in this way?" Are there instances in the scriptures in which God gives special and specific guidance to ordinary believing Christians? We know of instances where the apostle Paul mentions this happening to him, but where in the Bible are we instructed to seek after or expect to hear God speak to us in this way?

We know Rick Warren referred to John chapter 10 where Jesus said he is the Good Shepherd and his sheep hear his voice. However, that was part of a metaphor. It was not meant to be literal. Jesus is not prescribing a method of ongoing divine communication from that day forward.

Again, there are Christians who want God to speak to them as they experience a personal relationship with him, especially as they are encouraged to expect this from some faith leaders. Many are being set up to want a supernatural experience with God to happen regularly. Going back to what I said earlier, we are experiencing God speaking to us when we read and study the scriptures. This is like a supernatural experience. The Word of God has a way of transforming our lives. God speaks personally and powerfully to us through his Word!

Conclusion

The emphasis in preaching that we need to listen for the voice of God in our minds does not appear to be a message that is broadly preached. I only hear this emphasized in certain church denominations. But in those churches, one hears it a lot nowadays. I don't remember this being so twenty years ago or more. Since it is being forwarded by some prominent pastors, I thought it worthy of addressing in this book.

CHAPTER 15

Is God in Control of Everything?

The Sovereignty of God versus the Free Will of Man
has been characterized as one of the great debates
in the Christian community for centuries.

I remember going to college in the early 1970s and hearing people say the term "God is in control." I remember having difficulty understanding how that can be so. It was something I could not get my mind around. I don't remember it being mentioned during church services and church activities while I was growing up.

Many years later, I remember when my oldest son was attending college and told me about how some of his friends were Calvinists and believed in Calvinism's version of predestination. He introduced me to the book by Norman Geisler called *Chosen But Free: A Balanced View of Divine Election*. This was very enlightening and did a very good job of explaining the various perspectives of Calvinism.

A few years later, my younger adult son began attending a Calvinist-oriented church in the Atlanta area after he graduated from college. He would share with me what he was learning about Calvinism. I could tell he was being drawn to its doctrine, largely because of the dynamic pastor of that church. This motivated me to do a fair amount of research into Calvinism in terms of reading books and articles, listening to sermons by Calvinist pastors, and talking to many of my seasoned Christian friends about it. Fortunately, my son became dissatisfied with this church and its doctrines and left to attend a non-Calvinist church.

Soon after this, I began encountering Calvinist beliefs being expressed in my extended family, through some sisters (I have five of them), nieces, and their spouses. I would hear "God is in control" regularly uttered as well as other Calvinist themes during our times together.

At the non-Calvinist congregation we attended in Atlanta, our worship leader would regularly say, "God is in control. He's still on the throne." I've also heard many others in that congregation say God is in control. In the current non-Calvinist congregation we attend, I've also heard many say the phrase "God is in control." I think saying this phrase is becoming even more prevalent today.

In my personal studies on Calvinism, I've learned how the term "God is in control" comes out of the concept of the "sovereignty of God."

I know there are many people who use the term "God is in control" who are not Calvinists. Some of these are people who know little to nothing about Calvinism. I believe much of this is the result of how Calvinistic themes are infiltrating many non-Calvinist churches through Christian contemporary songs, Christian books and literature, the Internet among other ways.

There are also many ministers and Christian leaders who prominently use the phrase "God is in control" who are not Calvinists, but who believe the extreme concept of God's sovereignty. Charles Stanley, Max Lucado, and pastors and ministers from all kinds of churches preach this message. And yet I never hear them fully explain what they mean by it and how it fits with the realities of the world we live in.

So all of this is what has caused me to pursue a personal study to find answers to the many questions I've had about Calvinism and the sovereignty of God, especially in context of the concept of the free will of man. Exploring this subject has been an interest of mine for many years. I have read many books over the years and researched the pros and cons of the Calvinist doctrine. I am one who has studied this topic a fair amount and have thoughts and insights to share which I believe can be helpful to others.

The Free Will Controversy

About fifteen years ago, I was listening to a Christian radio station in Atlanta, and a person being interviewed made the comment that there is no such thing as free will mentioned in the Bible. It was clear to me he was saying man's free will as a concept is not supported by the scriptures.

Calvinist Arthur Pink in his book *The Sovereignty of God* has declared that "free moral agency is an expression of human invention" and believes the sinner's will is free in only one direction, namely in the direction of evil. Calvinist Charles Spurgeon in his book *Free Will: a Slave* has said, "Free will is nonsense."

The notion of free will is at odds with the notion that God is in control of everything. Calvinists who hold to the extreme view of the sovereignty of God are at odds with free will believers. There has been an ongoing debate regarding the concept of the sovereignty of God and the free will of man for centuries. It has been characterized as one of the greatest debates of all time.

The Christian community is highly divided by this debate. Differing views are strongly held. However, both viewpoints can't be true. This discussion requires one to make a decision on which perspective to believe. What is in line with truth is all that really matters. Any journey seeking truth should be guided by the whole of scripture and supported by reasonable thinking.

The reality is, the search for truth takes well-meaning people down differing paths. I suspect this is the way things have been since the time of Christ.

The Meaning of the Sovereignty of God

We would do well to try to come to a common definition of what we mean by the concept "the sovereignty of God." I think it would also be helpful to understand what Calvinists mean when they use this term. This will help us better formulate our freewill views and highlight how we need to be careful in choosing the words we use to describe our Christian beliefs.

We do not find in the scriptures a specific definition of God's sovereignty like we do for a definition of *faith* as found in Hebrews 11 and *love* as found in 1 Corinthians 13 and elsewhere. What we must therefore do is look for other ways to understand this concept.

As we look at what the word *sovereignty* means, we can first go to the Webster's dictionary. There it is defined as the following:

- first in rank, above or superior to all others, supreme
- supreme in power, rank, or authority
- holding the position of ruler, reigning

Since there are no scriptures which specifically define God's sovereignty, we then need to look for scriptures which reflect God's greatness and sovereignty. See the following for some of these.

- In the beginning God (Gen.1:1)… Before there was anything else, there was God.
- In the beginning was the word…and the word was God (John 1:1).
- God created the heavens and the earth (Gen. 1:1).
- For by him all things were created: things in heaven and on earth (Col. 1:16).
- He is called the Alpha and Omega—the beginning and the end (Rev. 22:13).
- God was there before the beginning of all time (2 Tim. 1:9).
- He is alone immortal (1 Tim. 6:16).
- He is before all things, and in him all things hold together (Col. 1.17).
- There is "one God and Father of all, who is over all and through all and in all" (Eph. 4:6).
- God is Omniscient (knows all things)—(Ps. 147:5; Isa. 46:10; Heb. 4:13; Rom. 11:33).
- God can do all things (omnipotent—all powerful).
  o God created everything.
  o God does miracles.

o   God does whatever pleases Him (Ps. 135:6).

o   Nothing is impossible with God (Luke 1:37; Matt. 19:26).

■   Regarding nothing is impossible with God: God can do whatever is possible to do—he won't act incongruent to his nature and attributes, he can't lie, he doesn't change (immutable), he won't make a square a circle, he won't make a triangle with two sides...

• There is no one else like God (Isa. 46:9–11).

• King of Kings and Lord of Lords (1 Tim. 6:15–16; Rev. 19:16).

It is from passages like these that the concept of God's sovereignty is generated.

One of the premier Reformed theology's scholars was *R.C. Sproul.* In his book *What is Reformed Theology?: Understanding the Basics,* he states, "If God is not sovereign, then he is not God. It belongs to God as God to be sovereign.

By sovereign, Sproul means "God is the absolute determiner and controller of everything down to the minutest details."

R.C. Sproul, in his book *Chosen by God,* states, "If there is one single molecule in this universe running around loose, totally free of God's sovereignty, then we have no guarantee that a single promise of God will ever be fulfilled."

Calvinist Paul Helm in his book *The Providence of God: (Contours of Christian Theology)* expresses his high view of God's sovereignty: "Not only is every atom and molecule, every thought and desire, kept in being by God, but every twist and turn of each of these is under the direct control of God."

Free will adherent and university professor *Roger Olson PhD,* who wrote the book *Against Calvinism: Rescuing God's Reputation from Radical Reformed Theology,* summarizes what he understands extreme Calvinists believe about God's Sovereignty:

> The total, absolute, meticulous sovereignty of God in providence by which God governs the entire course of human history down to the minutest details and renders everything certain so that no event is fortuitous (happening by chance) or accidental but fits into God's overall plan and purpose.

Charles Stanley, who is not a Calvinist, has recently (in a televised sermon aired on February 2020) stated his definition of the sovereignty of God through the "In Touch Ministry" featuring his preaching at his church in Atlanta. He stated the following:

> The Sovereignty of God means that God rules over all things and all people at all times. God absolutely rules over all circumstances of life. He is in control of everything. He knows everything past, present and future. If we don't believe in this view of the Sovereignty of God, we don't believe in the Bible.

To be omnipotent does not have to mean that God exercises his power to control all that happens. He can utilize his power even when he gives (delegates) to man a certain amount of power and responsibility. It is not incongruent with God's sovereignty that he can decide to self-limit himself or his activity. God's sovereignty does not have to mean he determines every last detail and orchestrates everything that happens.

And so the question is "Is the notion of the free will of man and the sovereignty of God compatible?" Can they both exist? Many believe they can both exist at the same time given the notion that God delegates a certain amount of responsibility and power to man. Otherwise they appear to me to be in contradiction with each other, thus violating the law of noncontradiction. (See the upcoming chapter regarding "Logic—the Basis for Relating to Others and to God" for more on this.)

The Bible presents God as the superior power who does not cling to his rightful authority to dominate but steps back to give room for man to function. As stated in earlier chapters, that is why he created man as he did in the first place.

We must remember that God made man in his image. He made man with free will. Once he did so, he can't take it back. Having free will is just the way God made us. The scriptures are all about harnessing the free will we have so that the choices we make conform to the will of God.

God gives man free will to make independent decisions. God invites mankind to have dominion over the world and be responsible for their lives. Free will is what enabled Adam and Eve to sin.

The Free Will of Man

If God is in total control and if all of our choices are determined by God, how can we be genuinely free? If we do not choose freely, how can God hold us accountable for our actions? In other words, we can't be blamed for that which we had no choice. Free will is the God-given ability for mankind to make independent choices in our lives. It means we could have always chosen to do otherwise. It means that we can make choices independently of God's control, and thus we assume responsibility for those choices. We are free when we are not constrained to act contrary to our desires. The truth is, apart from free will, there is no depth of relationships.

Edgar Mullin said in 1925 in the "Baptist Beliefs" publication the following about free will:

> Free will in man is as fundamental a truth as any other in the gospel and must never be canceled in our doctrinal statements. Man would not be man without it and God never robs us of our true moral manhood in saving us.

Bruce Reichenbach writes in the book *Predestination and Free Will: Four Views*, edited by David Basinger and Randal Basinger, the following:

> Scripture does not discuss human freedom per se (though it does discuss freedom in relation to other aspects of our lives, for example the law and sin). But it is filled with instances of posed choices which presuppose freedom. From Adam and Eve's option to obey or disobey (Gen.3) to Moses' presentation of a similar option to Israel (for example, Ex. 32 and 33) to Joshua's famous final speech concerning service (Josh 24) to Jesus' presentation of the broad and narrow ways (Mt 7:13–14) significant choices are posed. Further, as Christians we believe that we are under certain moral obligations, not the least of which is to love God and to love our neighbors as ourselves. But commands to act properly and the sanctions imposed on improper conduct only make sense if humans have freedom. God places before us his obligations and at the same time has created us free to accept or reject them.

The idea of mankind having independent free will is a concept which runs throughout the scriptures. We understand this by deduction, not direct pronouncement. The scriptures don't use the phrase "free will" outright, but we see free will playing a role in the major stories involving the experiences of key biblical figures. We see the necessity of free will when the authority figures in the scriptures give us commands, admonitions, and standards to live by as we follow Christ.

God gives people moral responsibility that can only be exercised with free choice. Without free will, we would not be responsible or accountable for our actions. Without free will, we could not freely love God. Freedom is a condition of love. We are to love God with all our heart. This can't come from being forced to do it. God does not force anyone to love him or to accept his love. Force cannot produce love. True love can only come voluntarily from the heart.

Nowhere does the Bible state that God's sovereignty requires that man has no power to make genuine choices, moral or otherwise. Nowhere in the scriptures does God have a sense of not being sovereign and all-powerful even though he created man with free will.

If God is in control of everything, then why should anyone be blamed for anything? If God is in control of all events, then how can I be responsible for anything that happens—even my evil actions? This extreme view of God's sovereignty eliminates our responsibility.

God appeals to human reasoning all the time. This underscores the assumption that people have free will and must be addressed using logic and persuasion, not power and control. The command central for regulating the thoughts and behaviors of human beings is our mind. It does not occur from an external force controlling us. Without the power to make genuine choices, a person could not be a morally responsible being, accountable to his or her creator. Without the power of choice, a person is not respected as a rational being.

It can be argued that making humans with free will is God's most marvelous and consequential work. It is indeed the gift that makes possible every other gift from God. Without the power to choose, man could not consciously receive any moral or spiritual gift from God. In Ephesians 2:8, we are told that salvation is a gift. By its very nature, a gift can be rejected. A gift must be received by an act of the will. If a gift is forced upon a recipient, then it is not a gift.

Logic tells us that extreme Calvinist positions must be rejected because they are contradictory. Opposites cannot both be true at the same time and in the same sense. (This is the law of noncontradiction, and this will be addressed in chapter 17.)

Norman Geisler and Frank Turek in their book *I Don't Have Enough Faith to Be an Atheist* address many dimensions of Christian apologetics which is a discipline focused on defending the Christian faith. Inherent in this discipline is that we can use reason and evidence to inform our faith…that God has made man with the ability to think, analyze, and make decisions. This is all about free will.

Consider what they say about man's freedom to make choices to accept or reject the truth about whether God exists:

> One beauty of God's creation is this: if you're not willing to accept Christianity, then you're free to reject it. This freedom to make choices—even the freedom to reject truth—is what makes us moral creatures and enables each one of us to choose our ultimate destiny.
>
> In other words, *God has provided enough evidence in this life to convince anyone willing to believe, yet he has also left some ambiguity so as not to compel the unwilling.* In this way, God gives us the opportunity either to love him or to reject him without violating our freedom. In fact, the purpose of this life is to make that choice freely and without coercion. For love, by definition, must be freely given. It cannot be coerced.

C. S. Lewis states in his book *Mere Christianity* the following:

> If a thing is free to be good it is also free to be bad. And free will is what has made evil possible. Why, then, did God give them free will? Because free will, though it makes evil possible, is also the only thing that makes possible any love or goodness or joy worth having.

Free Will Is Important and Widely Accepted

As we see from the above, free will is essential to so many spiritual obligations and commands. Free will is associated with fulfilling the greatest commandment and the second greatest commandment—to love God with all our being and to love our neighbors (Matt. 22:37–40). It seems quite obvious that this necessarily then elevates the importance of free will.

It would also seem logical that free will is associated with fulfilling all of the scriptural admonitions for us to behave in certain ways, have certain attitudes, have spiritual qualities, and do spiritual deeds.

As I talk to those *not* familiar with the tenets of Calvinism, I get the sense that they view it very strange and even incredible that we would have to examine and defend the notion, function, and validity of free will. To most, free will seems so obvious. They acknowledge that free will plainly follows human beings' cognitive abilities, including having intelligence, imagination, creativity, abstract thinking, analyzing options, and making decisions. These are elementary or basic concepts which apply to everyday life as well as to religious practices for the common person. These are concepts which seem so logical and reasonable.

We should not have to promote or affirm God's working in our lives as replacing or taking away basic and sensible functions of the human mind. The scriptures are based upon the reality that we humans can use our minds to understand teachings and admonitions. With open minds and willing hearts, we can be persuaded to accept the truth, come to faith, and embrace the offer of salvation presented to all through Christ. It just seems so obvious that one should not build a theology opposed and contrary to this.

God Does Not Exercise Control of Everything

We live in an age where Calvinism is expanding and its doctrinal language is spreading into all kinds of faith traditions. (It is interesting to note that much of the growth of Calvinism seems to be among men versus women.) Often we hear comments like "God is in control" as if he controls all aspects of our lives. We hear the phrase "Let go and let God" as if we need to just get out of the way so the Holy Spirit can do the work. We hear that "everything happens for a purpose" as if God has his controlling hand in every single thing that happens. These kinds of statements cause many to question how this can be so. How are these sentiments congruent with the responsibilities assigned to believers in the scriptures?

Jason Clark wrote the book entitled *God is not in Control: The Whole Story is Better than You Think* in 2017. For over twenty years, Jason served in pastoral roles as a worship leader, family pastor, and director of ministries. He posits in his book that God is not about control but love. He states the following in his book:

> I believe God is sovereign, having supreme power and authority.
>
> If Jesus is the true and fullest picture of what God is like, then Jesus is also the true and fullest way to discover God's nature, His sovereignty.
>
> Jesus was a perfect demonstration of God's sovereignty and He revealed it as love.
>
> Never once did sovereign Love establish the Kingdom of heaven on earth through acts of sovereign control.
>
> No one was ever compelled into servitude, browbeaten into following Him, or strong-armed into loving Him.
>
> Jesus never once compromised free will.
>
> Please understand this, sovereign Love never once revealed, through his actions and words, a desire or interest in controlling us.
>
> When I look at God through the revelation of Jesus, I don't see a God who seeks control. Quite the opposite, I see a God passionate about redeeming and empowering and setting free.
>
> God is sovereign and God is in control are two different thoughts, they are two totally different things.
>
> For much of my life I believed God's sovereignty was defined by the simple and yet absolute idea of control. Because of that, I unknowingly complicated His goodness.
>
> "God is in control" is a statement often used when we have no idea what else to say. For

many it's a heartfelt declaration of faith when
we don't understand, it's offered with the sincere
intent to help someone through sorrow or loss or
brokenness. It's the expression meant to encourage someone through disappointment. It's an
attempt to describe the goodness of God so those
who are suffering can be comforted. The heart
behind this expression typically comes from a
genuine desire to reveal the goodness of God.

The problem is, "God is in control" and
"God is good" are two different and often vastly
conflicting thoughts.

I would humbly suggest that God is either
good, or He is in control, but He can't be both.

I share these comments by Jason not to challenge them but as
an example of what many people understand as facts about how Jesus
related to people. His statements highlight obvious problems which
exist with the false notion that God is a controlling God. These
thoughts compel us to ask if God is truly in control of everything,
"how can he allow bad and terrible things to happen?" Being sovereign and good are concepts which clash if God is in control of everything that happens.

Contrary Responses to the Extreme Sovereignty View

The following are some of the concerns raised in response to the
extreme view of God's Sovereignty.

- The extreme sovereignty of God teaching slanders God
  and makes God the author of all evil and terrible things.
- If God indeed does terrible things, he would be perceived
  as a monster. Civilized nations would prosecute God for
  doing such terrible things and convict him.
- Christians who say that God is in control of everything
  are accusing God of doing all sorts of horrible things. At

the same time, they obviously see that these same things are criminal when done by a human being. How does this make sense?

- This is a doctrine that negates the goodness of God and the love of God.
- Only religion can convince people that something that is evil is good.
- We are to believe that God loves you and then gives you cancer, disease, devastation, rape, murder, etc.
- If God is responsible for all the evil and suffering in the world and God predestines people to hell, then God is not much different than Satan if he wants many to go to hell.
- How is it possible to have an intimate relationship with someone you think might potentially cause you harm, even great harm? Your guard will always be up. Apply this to our relationship with God.
- It is very difficult to have a healthy relationship if one is being controlled by another. Control usually requires coercion. The Calvinist view is that God does control everything in our lives...it is not something that is optional. Under those conditions, how can we have a healthy relationship with God?

Norman Geisler in his book *Chosen But Free: A Balanced View of Divine Election* has much for us to think about if we accept the extreme notion of the sovereignty of God. Here he highlights contradictions with the Calvinist view point on free will.

> Some believers have been known to excuse their sin, claiming, "The devil made me do it!" But the problem here is even greater, because logically one cannot stop at this point. For if God is in sovereign control of all things as extreme Calvinists believe, then instead it would appear that, ultimately, "God made me do it."

This response claims that free choice is simply doing what we desire, but that no one ever desires to do anything unless God gives him the desire to do so. If all of this were so, then it would follow that God would be responsible for all human actions.

If it were true, then the Bible should say that God gave Judas the desire to betray Christ. But it does not. Rather, it says, "The devil had already prompted Judas Iscariot, son of Simon, to betray Jesus" (John 13:2).

If free choice is doing what one desires, and if all desires come from God, then it follows logically that God made Lucifer sin against God. But it is contradictory to say that God ever could be against God.

If God Controls Everything, How Does He Do It?

So when we hear people say, "God is in control," how does God accomplish this? Where in the scriptures does it clearly state that God controls everything that happens? Where in the scriptures is this concept explicitly and directly explained to us? If this is such an important truth for us to understand, surely the scriptures would speak to this often and unambiguously. If true, this concept is huge for how we understand our experiences in life and how God would be connected to them. A concept like this should not be left to such debate, question, uncertainty, and confusion.

Yes, we see God acting mightily in scripture to bring about his will in both the Old and New Testaments. He uses great men of faith to affect the circumstances needed at the given time. Often these great men of faith are common people in the community. Consider the apostles. However, this does not have to mean that God works at all times by being in control of everything. We know nothing about the thousands, millions, or even billions of common people who lived over the ages.

Consider the great abilities God has given to man. We know man has been created in God's image. Man has a brain and can make decisions on what to do. We know that much of what man decides to do is influenced by the heart of man. Therefore, the question arises, "Does God then control the mind and heart of man?" Are we to assume that God controls all our thoughts and all our decisions? Is this even minutely alluded to in the scriptures? Can we even fathom how this can happen?

Conclusion

As has been mentioned by Jason Clark earlier, Jesus does not operate from coercion or force. We don't see Jesus trying to control anyone. This should give pause to anyone espousing those claims.

As we see from the New Testament scriptures, God primarily influences man through the Holy Spirit. Yes, we have seen in the Old Testament how he has partnered with the physical and meteorological realities of the earth to impact man. He's dealt with Satan and demons. We've seen the burning bush, the parting of the Red Sea, fire from above, manna from above feeding the Israelites, the walls of Jericho come falling down, etc. We've seen God do mighty acts in the Old Testament to show the world how great he is in every way.

In the New Testament, we've seen Saul (Paul) struck by a bright light, causing temporary blindness and Jesus speaking to him, saying, "Why do you persecute me?" We see demons forcing pigs to jump off cliffs into water and dying. We see Jesus doing many miracles. We see God causing earthquakes and God speaking audibly to Jesus at his baptism. We see God raising Jesus from the dead after his crucifixion. We see God giving extra powers to his apostles so they can do miracles.

All of this shows that God has a specific plan for how he wants to redeem and reconcile all of us back to him after the fall of Adam and Eve. This is a plan that was in effect before the creation of the world. Over the years, God has interrupted the lives of certain key figures he has chosen to implement his plan. Jesus is the apex of that plan with his death, burial, and resurrection that saves mankind.

However, for the common human being today, most of us would agree that God works in our lives through the Holy Spirit. God wants all people to be saved and be in a relationship with him. God wants people to come to faith in Jesus as our savior and Lord, to live our lives faithful to him and allowing the Holy Spirit to influence our way.

CHAPTER 16

⸻ ℘ ⸻

Does God Have a Specific
Plan for Our Lives?

For I know the plans I have for you," declares
the LORD, "plans to prosper you and not to harm
you, plans to give you hope and a future.
—Jeremiah 29:11

As with many topics, this one is also very controversial in the sense that there is much disagreement about God's involvement in orchestrating people's lives and how to interpret various scriptures related to this. Some will make the case that God has a preordained specific plan for everyone's life based on the Jeremiah 29:11 scripture. In fact, in recent years, this verse has been used on plaques, cards, and in many other ways in Christian bookstores and other places to offer emotional comfort to people. It's one of those phrases Christian people regularly quote.

On the other hand, there are many others who will say that yes, God cares about each person individually but only has a general plan for people designed to help them live their lives with purpose and meaning. This plan relates to the plan of salvation and the hope of life in heaven with God after we pass on from this life on earth. This plan also has moral and ethical demands for how God's people are to act. This plan relates to the attitudes and caring hearts we are to have for those in need. This plan provides guidance on how we should live our lives in ways pleasing to God and to spread the message of the gospel. (Good news!)

Questions

There are many questions about the notion of whether God has a specific plan for our lives. Some of the questions are the following:

1. What do people mean when they say God has a plan for my life?
2. Where is the scriptural support for such an idea, especially in the New Testament?
3. Does the idea that God has a plan for one's life apply to all people or just to Christians? Would it apply to all Christians?
4. Is this a plan that God communicates to each person in advance to let them know about what it is?
5. Is this a plan that just automatically happens without us knowing about it?
6. Is this a plan that is specific and adapts to a person's life changes throughout the years? For example, is the plan very detailed to include who we are to marry, what career and jobs we are to have over the years, how many children we will have, where we will live during our lives, including moves we make, etc.?
7. How specific does this plan become? For instance, is it about every detail of our lives or only the major issues in our lives? How do we know? What determines the level of specificity?
8. Is this a plan that a person is preordained to follow and can't vary from? In other words, is this a plan that will happen no matter what a person does? If there is such a plan, can a person get off-track with the plan God has for them? If so, will the person know when this is happening?
9. Is this concept predicated upon the notion that God is controlling everything that happens? Is everything that happens to a person a part of God's plan for them?

10. If God has a plan for my life, should I do any planning myself?
11. Does a person's free will have any impact on whether or not God does specific planning for their lives?

These questions reflect how challenging a topic this is. I'm not sure how well these questions can be answered, especially with scripture. If they can't be answered with scripture, we should be very cautious about moving forward with this idea.

I suspect that most who believe God has a specific plan for their life also believe God is in control of everything that happens. These concepts seem to be intertwined. If God is in control of all, then having a specific plan for what people do in their lives could then follow. However, if mankind indeed has been given independent free will, people are able to make their own plans for how they live their lives. These plans can conform to the will of God and the admonitions in scriptures for how we should live our lives.

God's Overall Plan Began before the Earth Was Created

As we've seen earlier, God had a plan for the world before the world was created. This plan was associated with his relationship to mankind and his desire that a way be secured where we could be saved and live with him in eternity. In the Old Testament, God's plans centered around using the covenants he made with the nation Israel. We also know that God's initial plan with Abraham had provisions for eventually including all people (including Gentiles, all non-Jewish people) in the invitation to having a life in eternity with God. With the New Covenant, the last and enduring covenant, Jesus fulfilled this plan offering us all eternal life.

See the following scriptures relating to this plan God established before the creation of the earth.

> ⁹ He has saved us and called us to a holy life—not because of anything we have done but because of his own purpose and grace. This grace

was given us in Christ Jesus before the beginning of time, [10] but it has now been revealed through the appearing of our Savior, Christ Jesus, who has destroyed death and has brought life and immortality to light through the gospel. (2 Tim. 1:9–10)

[18] For you know that it was not with perishable things such as silver or gold that you were redeemed from the empty way of life handed down to you from your ancestors, [19] but with the precious blood of Christ, a lamb without blemish or defect. [20] He was chosen before the creation of the world, but was revealed in these last times for your sake. (1 Pet. 1:18–20)

[3] Praise be to the God and Father of our Lord Jesus Christ, who has blessed us in the heavenly realms with every spiritual blessing in Christ. [4] For he chose us in him before the creation of the world to be holy and blameless in his sight. (Eph. 1:3–4)

[24] Father, I want those you have given me to be with me where I am, and to see my glory, the glory you have given me because you loved me before the creation of the world. (John 17:24)

The above scriptures relate to the general plan God has with people which started before the creation. We have already made the case that this plan involved the strategic use of a small number of people. In the Old Testament, God had a process of establishing partnerships with a few specific key people to implement his overall plans from the very beginning.

Planning Is Important

We know how important the planning process is for many businesses and corporations. This kind of planning occurs regularly and is crucial in keeping an organization relevant into the future. This highlights a reality; planning is about the future.

Making plans in our lives is one of the most powerful and effective ways to attain what one wants. We make plans to help us find our way forward. Some do well with this and others don't. We know that some people do not make plans. It they don't, then how can they know where they are headed and when they will arrive at their destination? As Benjamin Franklin has said, *"If you fail to plan, you are planning to fail."*

Planning our lives gives us an amount of control over our lives. If we create a plan, then we get to make choices and decisions rather than leaving things up to chance, or worse, letting others make decisions for us. When we have a plan, then we are in charge of where we are going, making it easier for us to get exactly where we want to be. For instance, if someone wants to be a medical doctor, they then can go down the path that leads to this becoming a reality, such as the proper education, making the right grades, choosing the right specialty, working out the financial means to accomplish it, etc.

The plans we have can help us to visualize a bright future. We may not be able to see ourselves living our ideal future life unless we plan on how we will be able to get there. It's amazing what we can envision when we have the right plans in place.

In many ways, it appears that many people have common plans and aspirations. Maybe this comes from cultural influences and our human nature. In America, we see many whose plans for their lives include achieving the following goals (we may call this the American dream):

- getting the right education
- pursuing careers that match one's skills, abilities, and personalities
- having good jobs that pay well
- finding the right person to marry
- buying a home and then buying additional upgraded homes
- having nice cars to drive

- having and raising children
- having good health and having health insurance
- having good friends
- having fun, interesting, and rewarding hobbies
- taking fun and interesting vacations
- having a nice church to be involved with in many ways
- helping others less fortunate and in need
- enjoying grandchildren
- saving for retirement and having a relaxing, fun, and productive retirement

It seems likely that many, if not most, in America employ this basic plan in their lives, almost like accepting this plan without questioning it.

Then there are others who seem to disengage from this plan (and planning) and drift along through life like a sailboat on the seas without a rudder…just going where the wind blows.

The scriptures point to the wisdom of planning. For example:

- Isaiah 32:7–8: "Scoundrels use wicked methods, they make up evil schemes to destroy the poor with lies, even when the plea of the needy is just. 8 But the noble make noble plans, and by noble deeds they stand."
- Luke 14:28–30: "28 Suppose one of you wants to build a tower. Won't you first sit down and estimate the cost to see if you have enough money to complete it? 29 For if you lay the foundation and are not able to finish it, everyone who sees it will ridicule you, 30 saying, 'This person began to build and wasn't able to finish.'"

Throughout the book of Proverbs, the need to plan is seen.

- Proverbs 11:14: "For lack of guidance a nation falls, but victory is won through many advisers."
- Proverbs 15:22: "Plans fail for lack of counsel, but with many advisers they succeed."

- Proverbs 21:5: "The plans of the diligent lead to profit as surely as haste leads to poverty."
- Proverbs 20:18: "Plans are established by seeking advice; so if you wage war, obtain guidance."

Biblical planning should be done in a prayerful spirit, asking for God's guidance. It is not an activity that is done independently from God.

- Proverbs 3:5: "Trust in the LORD WITH ALL YOUR HEART AND LEAN NOT ON YOUR OWN UNDERSTANDING; ⁶in all your ways submit to him, and he will make your paths straight."
- James 1:5: "But if any of you lacks wisdom, let him ask of God, who gives to all generously and without reproach, and it will be given to him."

As we've seen earlier in this book, we are told in Genesis 1 that God created the heavens and the earth over a period of time. This reflects incredible planning by God. He is a planner, and as people are made in his image, we are planners also.

Differences of Opinions Are Widespread

Again, the notion that God has a specific plan for each person's life is an idea that is as controversial as there are people who agree and disagree. Those who disagree understand the scriptural endorsement of the value of planning as mentioned in the above section. They also believe that the scripture of Jeremiah 29:11 is taken out of context if it is used to apply to ourselves today. It was written to a particular group of people (the Israelites) in a particular place at a particular time. It's been described as one of the most misunderstood verses in the entire Bible.

Here's the entire passage.

> "This is what the Lord says: "When seventy years are completed for Babylon, I will come to

you and fulfill my good promise to bring you back to this place. For I know the plans I have for you," declares the Lord, "plans to prosper you and not to harm you, plans to give you hope and a future. Then you will call on me and come and pray to me, and I will listen to you."

Many who believe God has a specific plan for their lives point to Jeremiah 29:11 as the evidence that God does have a specific plan for everyone. Again, the problem is, this verse isn't written to us. It's written to a group of people, the nation of Israel, thousands of years ago.

Jeremiah was a prophet, God's spokesman, who was given a message to communicate to the nation of Israel. During this time, the Israelites were living in captivity in Babylon. They were slaves and were treated very badly. Life was very hard on them.

They were looking for answers and searching for hope. During this time, there were false prophets going around, teaching that God was going to free them soon. If you read the surrounding verses, you will find where God denounces these false teachings and gives the Israelites some pretty tough news. They aren't going to be freed for another seventy years.

So this verse is about a plan to be manifested in the future. We should take note that many of the people hearing this message would die in captivity. Therefore, this prophecy would not personally impact the condition of their lives. It is more about their children and their future relatives.

This verse is a word from God about the future, not so much a word given to encourage the people over the short term. It's a promise that God's people will prosper again. In this context, we can see how many can be misguided in applying it as a specific plan God has for everyone today.

God's Plan for Everyone

We can understand that God's plan for everyone is aligned with the notion of how God works in the world. It is a plan based upon the partnership Christians have with God in implementing his will in the world and in our lives. This plan is based on the freewill efforts of each of us to voluntarily devote ourselves to following Christ and obeying the admonitions in the scriptures for how we are to live our lives. God joins us with our efforts through the work of the Holy Spirit.

We can also understand that God's plan for everyone is found in the New Testament scriptures. It is alluded to in a variety of passages where we are admonished how to live out the Christian life. All of this represents a general plan of God's will expressed for all people. It has to be. A book for all people does not single out one person for a specific message. In the scriptures, God does not tell one person something about what his will is and tell another person something different. God's general will is all the same for everyone.

God's plan for us is about the future. It encompasses a vision of the future where we live our lives in harmony with God's purposes and will. Again, this plan has many specific variables which are the same for everyone. Therefore, we can consider this a general plan for our lives with specific requirements. This is a plan about process, how we respond to God along life's journey, how we obey God, and how we choose to live according to his principles and values. It is not a plan that maps out and predetermines all the exact details of our life's activities and accomplishments along our journey.

God's plan for our lives includes the following variables:

1. God wants each of us to come to know him and accept his offer of salvation (2 Pet. 3:9). God wants all to be saved (John 6:40).
2. God wants us to love him with our whole being (heart, soul, mind) and love one another (Matt. 22:37–38).
3. God wants us to do justice, love, kindness, and walk humbly with him (Micah 6:8).

4. God wants us to do everything we do for his glory (1 Cor. 10:31).
5. God wants us to set our hearts on things above (Col. 3:1) and to put to death whatever belongs to our earthly nature (Col. 3:5–11).
6. God wants us to exhibit the fruit of the Spirit: love, joy, peace, patience, kindness, goodness, faithfulness, gentleness, and self-control (Gal. 5:22–23).
7. God wants us to forgive others with whom we have a legitimate grudge (Matt. 18:21–35).
8. God wants us to do good works (Eph. 2:10).
9. God wants us to remain in Jesus and bear much fruit (John 15:5–8).

As you can imagine, this list could go on and on. Can you see how God would be glorified if we do what was just mentioned?

Again, I believe God has made us all with certain kinds of skills, abilities, and personalities he wishes for us to use as we engage with life. For Christians, God also gives us manifestations of the Holy Spirit to use for the common good (1 Cor. 12:7).

As we devote our lives to God, we will seek to live our lives according to his will. As I mentioned earlier, we follow the directives and admonitions we have for our lives as found in the scriptures. By following God, we will be prospered spiritually in many ways. However, this prosperity is not focused or based on the material things of this life but spiritual.

This is a different concept than what many others in the *prosperity gospel* movement believe—what many call the *Word of Faith* movement. People in this movement, and certainly others, mistakenly believe God is in control of all that happens and has their lives all planned out from the very beginning to the end. By believing this, many will likely find themselves dismayed, confused, and wondering why things happened when difficulties, frustrations, and tragedies come their way.

Summary

Again, we know Christians have all kinds of ideas as to how God is involved in our lives. Some of this comes from the differing doctrinal affiliations of people. Coming to a conclusion on what one believes about how God is involved in plans for our lives should take into consideration what has been stated in this chapter.

The diversity of thought on this comes from many faith traditions. As we all likely know, even within the same church affiliations, people see and understand things differently! As I was writing this chapter, I saw a drama advertisement from the Saddleback Church in Southern California where Rick Warren is the senior pastor promoting their upcoming Sunday school theme. It will be on Jeremiah 29:11.

I find it difficult to logically and biblically understand that God would make specific plans for people's lives. Based on my understanding of scripture and my worldview, I can only wrap my head around the idea that God has general plans for us that relate to the way we commit our lives to him and change our perspectives to follow his ways. This is the way we engage in a partnership relationship with him.

If one were to believe that God has a specific plan for everyone who is a believer, what then are we to think when Christians endure terrible mistreatment, such as rape, physical abuse, vicious diseases, etc.? Do some events catch God off guard? What are we to think when Christians die as a result of being electrocuted or an accidental drowning? Was God looking the other way? What about those who die early in life due to a house fire or car accident? Are we to believe all this was God's plan for them? I don't see how any of these incidents fit with God having his hand in them because of what I know about God's nature as being a loving and merciful God who is kind to all people. See chapter 18 for a deeper discussion on this.

Again, I think God made plans for mankind when he created the heavens and the earth and then created mankind. I believe the plans for people are general plans and not specific plans based on God controlling or orchestrating everything. God works in partnership with believers who use their skills, abilities, and free will to follow the guidelines and commands of scripture.

CHAPTER 17

— ❧ —

Logic—the Basis for Relating to Others and to God

Critical thinking is a desire to seek, patience to doubt, fondness to meditate, slowness to assert, readiness to consider, carefulness to dispose and set in order; and hatred for every kind of imposture.
—Francis Bacon (1605)

Logic is the basis of all thought. Logic is basic to human activity. We use logic to do most everything. Logic governs much of what we do. The reality is every person thinks. The problem and challenge we have is that not all people think correctly. Every person should be reasonable. Unreasonable people cannot be dealt with rationally. Using reason and logic would not work with them.

Given all of this, Norman Geilser and Ronald Brooks in their book *Come Let us Reason: An Introduction to Logical Thinking* make the clear case that logic is very important in our lives. They state that logic can be defined as a way to think rightly so that we can come to correct conclusions and find truth by understanding implications and the mistakes people often make in thinking.

Logic gives us rules to govern the way we think and the ability to make good decisions, to draw right conclusions, and live life most effectively. Without logic, there can be no rational discussion of anything. One could not even put a sentence together without a logical order.

In 1 Peter 3:15, the Bible urges us to give the reason for the hope that is in us. "But in your hearts revere Christ as Lord. Always be prepared to give an answer to everyone who asks you to give the reason for the hope that you have. But do this with gentleness and respect." Giving a reason for our faith would be useless if it were not a logical reason that we can expect others to accept on rational grounds.

God Is a God of Logic

God is a rational being, and the principles of good reason flow from his very nature. We must understand that the basis of all logic is that some statements are true and others are false. We must seek to honestly and humbly pursue truth. False understandings can have serious consequences.

Being logical is a primary attribute of God. It is part of God's nature. God cannot do away with, defy, or violate the laws of logic (see these listed below). He wouldn't be logical or rational if he did. The laws of logic are essential for man to have knowledge and understanding. There can be no contradiction within God. God's greatness and his ways being so much higher than ours does not mean they are contrary to logic, nor are they intended to provide roadblocks to understanding what is important in life.

God cannot speak to us in illogical ways. We could not deal with a God who is irrational or illogical. Without logic, we could not discover the truths about God. Indeed, the study of theology requires a rational discourse about God. We could not understand God if he were not logical.

God acts in logical ways at all times. Similarly, he has created mankind as rational beings who should act in logical ways at all times. That is one of the major ways mankind reflects the image of God.

Because of this, it naturally flows then that the scriptures should be logical. A God of logic won't speak to us through scriptures which are not based on logic. Because of this, we should be able to use logic as we examine the meaning of the scriptures. It is only reasonable for this to be the case.

The Three Basic Laws of Logic

Logic is built on three basic undeniable laws. They are self-evident and self-explanatory. There is no way around them.

In the Christian worldview, we have an absolute, objective standard for correct reasoning: God. The laws of logic were created by God when he created the world. They were part of creation because they have always been a component of the character of God. Laws of logic reflect the way God thinks and are rooted in his nature. Laws of logic are the rules of correct reasoning. Not only do they reflect the way God thinks, they determine the way we must think if we are to think correctly.

1. *The law of noncontradiction* (A is not non-A) says that no two contradictory statements can be both true at the same time, in the same sense and in the same place. A statement cannot be true and false at the same time. This law draws the line between what is true and what is false. For instance, a statement such as "it is raining" cannot be true and false at my house at the same time.

2. *The law of identity* (A is A). If any statement is true, then it is true. That is, if p is true, then p is true. It is an obvious rule, but one that is never violated. The law of identity says that everything is itself and not something else. For example, my dog is not my dog and your dog at the same time. My dog is my dog, period.

3. *The law of excluded middle* (either A or non-A). The law of the excluded middles says that a statement such as "it is raining" is either true or false. There is no other alternative. Think of it as claiming that there is no middle ground between being true and being false. Every statement has to be one or the other. That's why it's called the law of excluded middle, because it excludes a middle ground between truth and falsity. A cannot equal non-A.

Laws of logic are the rules of correct reasoning. Laws of logic are also called rules of inference. We often have to come to conclusions making logical inferences. Correct reasoning can never violate a law of logic. There are many laws of logic. However, the three above are considered the most basic or primary.

The laws of logic are neither arbitrary inventions of God nor principles that exist outside of God's being. The laws of logic are not like the laws of nature. God may violate the laws of nature (say, suspend gravity), but he cannot violate the laws of logic.

Just because a person may not understand the logic of God does not mean that God is being illogical. God never behaves illogically.

So in defending a point of view, it is not sufficient to say that the issue doesn't have to make sense and that God will show us why when we are in heaven with him.

The Nature of the Laws of Logic

Laws of logic are universal, invariant, abstract rules of thought that govern all correct reasoning. Let's examine each of these adjectives one by one.

First, laws of logic are *universal,* meaning they apply everywhere in the universe. The law of the excluded middle works just as well on Earth as it does on Mars. The laws of logic apply equally well everywhere in the universe.

Second, laws of logic are *invariant,* which means they do not change over time. Many things do change over time. People change with age, and cars only last so long. But laws of logic do not change over time.

Third, laws of logic are *abstract,* meaning they exist in the mind. An abstract principle has no physical substance. You can think a law of logic, but you cannot touch one.

Conclusion

I believe a discussion on the principle of logic is important in many respects. It gives guidance to how we filter through much of what Calvinists present as their doctrine. As we have seen already, much of that is contrary to logic.

For example, it's not logical that a God whose nature is love would predestine people to go to hell. The idea of predestination and God controlling everything also does not square with love and logic. It does not make sense that God would create the world and mankind only for mankind to do only what God causes mankind to do. Creating puppets is not the way to have a love relationship with people.

We could go on and on. The simple truth is that any doctrine must be based on logic. The same is true for much of the doctrine presented by the Word of Faith movement.

Basing our views on logic does not mean that we have to understand everything about God. It just means that what there is to be known about how God acts will be consistent with logic.

CHAPTER 18

⁂

Maintaining Faith in the Midst of Suffering

I have told you these things, so that in me you may
have peace. In this world you will have trouble.
But take heart! I have overcome the world.

—John 16:33

The widespread prevalence of evil, pain, and suffering is said to be the number one reason atheists cite for rejecting faith in God. This must mean Christians are not presenting credible explanations for them.

The topic of understanding evil, pain, and suffering I believe is a subject that is a challenge for most people, including Christians. If you were to ask a group of Christians about what topic they would like addressed in class or in a small group, one of the first ones mentioned would be how to establish a credible and persuasive biblical response to the question of why there is so much evil, pain, and suffering in the world. This has been my experience.

This issue has bothered many people throughout the generations. The fact that it continually remains a highly preferred topic to be discussed reveals that many people just have not come to a point where they have a sense of confidence they have the understanding they need.

The question is "Why does this topic remain so unfinished and unresolved?" One reason could be the many differing explanations provided by well-meaning Christian people and Christian scholars. They make all kinds of statements to provide some kind of explanation about why God has allowed something horrible to happen. Often, these explanations are misguided and incorrect. People need to be careful to first understand the doctrinal position of those trying to explain this. Calvinist-oriented explanations fall within this warning of caution as they are troubling to many.

On a more positive note, I've noticed that in recent years, there have been many books written on this topic which are compelling and worth reading, not written from the Calvinist viewpoint.

Reasonable Explanations Are Needed

Calvinist Jerry Bridges has written a book called Is *God Really in Control?: Trusting God in a World of Hurt*. In this book, he gives an example of a complaint uttered by a confused person trying to understand why God allows people to suffer so much. The following is what the person said to him:

> God, if there is a God, should be ashamed of himself. The sheer enormity of the Asian tsunami disaster, the death, destruction, and havoc it has wreaked, the scale of misery it has caused, must surely test the faith of even the firmest believer... I hope I am right that there is no God. For if there were, then he'd have to shoulder the blame. In my book, he would be guilty as sin and I'd want nothing to do with him.

Many Calvinists have a hard time explaining their viewpoint on this topic because they have to say something they know many people won't like to hear. They believe that since God is in control of everything that happens, God has his hand in causing and allowing all the evil, pain, and suffering in the world. This causes people to react like the person above. I have found the explanations provided by Calvinists are unsatisfying to most people I know.

The above relates to one of the points Jason Clark made in his book *God is not in Control: The Whole Story is Better than You Think*, which we looked at earlier. He said the following:

> The problem is, "God is in control" and "God is good" are two different and often vastly conflicting thoughts. I would humbly suggest that God is either good, or He is in control, but He can't be both.

This is one of the major problems with the belief that God is in control of everything. How does God *not* get the blame for the terrible things that happen if he is permitting, causing, and controlling everything? It doesn't make sense to say a loving God who is in control of everything permits evil actions to be done to innocent human beings.

We can be clear and certain that one of the primary attributes of God is love. And because of this, logic tells us that God would not cause or allow terrible and devastating things to happen to those he loves if he could do something about it. This is obviously contrary to love. This idea that God is in control of all of this and wanting these bad things to happen seems clearly bizarre to me. What about you?

Evil, Pain, and Suffering Is Everywhere

Maintaining faith in the midst of suffering is a topic that is always relevant. I have long had an interest in Christian apologetics and, in particular, how we as Christians deal with the reality of there being so much pain, suffering, and evil around us. This is something that will impact all of us throughout life.

The truth is suffering is everywhere. It is unavoidable, and its scope and impact can often be overwhelming at times. No one is immune from suffering. We are all sufferers, or we will be.

Over the years, I have seen how dealing with suffering and the adversities of life can create many challenges for both people of faith and those who are skeptics. I would like to briefly bring to light some important perspectives regarding this issue as we try to know what to say to the skeptics among us. I also hope to provide some valuable encouragement to people of faith as we endure suffering in our own lives.

In *John 16:33*, Jesus tells his disciples, "In this world you will have trouble. Take heart! I have overcome the world." In this short statement, Jesus warns his disciples about a common experience they will face (troubles) and alludes to how they can cope with it (ultimately, through Jesus). I believe this scriptural message is relevant to all of us today.

The reality of suffering and evil is brought to our attention every single day if we watch the local and national news. Consider the following:

- Five children die every day in the United States as a result of child abuse and neglect. That number could likely be higher.
- Thousands die from traffic accidents, heart disease, and cancer each hour, leaving hundreds of thousands who will deal with the shock and grief of this.
- Many other medical illnesses (i.e., COVID-19) and natural disasters cause death, pain, and suffering in large numbers.
- Crimes of theft, rape, and murder leave much suffering in their wake.
- The betrayal of those we trust because of adultery and other personal moral failures is all around us, causing heartache and the breakup of families.
- Terrorist attacks in the US and all throughout the world.
- What is most troubling is when suffering is personal…we or our loved ones suffering and dying.

As you know, the list could go on and on. Suffering and evil are so pervasive that what I just recounted hardly makes us blink because we hear it so often.

A Crisis of Faith for Some

Hearing about this is one thing; experiencing it is another. The experience of suffering and evil brings many questions to people's minds and leads almost inevitably to the ultimate question: "Why did God allow this to happen?" That's because we want explanations for the difficult events in our lives. We often search to find purpose and meaning to the suffering and evil we experience.

Again, it's been stated by Christian apologists (defenders of the faith) that the number one reason why skeptical people struggle with coming to faith is because of the reality of so much suffering, pain, and evil that exists in the world. Also, many people of faith struggle with their own faith in the midst of personal suffering. I think personal suffering is the worst. Often, the experience of suffering and evil creates a crisis of faith for many. It's a time of faith testing. It can be a turning point in one's life for the better or for the worse.

I think of a situation in which a middle-aged woman who has been a member of the church all her life was thrown off balance because of the unexpected death of her husband. This is a woman who had been on the church staff for many years. Her husband had a rare medical complication associated with a minor health issue that led to his untimely death. This woman is struggling with God and why he would allow that to happen. It created a crisis of faith for her that has lingered on in her life years after her husband's death.

I know there are many like her who struggle with faith when devastation hits. Doubts in the mind can grow with pain in the heart. At the time our hearts need comfort, our minds are also looking for answers.

Given all of this, we all know we have a big challenge in learning how to maintain a life of faith in the midst of adversity and suffering.

The Bible Speaks to Suffering

We need to realize that one thing is for certain. The Bible does speak a great deal about suffering. In fact, suffering is one of the major themes of the scriptures. It is referred to and spoken about often throughout both the Old and New Testaments.

We know that one of the great men of God, the apostle Paul, was someone who was well acquainted with suffering. In *2 Corinthians 11:16–33*, he talks about his sufferings and why he even boasts about his suffering.

> I have been imprisoned more frequently, been flogged more severely, and been exposed to death again and again. Five times I received from the Jews the forty lashes minus one. Three times I was beaten with rods, once I was stoned, three times I was shipwrecked, I spent a night and a day in the open sea, I have been constantly on the move. I have been in danger from rivers, in danger from bandits, in danger from my own countrymen, in danger from Gentiles; in danger in the city, in danger in the country, in danger at sea; and in danger from false brothers. I have labored and toiled and have often gone without sleep; I have known hunger and thirst and have often gone without food; I have been cold and naked. (2 Cor. 11:23–27)

How many of us would like to exchange life experiences with the apostle Paul?

Paul refers to his suffering in other passages also. And so, we know that he's been through some very difficult, painful, life-threatening, and undeserved hardships. If anyone has the authority to speak on suffering, it is the apostle Paul. And yet it is interesting to note that Paul does not complain about his suffering nor struggle with his faith because of his suffering. We should ask ourselves, "Why?" How can that be? I believe it is because he understood the broader purpose and value of suffering.

A Broad Purpose of Suffering

Paul speaks to this purpose in Romans 5:3–5. He states, "We also rejoice in our sufferings because we know that suffering produces perseverance; perseverance character; and character hope. And hope does not disappoint us, because God has poured out his love into our hearts by the Holy Spirit, whom he has given us."

This scriptural insight is for us. Now we know it's counterintuitive to think of rejoicing in our sufferings. Our natural inclination is not to say, "Hey, let's rejoice and boast about the trauma and heartache in our lives." No, I don't believe Paul is referring to having a pleasant time as we experience our pain and suffering. He wants us to see beyond our pain to a greater purpose.

In rejoicing, I believe Paul wants us to find a sense of contentment about our sufferings based on a deep relationship with Christ and the hope we have for eternal life, *not* from a sense of contentment based upon our circumstances. He wants us to see how suffering can relate to our goal in life, the hope we have of a home in heaven and all that entails. It's like what Jesus said in *John 16:33*. Take heart. He has overcome the world.

Also, I think it's worth noting that we are not given a basis here to expect an explanation for our suffering. We are given an encouragement to accept our suffering and see beyond our pain.

We know that trials and troubles in life can either make us or break us, so to speak. Either way, we will not remain the same. We are all tested and changed by our trials. What's important, though, is not *why* we have difficulties, but *how* we respond to our difficulties. The apostle Paul is telling us that our trials can work for us and not against us. However, only we can determine this course by the choices we make.

Endurance, Character, and Hope

In Romans 5, Paul is telling us that trials are actually good for us because they produce benefits. They help us develop in three areas. One is *endurance*, another is *character*, and another is *hope*.

The idea of *endurance*, what we also call *perseverance*, is the ability to carry on when we are facing trials and sufferings in life. By enduring and not quitting, we become victorious. The enduring here is about maintaining our faith. As the song says, "Faith is the Victory." It is said that when you are face-to-face with difficulty, you are up against a discovery! This relates to how we can grow and learn through our difficulties if we will endure. There is a lot to discover in life!

Another benefit of suffering is how it develops our *character*. The truth is, it is often *in* the difficulties of life where we learn a great deal about ourselves and have our character tested and strengthened. We know that the troubles of life have a way of exposing what's in our heart, revealing our character. We need to use the insight gained from this to help us grow as we know God cares about our hearts. He wants our heart. He wants our commitment. He wants our endurance. He wants us to have an enduring faith.

The third benefit of suffering Paul mentions relates to our *hope*. It is when we truly place our hope in Christ that we become victorious over our difficulties. It is because of our hope that we have a reason to endure and stay true to our faith. Hope gives us a purpose and keeps us focused on what is most important, not the pain, but the end result. For Christians, that is a home in heaven with the Lord.

The truth is, there are no victories without battles. Our endurance, character, and hope develop as we are tested by the experiences of life. These experiences can draw us closer to God, or they can push us away from him. Again, it is up to us to choose the course we take.

Suffering can play a role in changing our lives. It can humble us. It can show us how fragile we are. It can remove our blind spots to see reality better, and it can remind us how vulnerable we are. Suffering can cause us to examine ourselves, to see our weaknesses and strengths and can reveal any impurities in our faith which need to be addressed.

Not only is suffering a way to know ourselves better, we should look at suffering as a way to know God better, to draw closer to God as never before and as a way to see how God could use us in service to him because of what we've experienced. It is by enduring the experience of suffering that we are enabled to provide comfort to others. Most often, we relate best to things we've experienced ourselves. It is because of what we have learned when we have suffered that we can comfort others in their suffering.

So it can be said that suffering is a significant part of the human story. It's part of what leads to our destiny.

Atheism's Viewpoint to Suffering and Evil

As I mentioned earlier, one of the greatest challenges many skeptics have in coming to faith in God is the presence of evil and suffering in the world. Atheists and agnostics like to argue on the question "If there is a God, why is there so much evil in the world?" They would make the case that the presence of such great evil in the world is evidence there is no God. So it's like them saying that God and evil cannot coexist, that evil has to exist without God.

The Christian Response to Atheists

In response to this line of thinking, one Christian author emphasized an opposite viewpoint, simply stating, "No God—no evil." His point is that *if* there is no God, there is no such thing as evil. That is because without God, evil doesn't exist because evil relates to morality (Rice Broocks in his book *God's Not Dead, Evidence for God in an Age of Uncertainty*).

Morality only exists if there is a moral law giver. The fact is, God can only be the one with the authority to impose a moral law on everyone. The awe-inspiring, sovereign God of the universe is the only one who has the moral authority to impose rules on everyone. Without God, it just comes down to the opinion of the individual. If that is the basis of morality, then anything goes. If anything goes, there is no basis for defining anything as evil.

And so Christians would assert that the presence of evil does not disprove the existence of God. On the contrary, it helps provide evidence *for* the existence of God.

Many would agree that the reason why acts of evil are gradually becoming more common is because of the decreasing presence of the knowledge of God in society. It can be said that the knowledge of God is an immune system to the soul…that the less of this knowledge in people's minds, the more evil rises in any culture. Again, the existence of evil is not evidence of God's absence in the world but evidence of his absence in the lives of some people.

Yes, the Bible speaks much about pain and suffering. The apostle Peter relates to this in *1 Peter 1:3–9.*

> [3] Praise be to the God and Father of our Lord Jesus Christ! In his great mercy he has given us new birth into a living hope through the resurrection of Jesus Christ from the dead, [4] and into an inheritance that can never perish, spoil or fade. This inheritance is kept in heaven for you, [5] who through faith are shielded by God's power until the coming of the salvation that is ready to be revealed in the last time. [6] In all this you greatly rejoice, though now for a little while you may have had to suffer grief in all kinds of trials. [7] These have come so that the proven genuineness of your faith—of greater worth than gold, which perishes even though refined by fire—may result in praise, glory and honor when Jesus Christ is revealed. [8] Though you have not seen him, you love him; and even though you do not see him now, you believe in him and are filled with an inexpressible and glorious joy, [9] for you are receiving the end result of your faith, the salvation of your souls.

Yes, the stakes are high. We must realize that maintaining a strong and enduring faith is the key. Our faith gives us the victory, the salvation of our souls.

How We Understand Suffering

We know there can be many reasons for suffering and evil in the world. It comes because we live in a fallen world, because of the sinful choices we make, and because of the poor choices of others who do terrible and evil things outside of God's will. These explanations are likely the most accurate even though they may not provide much comfort.

We know the Bible does *not* promise we will fully understand the reasons for suffering or that suffering will come to full resolution or a happy ending in this life. I think at best we will only have partial answers to our questions. I propose we not spend much time looking for God-caused reasons.

The stories in the Bible of the great people of faith show us that having enduring faith through times of difficulty is what God is looking for from us. The most prominent example of this is found in the book of Job in the Old Testament. He endured his suffering without getting an explanation for why he was suffering. Indeed, God chastised him for even asking for an explanation.

And so while Christianity never claims to be able to offer a full explanation of the reasons behind instances of evil and suffering, it does have a final answer to it. James relates to this in *James 1:12*: "Blessed is the man who perseveres under trial, because when he has stood the test, he will receive the crown of life that God has promised to those who love him."

The Bible teaches us to look forward to the final judgment as a decisive answer from God to human suffering. We know we are promised in heaven a place where there will be no more suffering. It will be our crown of life!

I hope we can all affirm what Paul says in *Romans 8:18*: "I consider that our present sufferings are not worth comparing with the glory that will be revealed in us."

Paul is saying our future inheritance, the hope we have in heaven, vastly outweighs the negative impact of our present sufferings, and this should help us cope with our sufferings.

Conclusion—Stay Connected to Spiritual Family

Hopefully, this message provides some comfort to all of us. One of the great blessings of being in the family of God is that there are those who can encourage us in our difficult times. How sad it is when people don't have a Christian family to support them through the trials of life. Regardless of the hardship we experience, we need to remain connected to our family.

Also, as a professional counselor myself, I can attest to the value of seeking Christian professional counseling when personal issues are great and overwhelming. Seeking counseling should not be considered a sign of weakness but of strength. We all should do what it takes to grow and mature through the challenges of life. This is when we can use our experiences to help others.

CHAPTER 19

Conclusion

So have you been challenged? Would you say this book has caused you to think deeper about what a personal relationship with God means? Did you find yourself wanting to do further study on topics and issues which were raised in this book? If so, I've accomplished one of my purposes for writing it.

Our journey together started with acknowledging how the broad Christian community is so divided about its deeply held beliefs. There seems to be a narrowing of consensus among many groups, denominations, and movements about interpretation of scripture and how God works in people's lives today. The result of all this is confusion for people who want to know how to have a genuine relationship with God.

There are many who think they have found the truth and are connected to a church or movement, which is providing them with proper guidance, when in fact, they are connected to heretical groups. Just because one is associated with large churches does not mean they have found a place that teaches the complete truth of the scriptures. Being among a large number of followers does not provide a sense of security that one is in a good place.

Why can so many people be misguided? There are many possible reasons. However, one of the solutions is to question things, research issues, and ensure as best as one can that one is in a biblically based church, where truth is more important than emotional experiences.

I know I've challenged some doctrines which are held onto fondly by a large number of followers. I hope everyone can at least see that any doctrine I criticized was done with sufficient and reasonable objections which were well thought out and supported clearly with scripture and logic. What I focused my critique on are issues which are causing great confusion among believers and those who are considering a relationship with God.

I think many of the questionable doctrines addressed in this book are causing disappointment in people because they inevitably lead to expectations about God which will go unfulfilled. I also believe false ideas on how God works today are creating situations in which God is getting blamed for what he does not deserve. Many issues related to this have been addressed in this book. I hope we all can agree that truth matters and that truth matters a great deal. We should always dig deep to find the truth. False beliefs get us nowhere.

It's a real shame that so many Christian groups can have differing views on some of the most important issues. Not everything rises to the level of importance as some critical issues do. I think one of the most critical issues is about how we become a Christian. I hope most will agree that we should get this right and base our understanding of this solely on scripture which is clearly and simply stated. We should have the whole of scripture come to bear on an issue like this (and others). However, I often see where groups or denominations only focus on some scriptures and leave out others. When needing to be clear on something critical, ask for book, chapter, and verse and look for all of the passages associated with the topic.

I find that Calvinists, in particular, go back to the Old Testament a great deal to build their doctrinal beliefs. They love to quote Psalms. However, as I understand it, many say we should take caution in using the Psalms for establishing doctrine as they are a collection of songs and poems. Many are not to be taken literally.

What I hope you have found in this book is how important a quality and intimate relationship with God is for each person. For those from a skeptical perspective, I hope you have seen compelling reasons to believe in God and have come to understand how God, from the very beginning, set the world up for him to have a loving relationship with everyone.

I hope I have convincingly provided clarity as to the partnership relationship God seeks to have with all of us. This is an important concept to understand and accept. This partnership doctrine directly challenges those who mistakenly believe God wants to control everything that happens and expects us to just get out of the way so he can meet all our needs and solve all our problems. Instead, God takes delight in how we use our considerable talents and abilities. He is glorified by our accomplishments as these are a reflection of him and how he made us in his image. The partnership relationship we have with God also encompasses an appreciation for how God helps us and works with us through the indwelling Holy Spirit given to us when we are born again.

We've addressed some issues with which many have had long-term concerns, such as understanding a biblical view of evil, pain and suffering, and how to maintain a relationship with God through the tough times of life. We've examined issues which help us come to clarity on how God speaks to us today and how we can take comfort in the notion of God being with us at all times.

Balanced Information Needed on the Internet

As I was doing research for writing this book, I did a lot of searching on the internet. It was very disturbing to me that about all I could find easily were writings from the Calvinist perspective. I would say it seemed that 99 percent of searches took me to Calvinist-oriented sites. I not only looked at the first page of a Google search in the *organic* section (where there are no advertisements and pay-per-click listings). I went several pages deeper. Still, I rarely found a non-Calvinist site. Why is this so?

Having been involved with search engine optimization (SEO) efforts for the nonprofit agency in Atlanta I served with as the executive director, I am very familiar with how difficult and challenging it is for information to be found on the first page of a Google search. My agency was trying to promote our work in adoption services. We paid a company to help our agency to be found in searches. If people can't find us on the first page of an internet search, it's like we don't exist.

I wonder why non-Calvinist groups are not working harder to get their scholarly writings (similar to relevant topics like I've put in this book) placed on the internet with the proper SEO work so they can be found. The Calvinists are dominant in reaching out to people in this marketplace of ideas right now. This is not good.

An important way to reach out to the community and the world is through the internet. That is where many are searching for information. Somehow, a concerted effort needs to be made to provide alternative viewpoints. This is a clarion call for this! Who can do it? How can it be done? Do new ministries need to be spawned to take this challenge on? There needs to be widespread effort by many Christian universities, religious institutions, and churches to accomplish this. Alternative viewpoints to Calvinist teachings need to be produced and be easily found on the internet.

I hope you will read the appendixes I've included. There is some important information there and also some references to additional material of interest.

God bless you all!

Notes

Introduction

- Philip Yancey, *Reaching for the Invisible God: God: What Can We Expect to Find?* (Grand Rapids: Zondervan, 2000) 215.

Chapter 1—Confusion Abounds in How to Have a Relationship with God

- Andy Stanley, *Irresistible: Reclaiming the New that Jesus Unleashed for the World* (Grand Rapids: Zondervan, 2018) 72, 95, 103–104.
- Philip Yancey, *Reaching for the Invisible God* (Grand Rapids: Zondervan, 2000) 15, 18, 64, 65.

Chapter 2—Relationships Matter with Others and with God

- J. Paul Getty, https://www.brainyquote.com/quotes/j_paul_getty_150862.
- Gordon Fee and Douglas Stewart, *How to Read the Bible Book by Book: a Guided Tour* (Grand Rapids: Zondervan, 2002) 14.

Chapter 3—God's Covenant Relationships

- The Bible Project, The Covenants: https://bibleproject.com/blog/covenants-the-backbone-bible/.

Chapter 4—Does God Exist? Compelling Reasons to Believe

- Philip Yancey, *Reaching for the Invisible God: God: What Can We Expect to Find?* (Grand Rapids: Zondervan, 2000) 41.
- Norman L. Geisler and Frank Turek, *I Don't Have Enough Faith to Be an Atheist* (Wheaton, Crossway, 2004) 20.
- Rice Broocks, *God's Not Dead: Evidence for God in an Age of Uncertainty* (Nashville: W. Publishing, 2013) 9.

Chapter 5—Entering into a Relationship with God

- Harold Shank, *Listen and Make Room* (Abilene, TX: Abilene Christian Press) 39.
- Andy Stanley, *Irresistible: Reclaiming the New that Jesus Unleashed for the World* (Grand Rapids: Zondervan, 2018) 23–24.

Chapter 6—The Challenges in a Relationship with Our Creator

- Philip Yancey, *Reaching for the Invisible God: God: What Can We Expect to Find?* (Grand Rapids: Zondervan, 2000) 41.
- Roger Olson, *Against Calvinism* (Grand Rapids: Zondervan, 2011) 23.
- Jerry Bridges, *Is God Really in Control?: Trusting God in a World of Hurt* (Colorado Springs, NavPress, 2006) 18, 19, 20, 21, 27, 36.
- John MacArthur, John 3:15-21, https://www.gty.org/library/sermons-library/43-17/belief-judgment-and-eternal-life.

Chapter 7—What Does an Intimate Relationship with God Mean?

- Barna Group, What do Americans Believe About Jesus: 5 Popular Beliefs, https://www.barna.com/research/what-do-americans-believe-about-jesus-5-popular-beliefs/.

Chapter 8—Comparing Human Relationships to One with God

Chapter 9—Created in God's Image for a Special Relationship

- Christianity.com, *The Image of God: "Imago Dei"* https://www.christianity.com/wiki/bible/image-of-god-meaning-imago-dei-in-the-bible.html.
- The Bible Dictionary, *The Image of God*, https://www.biblestudytools.com/dictionary/image-of-god/.
- The Bible Project, *The Image of God,* https://bibleproject.com/explore/image-god/.
- Genetics Home Reference, *What is DNA*, https://www.biblestudytools.com/dictionary/image-of-god/.
- Mike Cosper, *Imago Dei: God's Image, God's People, God's Mission* (Nashville: LifeWay Press, 2019).
- Paul Copan, *Is God a Moral Monster? Making Sense of the Old Testament God* (Grand Rapids, Baker Books, 2011) 29.

Chapter 10—Our Relationship with God—a Partnership

- C. S. Lewis, *The World's Last Night and Other Essays* (New York: Harcourt, Harvest Books, 2002), pp 8-9.
- Philip Yancey, *Reaching for the Invisible God: God: What Can We Expect to Find?* (Grand Rapids: Zondervan, 2000) 59, 182.
- Paul Copan, *Is God a Moral Monster? Making Sense of the Old Testament God* (Grand Rapids, Baker Books, 2011) 39.
- Jerry Bridges, *The Pursuit of Holiness* (Colorado Springs, NavPress, 2006) 78–79.

Chapter 11—Ways We Can Learn about God

Chapter 12—Our Relationship with the Holy Spirit

- Mark Batterson, *The Circle Maker: Praying Circles Around Your Biggest Dreams and Fears* (Grand Rapids: Zondervan, 2016).

Chapter 13—God is with Us All the Time

- M. Scott Peck, MD, *The Road Less Traveled: A New Psychology of Love, Traditional Values and Spiritual Growth* (Simon and Schuster: New York, 1998) 1.
- *Pearl Harbor*, Disney Studios, 2001.

Chapter 14—How God Speaks to Us Today

- Rick Warren, *Understanding How to Recognize God's Voice*, found at the following link: https://www.youtube.com/watch?v=-827QmRDjUA.
- Charles Stanley, "How Can I Hear God's Voice," found at the following link: https://www.youtube.com/watch?v=V4ocm31RJ7g.

Chapter 15—Is God in Control Everything?

- Norman Geisler, *Chosen But Free—A Balanced View of Divine Election* (Bloomington: Bethany House Publishers, 2nd edition, 2001) 19, 20, 21.
- Arthur W. Pink, *The Sovereignty of God* (Grand Rapids: MI: Baker Book House, 2nd printing, 1986) 143.
- Charles H. Spurgeon, *Free Will—A Slave* (McDonough, GA: Free Grace Publications, 1977) 3.
- R.C. Sproul, *What is Reformed Theology?: Understanding the Basics* (Grand Rapids: Baker, 1987) 141.
- R. C. Sproul, *Chosen by God* (Wheaton, IL, Tyndale, 1988) 27.

- Paul Helm, *The Providence of God: (Contours of Christian Theology)* (Downers Grove: InterVarsitiy Press, 1994) 22.
- Roger Olson, PhD, *Against Calvinism: Rescuing God's Reputation from Radical Reformed Theology* (Grand Rapids: Zondervan, 2011) 40.
- Edgar Y. Mullins, *Baptist Beliefs* (ValleyForge, PA: Judson Press, 4th ed. 1925) 27.
- David Basinger and Randal Basinger (Editors), *Predestination and Free Will: Four Views,* (Downers Grove: InterVarsity Press, 1986) 104.
- Norman L. Geisler and Frank Turek, *I Don't Have Enough Faith to Be an Atheist* (Wheaton, Crossway, 2004) 31.
- C. S. Lewis, *Mere Christianity* (New York, Simon & Schuster, 1952) 53.
- Jason Clark, *God is not in Control: The Whole Story is Better than You Think* (Cornelius, NC: A Family Story, 2017) 8, 9, 10, 14, 15, 19.
- Norman L. Geisler, *Chosen But Free—A Balanced View of Divine Election* (Bloomington: Bethany House Publishers, 2nd edition, 2001) 19, 20, 21.

Chapter 16—Does God Have a Specific Plan for Our Lives?

Chapter 17—Logic—the Basis for Relating to Others and to God

- Norman L. Geisler and Ronald M. Brooks, *Come Let Us Reason: An Introduction to Logical Thinking* (Grand Rapids: Baker Academic, 1990) 13, 19.

Chapter 18—Maintaining Faith in the Midst of Suffering

- Jerry Bridges, *Is God Really in Control?: Trusting God in a World of Hurt* (Colorado Springs, NavPress, 2006) 13–14.
- Jason Clark, *God is not in Control: The Whole Story is Better than You Think* (Cornelius, NC: A Family Story, 2017) 15, 19.

- Rice Broocks, *God's Not Dead: Evidence for God in an Age of Uncertainty* (Nashville: W. Publishing, 2013) 42–43.

Chapter 19—Conclusion

The Word of Faith Movement

The Word of Faith movement is also known by other titles—including Word-Faith, Faith Movement, Prosperity Theology, the Prosperity Gospel, and the Health and Wealth Gospel.

It's called a movement because as a whole, it has no formal organization or authoritarian hierarchy which governs the movement. In contrast to a denomination with a formalized institutional structure, voluntary organizations are the norm within the Word of Faith movement. The Word of Faith movement is a loose collection of preachers and teachers who put great emphasis on worldly success and the power of a Christian to control their own future through positive thinking and positive acts.

The International Convention of Faith Ministries (ICFM), founded in 1979, provides an organizational link among member ministries by offering opportunities for networking, fellowship, and support among ministers. The ICFM also holds a yearly convention at which member ministries come together for revivals, seminars, and other church-related activities.

Founders

Evangelist E. W. Kenyon (1867–1948) is considered by many to be the founder of Word of Faith teaching. He began his career as a Methodist minister but later moved into Pentecostalism.

Most scholars agree, however, that Kenyon was an influence on Kenneth Hagin Sr., often called the father or *granddaddy* of the Word of Faith movement. Hagin (1917–2003) believed that it is God's will that believers would always be in good health, financially successful, and happy. A pivotal figure in the formation of today's movement, Hagin established and incorporated the Kenneth Hagin Evangelistic Association in 1963. Through his books and tapes, his radio and television broadcasts, and the Rhema Bible Training Center (1974) in Broken Arrow, Oklahoma, he helped expand the audience for these teachings. Hagin's efforts facilitated the transformation of the Faith message into the ideological basis of an international movement, as well as producing a second generation of Faith teachers. Since the first graduating class (1974–1975), the Rhema Bible Training Center has sent more than 16,500 new Faith Movement ministers out to establish new ministries throughout the world. Hagin's magazine, *The Word of Faith*, reports a monthly circulation of 540,000.

Hagin, in turn, was an influence on Kenneth Copeland. Copeland and his wife, Gloria, founded Kenneth Copeland Ministries in 1967 based in Fort Worth, Texas.

While Copeland is considered the current leader in the Word of Faith movement, a close second is TV evangelist and faith healer Benny Hinn, whose ministry is located in Grapevine, Texas. Hinn began preaching in Canada in 1974, starting his daily television broadcasts in 1990.

The Word of Faith movement got a major boost starting in 1973 with the founding of the Trinity Broadcasting Network, headquartered in Santa Ana, California. The world's largest Christian television network, TBN, airs a variety of Christian programming but has embraced Word of Faith.

Trinity Broadcasting Network is carried on over five thousand TV stations, thirty-three international satellites, the internet, and cable systems all over the globe. Every day, TBN takes Word of Faith broadcasts into the United States, Europe, Russia, the Middle East, Africa, Australia, New Zealand, the South Pacific, India, Indonesia, Southeast Asia, and South America.

In Africa, Word of Faith is sweeping the continent. *Christianity Today* estimates that more than 147 million of Africa's 890 million people are *renewalists*, Pentecostals, or charismatics who believe the Health and Wealth Gospel. Sociologists say the message of money, cars, houses, and the good life is almost irresistible to poor and oppressed audiences.

In the US, the Word of Faith movement and the Prosperity Gospel have spread like wildfire through the African-American community. Preachers T. D. Jakes, Creflo Dollar, and Frederick K. C. Price all pastor black megachurches and urge their flocks to think right to get their monetary and health needs met.

Some African-American pastors are worried about the Word of Faith movement. Lance Lewis, pastor of the Christ Liberation Fellowship Presbyterian Church in Philadelphia, said, *When people see that the prosperity gospel doesn't work, they may reject God altogether.*

Core Claims

The basic theology of the Word of Faith movement is a mix of orthodox Christianity and mysticism. Doctrines considered essential by historic Christianity are not necessarily considered essentials of the Word of Faith theology. Word of Faith teachers often redefine or reinterpret Christian essentials to fit them into their own peculiar theological systems. These reinterpretations are often derived from *revelation knowledge* (i.e., special revelations supposedly from God given specifically to Word of Faith pastors). Placing this *revelation knowledge* above scripture is one reason why Word of Faith teachers often blatantly contradict scripture. In short, the Word of Faith movement is not only unbiblical; it is completely heretical. Multitudes are being drawn into this counterfeit Christianity. This doctrine stands opposed to concepts Christianity has taught throughout its history.

The core claims of the Word of Faith/Prosperity movement are that God's desire is for all Christians to be happy, healthy, and wealthy. These teachers often claim that God allows a person to *speak* their desires into reality, as though they had a creative power similar to that of God. Sickness, poverty, and other struggles are seen as evidence of a lack of faith, or at least a poor application of it.

So therefore, the world's fastest-growing false religion tells us that our faith is a *force* and the words we speak have the power to create something new. The Word of Faith proponents promise we can obtain health, wealth, success, and more if we simply have enough faith. Biblical Christianity says no.

Their main teachings revolve around three key points:

1. "Positive confession"

They teach that words have power in and of themselves. If you believe it, think it, act like it, and say it, then God will give it to you. Some go as far as to say that since we can create with our words, we must carefully use them because we might accidentally create something! This is the heart of the Word of Faith movement, the belief in the *force of faith*. It is believed words can be used to manipulate the faith-force, and thus actually create what they believe Scripture promises: health and wealth. Laws which supposedly govern the faith-force are said to operate independently of God's sovereign will and that God himself is subject to these laws. This is nothing short of idolatry.

2. Little gods

If man is able to create with his words as God is able to create with his words, then the logical conclusion is that man must be a god. It is here where its theology strays further and further from Scripture. It claims that God created human beings in his literal physical image as little gods. Before the fall, humans had the potential to call things into existence by using the faith-force. After the fall, humans took on Satan's nature and lost the ability to call things into existence. In order to correct this situation, Jesus Christ gave up his divinity and became a man, died spiritually, took Satan's nature upon himself, went to hell, was born again, and rose from the dead with God's nature. After this, Jesus sent the Holy Spirit to replicate the incarnation in believers so they could become little gods as God had originally intended.

3. Limited God

Of course the "little god" doctrine leads to something even worse. If man is a god, then God Himself must be limited in some way. Thus, many of the Word of Faith teachers claim that God the Father has a body and is bound by laws which limit his ability to act.

While man is glorified, God is humiliated in the Word of Faith system. Copeland declares Adam was the copy—looked just like God. If you stood Adam beside God, they looked exactly alike. If you stood Jesus and Adam side by side, they would look and sound exactly alike. Following the natural progression of these teachings, as little gods, we again have the ability to manipulate the faith-force and become prosperous in all areas of life. Illness, sin, and failure are the result of a lack of faith and are remedied by confession, claiming God's promises for oneself into existence. Simply put, the Word of Faith movement exalts man to god status and reduces God to man status. Needless to say, this is a false representation of what Christianity is all about. Obviously, Word of Faith teaching does not take into account what is found in Scripture. Personal revelation, not Scripture, is highly relied upon to come up with such absurd beliefs, which is just one more proof of its heretical nature.

What the Scriptures Say

The Bible defines *faith* as "the assurance of things hoped for, the conviction of things not seen" (Heb. 11:1). Our "faith" cannot override the will or nature of God. But our faith that he is able to accomplish all good things for his glory is a necessity for prayer and petition to God. Without faith, it is impossible to please God.

Instead of stressing the importance of wealth, the Bible warns against pursuing it. Believers, especially leaders in the church (1 Tim. 3:3), are to be free from the love of money (Heb. 13:5). The love of money leads to all kinds of evil (1 Tim. 6:10). Jesus warned, "Watch out! Be on your guard against all kinds of greed; a man's life does not consist in the abundance of his possessions" (Luke 12:15). In sharp contrast to the Word of Faith emphasis on gaining money and possessions in this life, Jesus said, "Do not store up for yourselves treasures on earth, where moth and rust destroy, and where thieves break in and steal" (Matt. 6:19). The irreconcilable contradictions between prosperity teaching and the gospel of our Lord Jesus Christ are best summed up in the words of Jesus in Matthew 6:24, "You cannot serve both God and money."

APPENDIX B

Reasons to be Concerned about Calvinism

Many question if the debate about the truthfulness of the doctrines of Calvinism is worth the effort. There are many scholarly types on both sides of the issue. So who is right? Does it even matter? Do we need to care?

Many would say it doesn't make a difference if one follows the Calvinist doctrine or not, referring to what one may think about God's sovereignty, the TULIP, predestination, God's secret will, the effectual call, the elect, original sin, etc. That is because some say that even if one gets this doctrine wrong, they still are going to heaven with God because they do believe in Jesus Christ as their savior and Lord. However, I wonder if the many features and ramifications of reformed theology are well understood. Maybe, the lack of concern comes from not truly understanding the breadth and depth of Calvinist beliefs.

One must know that according to Calvinists, the acrostic TULIP represents what is known as the five points of Calvinism: total depravity, unconditional election, limited atonement, irresistible grace, and perseverance of the saints. According to Calvinists, if any one of these points can be shown not to be true or valid, then all of the points fall apart like a domino effect.

Does it matter how people understand the process of salvation? Calvinists have a vastly differing point of view than Arminians (named after Jacobus Arminius, 1560–1609) and generally represent non-Calvinists and free will believers. Does it matter how people understand the nature of God as a loving father of all?

Additional Concerns about Calvinism:

1. Distorts scripture, misuses scripture, and misapplies scripture. Relies heavily upon Old Testament/Old Covenant scripture to base its doctrine.

2. Incorrect doctrine on the most important concept of all—how to be saved. How could God be pleased that Christians would be confused about this?

3. Wrong teaching on God causing evil, suffering…everything. This is dangerous theology because it is untrue and can turn off people toward God. If God is controlling all that happens, then God is allowing bad things to happen when he could do something to stop them. Therefore, God gets the blame for causing all the bad things that happen to people, even the terrible, horrible events. God, therefore, becomes a monster.

4. The doctrine confuses people. It is very convoluted. It picks and chooses a variety of scriptures here and there to build its doctrine. The doctrine is not plainly and clearly revealed in scripture.

5. Goes against God's character revealed to us…love, kind, just, merciful, compassionate, etc.

6. Ignores scriptures contrary to its teachings. God wants all to be saved. Man is responsible for his choices and behavior. Repentance and baptism when coming to belief, not infant baptism with the original sin concept.

7. The incongruent nature of their doctrine. If the elect concept is true and predestination is true, then to be evangelistic would be cruel…talking to the nonelect about heaven which they can't have.

8. Takes responsibility for behavior off man. If no free will, this undermines the concept of morality and accountability.

9. Does truth matter? If it doesn't matter what we believe, then what we believe doesn't matter.

10. How can Calvinism be okay if it is wrong? If much of the doctrine is false, should we not speak up about it? How can false doctrine be helpful? Is this doctrine harmful? It does harm God's reputation.

11. Defend the vulnerable among us. There are many young-in-the-faith Christians and even other more experienced Christians who can be easily confused and drawn into this false teaching. Many who are not adept in knowledge and understanding can be easily swayed to believe the Calvinist doctrine. Those who have studied this and have a good grasp of its errors need to step up and help those who don't have this knowledge.

12. Defend the honor of God. If someone was telling lies about your earthly father whom you adored and believed in, would you stand up and confront those who are spreading the lies? What if the lies made your earthly father falsely appear to be a mean, hateful, and uncaring person? What would you do? Now what if someone you believed in who was seeking public office was being besmirched by those telling lies and distorting the truth about what this person stands for? Would you not go to his or her defense? And finally, what if there are those who are telling lies about God? Those who have the truth mixed up and are spreading falsehoods? Those who attribute actions to God which make him seem to be a monster? Would it not be appropriate and compelling to defend God as much as we can?

13. What if one of your children was being drawn to Calvinism?

Excellent Books to Read on the Concerns of Calvinism

- Dave Hunt, *What Love Is This—Calvinism's Misrepresentation of God* (Bend, Oregon: The Berean Call, 2006).

- Roger Olson, *Against Calvinism* (Grand Rapids: Zondervan, 2011).
- Norman Geisler, *Chosen But Free—A Balanced View of God's Sovereignty and Free Will* (Minneapolis: Bethany House Publishers, 2010).
- Leighton Flowers, *The Potter's Promise: A Biblical Defense of Traditional Soteriology* (Trinity Academic Press, 2017).

Interesting YouTube Messages Challenging Calvinism

- Why I am Not a Calvinist: With Dr. Leighton Flowers at the following link: https://www.youtube.com/watch?v=M-TCokZKX8U
- The 5 Points that Lead me out of Calvinism (with Dr. Leighton Flowers) at the following link: https://www.youtube.com/watch?v=M-TCokZKX8U
- Andy Stanley on Calvinism's Impact in the Local Church at the following link: https://www.youtube.com/watch?v=BWdoPMDD-pc
- Mike Winger: Why I think Calvinism is Unbiblical at the following link: https://www.youtube.com/watch?v=oxakEl8BYBE

Problems with Calvinism

Calvinism or reformed theology has a broad set of unique and specific doctrines and beliefs to define them. Those who are non-Calvinists also have specific doctrines and beliefs to define them. However, non-Calvinists do not have a universally used name or title as a common label for the group.

For Calvinists, this name or title comes from the French theologian John Calvin, a leader of the Reformation who lived from 1509 to 1564. Those known as non-Calvinists were initially known as Arminians. They are followers of the teachings of Dutch theologian Jacobus Arminius (1560–1609).

Interestingly, the Arminians first wrote their five points of Arminianism in opposition to Calvin's teachings. This was done after Jacobus Arminius had died, and it was written by the Remonstrants in 1610. In response, a few months later, the Calvinists wrote the five points of Calvinism at the Synod of Dort. Later came the Westminster Assembly (1643) and their proclamations.

The Westminster Assembly is often quoted among leading Calvinists today. However, these creeds, such as the Westminster Confession, were forced on the Independents, Baptists and other Christian groups in England by a Calvinist state church which refused to let these groups be a part of the meetings/discussions.

The Westminster Assembly was convened to reform the Church of England. The Westminster Assembly was convened by Parliament and was not a gathering of those representing all true believers, but only of the Calvinists who had gained the upper hand in Parliament. In essence, the Westminster Assembly established a state church with Calvinist beliefs.

So with this bit of church history, we see that initially, the debate was between Calvinists and Arminians or those we can call *free will believers*. Today, Calvinists prefer to go by the label *reformed theology*. Also, we must understand there are many versions of Calvinism. There are extreme Calvinists, moderate Calvinists, and those who have their own version of Calvinism. Many say that John Calvin would not even believe himself in a certain amount of modern Calvinist doctrines. John Calvin wrote much of his theology in what is known as his *Institutes of the Christian Religion*. He wrote these when he was twenty-five years of age.

Some of the leading Calvinists, both current and in the past, include R. C. Sproul, John Piper, Timothy Keller, John MacArthur, James White, John Gerstner, Jonathan Edwards, Edwin Palmer, Steven Houck, J. I. Packer, A. W. Pink, John Calvin, John Knox, David Wells, Michael Horton, and St. Augustine. Charles Spurgeon is often quoted, but both sides quote him. There are many more who could be considered for this list.

The past two decades have witnessed a resurgence of Calvinism among American evangelicals. This resurgence is especially evident within the Southern Baptist Convention, which historically has been and still is divided over the issue. However, it has also made its presence felt in Pentecostal denominations, such as the Assemblies of God, which do not have historic ties to Calvinism. According to adherents.com, the Reformed/Presbyterian/Congregational/United churches represent seventy-five million believers worldwide. The World Communion of Reformed Churches, which includes some United Churches (most of these are primarily Reformed), has eighty million believers.

For Arminians, we don't hear this title used much. There really is no commonly used title to reference this group. Many prefer to use the term *free will believers* as this aspect of non-Calvinism is a major point of distinction between the groups.

Calvinist Doctrine

The following will not be an exhaustive review of the Calvinist doctrine. It will highlight many aspects of their doctrine which are troubling to many in mainstream Christianity. All the doctrines of Calvinism are based on scripture, many by inference and not with explicit terminology. Most, if not all, of the questionable scriptural interpretations they cite to defend their beliefs can have alternative interpretations.

One will find that much of the Calvinist doctrine is based on a convoluted collection of scriptures gathered from here and there. They bounce around a lot and use a lot of the Old Testament/Old Covenant scripture to make their points. One won't find in the New Testament a clear and explicit explanation for many of their doctrinal stances. That is because Calvinists often twist and spin scriptures for them to say what Calvinists want them to say. After hearing what they say for many doctrinal stances, one often has to ask, "Where in the scriptures is this clearly stated?" For instance, there is no scripture which explains explicitly their idea of regeneration, infant baptism, predestination of specific individuals to salvation, and God only loving the elect enough so that he only saves them without giving the rest of humanity a chance to be saved.

There are many important and deep issues which divide Calvinists and free will believers. Many would say the deepest difference relates to how we understand the character of God. Freewill people believe there is much about Calvinism that goes against God's character, especially as we understand God's love for all mankind. Calvinists will go to great lengths to defend their position that God does not have to love all people the same to defend their stance that Jesus did not come to save all people, just the elect. I heard John Piper, in his sermon on John 3:16, strongly encourage everyone to read a book written by a Calvinist on how to understand why God did not have to love everyone the same by offering salvation to everyone. Why should we have to read a book to understand the simple concept that God so loved the world?

Calvinism and free will believers' positions are very different, and both can't be true. The fact is that people will have to make a choice between which of these views they believe is true. This must be based on the amount of evidence for the scriptural veracity of what is said and the logic behind their assertions. Even though Calvinists will try to explain away conflicts and contradictions, we must ask, "Are their responses really convincing?" Keep this in mind as you read about their TULIP.

Many Calvinists would say that the framework of the *Five Points of Calvinism* set forth clearly what the Bible teaches concerning the way to salvation. They would say that if you don't know the five points, you don't know the gospel. So this assertion brings the claims of Calvinism to a higher level.

The Five Points of Calvinism

Much, but not all, of the doctrine of Calvinism is centered on how people are saved. They explain it by the acronym TULIP:

- T—Total depravity
- U—Unconditional election
- L—Limited atonement
- I—Irresistible grace
- P—Perseverance of the saints

First, the Calvinist understanding of the TULIP will be presented, and then afterward, commentary challenging these notions will be presented.

Total Depravity

The first point is *total depravity*. Calvinism teaches that human beings are all born so corrupted and depraved by original sin that people are incapable of even using their minds to respond to God or exercising any good will toward God. As Scripture says, "There is none that does good, no not one" (Rom. 3:12). Another scripture says, "There is no one who seeks after God" (Rom. 3:11). Total depravity does not mean every person is as evil as it is possible to be. Rather, it means every part of us, including our reasoning ability, is so damaged by inheriting Adam's corruption that we cannot even conceptualize in our minds anything about what God wants from us.

Unconditional Election

The second point is *unconditional election*. It means, according to Calvinists, that *if* a person comes to Christ and is saved, it is because he or she was chosen by God to be saved. God selects some people out of the mass of humanity to be saved. Others are left to their deserved damnation. This is also known as *double predestination*. This is where God chooses some to save and others to damn. All of this is based on their notion of predestination.

Limited Atonement

The third point is *limited atonement*. Most Calvinists prefer to call it *particular atonement* because it says Christ died only for particular people. It does not mean that the value of Christ's death was limited. Rather, according to five point Calvinism, Christ bore the punishment only for the elect. This is the point some Calvinists choose to reject, calling themselves *four-point Calvinists* instead.

Irresistible Grace

The fourth point is *irresistible grace*. Most Calvinists prefer to call it *effectual grace*. The meaning is that saving grace extended by God to the elect cannot be resisted by the people. It is always effectual. Part and parcel of this is the idea that regeneration, being *born again*, happens *before* conversion. An elect person, predestined by God for salvation, will freely choose to repent and believe *because* he or she has already, perhaps unconsciously, been regenerated by the Spirit of God. The person is a new creation in Christ Jesus *first*, and only then are they converted. To Calvinists, regeneration precedes faith.

Perseverance of the Saints

The fifth point is *perseverance of the saints*. It means simply that a truly saved person cannot fall away and be forever lost. That is because he or she is one of God's elect and God would not elect a person and then allow him or her to fall from grace. This is sometimes called *once saved always saved* and *eternal security*. Many non-Calvinists believe this doctrine also but not because they believe the eternally secure person is sovereignly predestined by God. For instance, many free will Baptists simply believe God will not allow one of his children to fall forever away from his grace.

Commentary Challenging the Calvinist TULIP Re: Total Depravity

First of all, there are no words in the Bible that say *total depravity*. Nowhere do the scriptures use these words.

Calvinists believe in the idea of total depravity by saying that since man is dead, he cannot respond without God regenerating man first. To Calvinists, regeneration comes before faith. They believe that God is fully able to save without the aid of his creatures. They believe people do not seek God and have no fear of God before their eyes. They believe man does not have the ability to seek God or repent or have any faith without first being regenerated by God. When this happens and how it happens is never explained.

However, if regeneration takes place by God's sovereign act without any faith on man's part, what does believing the gospel accomplish? Why would a regenerated child of God need to be saved? The Biblical doctrine of salvation through faith in Christ and being united with Christ in baptism contradicts so-called "reformed theology."

The idea of spiritual death is a figure of speech used to describe the fallen state of mankind. However, people are not literally dead. Unsaved people can use their minds to make many decisions in all areas of life, including in the area of religion. If man is totally dead and can't respond, "How then can a person be held accountable for not responding to the gospel?" If man is totally incapable of good, then man cannot truly be remorseful or repentant. If man is totally incapable of good, then man cannot be faulted for his sins.

Re: Unconditional Election

First of all, there is no mention in the Bible of the phrase *unconditional election*. Nowhere do the scriptures use these words.

According to the Calvinist notion of unconditional election, God simply decides to save some, the elect, and then let's the rest to go to hell. What kind of love is this? The scriptures are clear that God wants all people to be saved. I count at least 39 passages of scripture clearly relating to the idea that God wants all people to be saved, including the following: John 3:14-18; John 6:40 & 47; John 11:25-26; Rom. 20:9-10 & 13; and 2 Pet. 3:9.

Re: Limited Atonement

Limited atonement also cannot be supported by scripture. It contradicts the love of God, making God one to show partiality (which is unscriptural), but also hateful toward the non-elect. Belief in limited atonement would make it cruel to share the gospel with those who are not part of the elect.

Each of the points of Calvinism's TULIP has proven divisive over the years, but none has proven more so than its teaching of limited atonement. In fact, this point is the reason there are *four-point* Calvinists.

Limited atonement is the idea that Jesus didn't die for the sins of the whole world. Instead, he died only for those persons Calvinists believe were chosen and predestined for salvation before the foundation of the world.

Re: Irresistible Grace

While Calvinists understand God's saving work as being his alone, freewill believers insist that each person has a part to play in this process—namely, receiving and believing in the gospel of Christ. The Bible is full of passages about appealing to people to believe and live godly lives.

Re: Perseverance of the Saints

This concept is not as controversial as the other parts of the TULIP are with free will believers. There are scriptures which seem to say that God won't let any believers to be lost. However, there are many warning scriptures which clearly indicate that a person can reject the faith and not remain faithful.

Additional Questions about Calvinism/ Reformed Theology

1. The scriptures mention a great deal about God's love for the world. This love is not only directed at the elect. Love is the nature and character of God (1 John 4:8, 16). "For God so loved the world" (John 3:16). A major problem with the whole system of Calvinism is the inconsistency and incongruence between God loving the world but only choosing to save some, the elect (those he predestined, chose before their birth), to go to heaven. All others, before

they were born, were predestined to go to hell. How can that be consistent with God's character? What kind of love is that? Is there just even one scripture that clearly states that God's love and grace are limited to just a select group?

2. Calvinists will quote the scripture in Romans 9:18 that God will have mercy on whom he desires. They will argue that God is not obligated to have mercy or save anyone. Others will argue that of course God is under no obligation to extend mercy or grace to anyone. By very definition, mercy and grace are completely without obligation. However, obligation is not the basis for extending grace and mercy but rather love and the desire to meet the sinner's need. Consider the following scriptures regarding God's mercy (Ps. 86:15, Micah 7:18 and 6:8, Eph. 2:4, and Rom. 11:32). These scriptures do not indicate at all that God limits His mercy and grace to a select group.

3. Only a Calvinist can believe God loves those he has predestined to eternal suffering. Wouldn't it be a mockery for God to plead with them to repent (as he does in the great commission Matt. 28:19–20) when he withholds from them the grace to do so? There are biblical and rational reasons why God, in his sovereignty, could give to all mankind the power of choice. Man's will is no threat to God's sovereignty. Instead, it brings greater glory to God, who *wins* the love and praise of those who are free to choose otherwise. Predestined, irresistible, and *forced* (no choice in the matter) is not love from the heart.

4. In the book of Romans, Paul mentions over and over again how the gospel is the power of God for salvation of everyone who believes (Rom. 1:16), to all who are of the faith of Abraham (Rom. 4:16), that Christ died for the ungodly and for us (Rom. 5:6, 8), and that Christ can bring life to all men (Rom. 5:18). Paul says we died to sin so that we may have a new life (chapter 6); and therefore, we do not let sin reign in our mortal body (Rom. 6:11). How is it

possible for us not to let sin reign if we are *dead* (i.e., total depravity)?

5. The Bible presents two sides to salvation: God's sufficiency and man's responsibility.

About the Author

Douglas Mead grew up in a suburb of Boston, Massachusetts. He attended college at David Lipscomb College in Nashville, Tennessee, for two years and then went to Abilene Christian University in Abilene, Texas, where he graduated with a double major in social work and psychology and a minor in Bible.

Doug spent his whole career working for Christian-based child and family service agencies. He first worked as a social worker for the Children's Home of Lubbock in Lubbock, Texas, for a couple of years and then went to the University of Texas at Arlington where he received his masters of science in social work degree (MSSW).

Doug then went on to work as the program director at a residential program for boys, Timothy Hill Children's Ranch in Riverhead, New York, for four years. He then served as the executive director of Christian Family Services of the Midwest in the Kansas City area for eleven years. That agency provided foster care, adoption, and counseling services. This is where Doug received his clinical license in social work and did a fair amount of marriage, family, and individual counseling. He then went to serve as the executive director of Georgia Agape, Inc., in Atlanta where he worked for twenty-one years. Georgia Agape provided foster care and adoption services.

During his working years in Georgia, Doug was very active in a statewide adoption advocacy group called the Georgia Association of Licensed Adoption Agencies where he served as president of that organization for several terms over the years. He also served on the board of directors of two child and family service organizations. One was a statewide advocacy and networking organization in Georgia called Together Georgia, previously named the Georgia Association of Homes and Services for Children. He also served on the board for the Christian Child and Family Services Association, a national advocacy and networking organization which is now called Network 1:27.

Over the years, Doug had been involved with churches in the communities where he and his family lived. He served as a deacon for two congregations, as a small group leader, and taught adult Bible classes. He also traveled to speak to churches each year to promote the work of the agencies he served. While in Georgia, Doug spoke over five hundred times in the pulpit to over a hundred congregations and taught many Bible classes. He also was a presenter at professional conferences on a variety of topics.

Prior to his retirement, Doug received several awards honoring his service and commitment to the field. One was the Distinguished Service Award from the Christian Child and Family Services Association. He also received the Lifetime Achievement Award from the Christian Child and Family Services Association. He received the Gail Bayes Lifetime Achievement Award from Together Georgia.

Doug has been married to his loving wife, Nancy, since 1976. They have two sons and daughters-in-law and four grandchildren. They both retired from their professional careers in 2016 and moved to Southern California where both of their sons' families live. They love retirement and the time they can spend with their grandchildren! Doug also is active in his local congregation, including teaching the adult Bible class from time-to-time. He also does pro-bono consulting for Agape Villages, Inc. in Northern California, a licensed and nationally accredited foster care and adoption agency. You can reach him at the following email address: goingdeeperwithgod806@gmail.com

CPSIA information can be obtained
at www.ICGtesting.com
Printed in the USA
BVHW081400120921
616610BV00002B/2